TROPICAL SKETCHES

OR

REMINISCENCES OF AN INDIAN JOURNALIST

TROPICAL SKETCHES

OR

REMINISCENCES OF AN INDIAN JOURNALIST

WILLIAM KNIGHTON

IN TWO VOLUME

VOL. I

GYAN

Published by

GYAN

Gyan Publishing House
5, Ansari Road
Daryaganj, New Delhi-110002
Phone: 011-47034999, 9811692060
E-mail: books@gyanbooks.com

Distribution Network
gyanbooks.com
India, USA, Canada, UK, Australia, France

ISBN : 978-81-212-4174-8 (Set)
ISBN : 978-81-212-4742-9 (HB)
First Published, London, 1855

2nd Impression 2020

Printed at: Gyan Press, Delhi.

Tropical Sketches Vol. I
Author: William Knighton

TROPICAL SKETCHES;

OR

REMINISCENCES OF AN INDIAN JOURNALIST.

BY

WILLIAM KNIGHTON, M.A.

AUTHOR OF "FOREST LIFE IN CEYLON."

IN TWO VOLUMES.

VOL. I.

LONDON:
HURST AND BLACKETT, PUBLISHERS,
SUCCESSORS TO HENRY COLBURN,
13 GREAT MARLBOROUGH STREET.
1855.

CONTENTS OF VOL. I.

PREFACE.

THE increased facilities of intercourse with Europe are rapidly producing innovations in India, and in Anglo-Indian life. Railways and the electric telegraph, a Civil Service no longer to be appointed on account of its family connections, and a public opinion in England bearing upon Indian Government, must, sooner or later, produce a complete revolution in the ordinary routine of Indian existence. These *Tropical Sketches*, therefore, will be, in a very few years,—nay, to a great extent, are now probably,—rather views of what has been than of what is; particularly in all that relates to newspapers and their offices.

Many of the following chapters were originally written in India, amid the scenes and circumstances which they describe. They have all been carefully revised, however, and, in fact, rewritten for the present work.

No man can have been the editor of a newspaper anywhere, without making many personal enemies. This is particularly the case in small communities, such as those of Colonial towns and the capitals of the Indian Presidencies. To such enemies a work issuing from the pen of the obnoxious editor will afford the long-sought opportunity of paying off old scores, of discharging the vials of that wrath which has long been pent up within the breast, uncomfortably and inconveniently.

I am perfectly aware, also, that whoever ventures to find fault with any portion of the system of Indian administration, will find many ready to assail him. Some, writing from honest conviction in honest defence of the government they admire or serve; others, to obtain the favour of the authorities, and thereby secure their own promotion or advantage. To the former I would simply observe, that, in the following pages, I confine my condemnation of Indian administration to that department in which I served—the Educational.

If I have written strongly on the subject, it is because I feel strongly. Mental philosophy and pure mathematics have been the subjects chiefly taught in the Government Colleges of India. The religion in which the students have been nurtured in infancy, Brahmanism, has been uprooted by the study of geography and astronomy, and no other religion has Government given them the opportunity of inquiring into or embracing. It was but a few months ago that the leading and oldest daily journal in Calcutta—the *Bengal Hurkaru*—wrote as follows:—

"It is a lamentable fact, that in no civilized country on earth has so little been done in the way of public instruction as in India, and even that little is more owing to private enterprise than to any endeavours on the part of Government to place education within the reach of the poor; moreover, the little that has been done—little, considering the hundred millions of the British subjects—has chiefly been done by Missionaries, almost entirely unaided by government."

The results of the system pursued in the Government Colleges have been such as might have been anticipated from the studies most patronised—great intellectual acuteness and a total want of moral principle, utter infidelity in religion, combined with an enthusiastic worship of reason and money.

Indeed, the members of the reformed Council of Education of Bengal seem to have partially discovered its defects. "Whilst we have trained scholars—" say they in a recent report; "whilst we have trained scholars in scores, who will integrate a difficult problem, no one has ever left our schools whom an officer making a road would employ as an overseer in preference to an English serjeant who can just read and write." Let the leading magazines and reviews in England which have said so much in favour of Government Education in India, particularly *Blackwood* and the *Dublin University*, ponder that confession—that and the following, both taken from the same report:—"The want of everything of a practical character in the educational course at present, appears to the Council to be its greatest defect. Everything that strikes the senses, one half of the whole circle of knowledge is, as it were, ignored in our present system of education." All honour to the Council of Education of Bengal for acknowledging its former deficiencies and shortcomings so candidly! Let it not be forgotten, too, that the system must have been a very bad one indeed, which could call down such a censure from the present Council upon the labours of its predecessors. My readers must not suppose, however, that the chief objection has therefore been removed. Far from it. The youth of India are still brought up without faith, without a religion, as in times past.

I am perfectly aware that all this will not prevent my being virulently attacked by certain Indian journals and Anglo-Indian patriots —"Venomous falsehoods," "Ignorant and malicious calumnies," "Ridiculous drivellings," "Absurd rhodomontade," "Vile aspersions," are some of the amenities of literature culled from Indian journals (such as the *Friend of India*) relative to what I have previously written; and similarly gentle remonstrances will doubtless be issued with reference to the present work. My justification is not for such as use those terms—for such as will not see, nay, possibly cannot see—but for that portion of the press and public of England which can and will see. Let but that press and that public receive these *Tropical Sketches* with as much favour as *Forest Life in Ceylon* was received, and I shall care little for the pop-gun salutes of anonymous correspondents in Indian journals, or the more formidable broadsides of their editorial columns.*

* For misrepresentation in Ceylon and India, I was prepared, but I confess I was not prepared for misrepresentation in New York. In Mr. Mitchell's paper, *The Citizen*, an account was given, early in the present year, of my description of Indian Coolies and their treatment on the coffee-estates, which was as far from the truth in its inferences, as it was from being a just representation of my views in its statements.

CHELSEA, *October*, 1854.

TROPICAL SKETCHES;

OR,

REMINISCENCES OF AN INDIAN JOURNALIST.

CHAPTER I.

THE COLONIAL NEWSPAPER.

"NOTHING, sir, can be more foolish," said my uncle. We were at the moment seated in his office in the Fort of Colombo, the thermometer at ninety degrees in the shade. He was one of those bald, apparently irascible but really benevolent, men, who wax red at the least provocation, and who constantly rub their shining phrenological developments, guiltless of hair, with their handkerchiefs, when excited.

He had just given me a long dissertation on the evils of that desire for change, which young men so often exhibit, and was now winding up his discourse. "Nothing, sir, can be more foolish. You give up a flourishing estate, bright prospects—" "The leeches and solitude, the coolies and the lonely bungalow," I added. "Pshaw! what are these?" was the reply; "trifles not worth naming. You give up, I say, the prospect of a fortune, and for what? to edit a miserable newspaper that nobody reads." "It has four hundred and eighty-seven subscribers," said I, interrupting him,—for, where the honour of the *Ceylon Herald* was at stake, I thought myself bound to take up arms. "Four hundred fiddlesticks!" quoth my uncle, waxing wroth, as he tried to puff his cigar again; but the light had long been extinguished, and the attempt was vain. "Four hundred fiddlesticks! it's easy to make out a case." "And then, with management, I see no reason why we should not have seven hundred subscribers in a short time. They say the *Observer* has more," I added. "With *your* management and with *your* pen," said he, "it must be a thousand soon;" and there he paused. I puffed my cigar, sipped a little more brandy and water, smiled, and said nothing.

I had but just completed my nineteenth year, when I first landed in Ceylon. Two years of jungle life, spent in the management of a coffee-estate, had made me melancholy, moping, dull, a bookworm, and a man of reverie. I determined I would stand it no longer. I had before me an offer to undertake the editorship of the *Ceylon Herald*, at a small salary, it is true, but then the salary was to increase with the circulation. I was in all the budding glory of twenty-one, and I had made up my mind to try my hand at leading articles for the future, leaving coffee estates and coolies, bugs and bungalows, to the poor denizens of the forest.

My letters from the jungle had always appeared in conspicuous positions in the Colombo papers—the italics, the notes of admiration and exclamation, the dashes and the Greek and Latin quotations, always carefully attended to. My contributions were evidently valuable, why then should not my leading articles succeed? I knew a great deal about coffee, much about horseflesh, more about elephants, and most of all about cigars, and I saw no reason why I should not succeed. When I had altered the ode* of Horace to suit the colonial secretary and Ceylon, asking him, in elegant Latinity, why he hastened to destroy the island, by loving it too well, had not the joke called forth an angry correspondence between Philos and Milos, as to the authorship? Why, then, should I not succeed?

Such were the reflections that passed through my mind—such the questions I asked myself, when my uncle observed, "With *your* management and with *your* pen, the number of subscribers will soon be a thousand." "I do not see why it should not," I answered inwardly, but a smile was the only external evidence of the thought. "Dr. Tweezer," said I, "assures me that the coffee-mania cannot last much longer—that the days of its success will soon be ended—and that it would be folly to trust to it alone." "Dr Tweezer

* The eighth ode of the first book, commencing—

"Lydia, dic, per omnes
Te Deos oro, Sybarin cur properas amando
Perdere?" &c.

has his money largely embarked in sugar-planting," was my uncle's reply, "no wonder he distrusts coffee." "Well, but, my dear uncle," I observed, determined to put an end to this unpleasant scene by soothing him, "Mr. Pinto, the Portuguese agent, looked after the estate very well before I came; he can return to it now, and I will run up often, to see how he gets on." "Well, well, you are determined on it, I see," said the old man kindly, "and must have your way as usual. I wish you every success with the paper, my boy; and, between us, we must see that Pinto minds what he's about—he will be honest as long as he's well looked after." So saying, my uncle gave a final polish to his head with his handkerchief, and threw the end of his cigar into the fire.

The office of the *Ceylon Herald* was situated in one of the narrow streets of the Fort of Colombo, a street principally occupied by Portuguese shoemakers and tailors, and the junior officers of Her Majesty's hundred and forty-fourth, then quartered in Colombo. The floor and the roof were both constructed of red tiles; those beneath our feet flat for walking-on, those above us curved, in order to lap over each other and exclude the rain. A small verandah formed a kind of vestibule to the office, the roof being supported by rude wooden pillars, once painted, although what colour they *had* been painted it would not be easy to discover by examining them. Of the large room which formed the front of the house, opening out on the verandah, a portion near the window was screened off to form the sacred chamber of the editor, whilst the part near the door, which was always open, was allotted to the solitary clerk who received the advertisements, watched their insertion, computed their cost, and made out the bills. In the adjoining chamber stood the type-cases of the compositors, so that the editor had but to pass from his little screened-off chamber into the adjoining room to discover his editorials cut up into convenient lengths, and being "done into" print by the swarthy fingers of Portuguese and Singhalese compositors. Over these reigned the head printer, Don Gonzalez Antonio de Perez, a Portuguese descendant, as black and ugly as the swarthiest borderer on Lake Tschad, in the centre of Africa.

I never knew the real name of Mr. Perez, as we called him, until he laid a note on my table one day, asking whether he, "Mr. Don Gonzalez Antonio De Perez," might have "the supreme felicity and honour" of seeing me, "when he consummated his nuptials with Miss Felicia Maria St. Anna Hernandez," as he expressed it.

Mr. Perez, I say, was the presiding genius of the dining-room; that is, of what had been the dining-room, but was now the compositors' office. In shirt-sleeves rolled up to the shoulder, revealing two slender black arms, and in pantaloons once white, did Mr. Perez administer rebuke and commendation as he listed to those beneath him. He prided himself on his knowledge of English, which, however, he spoke after the Portuguese fashion—he had been reading and misunderstanding Carlyle, and prided himself on being one of those intensely earnest, practical men, who cannot understand a joke, and who talk of their "mission." Of voluble tongue, fluent in English, in Portuguese, in Singhalese, he talked and worked incessantly, never for a moment idle, never for a moment at rest. An invaluable man under the circumstances, but obstinate as a donkey.

The compositors' office opened into a paved yard behind, in the centre of which stood a melancholy-looking jack-fruit tree, with a few dark, scanty leaves adorning its branches; so little green, so much black, about its trunk and limbs, that one might almost conclude at a glance it had been nourished with ink instead of water. In an apartment of the back premises, which had once been a kitchen, stood the printing-press, doubtless of a similar form to that which William Caxton, of venerable memory, had used when he set up his marvellous engine in Westminster, "hard by the cathedral," so clumsy, so awkward in its wooden massiveness, did it appear.

Brushes and buckets; piles of paper and of papers; dark, ink-bespattered boys, looking forward to a future intimately connected with the composing-stick, and two or three lazy, lounging Singhalese messengers, completed the furniture, animate and inanimate, of the *Ceylon Herald* office.

Totally ignorant of the mysteries of printing—innocent of the difference between a composing-stick and a galley, between Great Primer type and Diamond—I seated myself at the little table in the mysterious office, sole manager and director, editor, corrector of the press, accountant, cashier, treasurer, and letter-writer, of the newspaper and of the printing office.

When men take upon themselves employments and responsibilities, of the very nature of which they are ignorant, says some cynical critic (determined to put down this loose system of writing, these random sketches without statistics), they may expect to fail—no other result can be anticipated. Quite correct, O critic!—but, as applied to the present instance, altogether wrong; for, though I made many blunders—ridiculous blunders some of them—displayed much ignorance, and endured much sarcasm from the better-appointed *Observer*, I did *not* fail. The exception proves the rule, argues the critic, and thus we are both satisfied.

Fortunately, the paper was published but twice a-week, so that I had ample time to write leaders and correct the proof-sheets, to write letters to myself and answer them in the editorial columns, to note down answers to imaginary corespondents in my liveliest vein, and to go through all the other business of the editor of a "pushing" colonial newspaper. I have still, however, the liveliest recollection of the arduous labour involved in the correction of the press, of the way in which I was interrupted, in the midst of my profoundest articles, by the incessant talking of Mr. Perez, and the loud tones in which he reproved the habitual laziness of "black men," as he was fond of calling the Singhalese. The Portuguese descendants fared better at his hands — his heart, which opened to a pair of pantaloons, was cold as ice to the camboy.*

"Mr. Perez," said I, calling him one day, when I had been elaborating a would-be brilliant article on some local triviality, illustrated by quotations from Cicero and Bacon—"Mr. Perez, I really cannot get on, with the noise from the compositors' room. I have been obliged to lay down my pen twice," I continued—suiting the action to the word, and throwing the pen on the paper (I had cleaned it beforehand for the purpose)—"I have been obliged to lay down my pen twice in the course of this single

* The cloth wrapped round the legs of the Singhalese, like a scanty petticoat, is so called.

article, in consequence of the incessant loud talking."

"I shall see to him, saar," said Mr. Perez, showing his white teeth, in a condescending smile. "That new compositor, the Singhalese man, Hathacatarr, he's a plenty loud talker; he's a talker enough for twenty men. He doesn't understand when I go tell him, that's no way—work, I say, well first, talk after—but he's all the same as one lunatic, he hears, but does not see or comprehend."

And so saying, Mr. Perez returned to create more noise than ever. First, he attacked Hathacatarr in Singhalese, asking why he (Mr. Perez) and *his* office should be disgraced by a black jabberer who did not understand his work? A Portuguese compositor offered his opinion on the subject in choice Portuguese. Hathacatarr replied in Singhalese, and a countryman of his spoke in his defence; two new combatants joined in the war of words incontinently, and louder than ever rose the din and the confusion; whilst above all rang clearly the commanding voice of Mr. Perez, shouting, "Silence, saar!" to each in turn, without reference to distinction of race. Not only was my work put an end to, and an eloquent peroration nipped in the bud, in which "Justice and Truth, twin goddesses," were feelingly appealed to, but I felt convinced too that all work in the adjoining office was suspended for the time being. I, therefore, rose from my chair, coughed leisurely, walked slowly into the compositors' apartment, asked Mr. Perez whether the advertisement relative to the recent samples of coffee from Ruminacadde had been "set up" in fancy type, and walked about, when the question had been answered, looking particularly at nothing. The tumult was stilled, and did not break out again for a time; but I took care, for the future, to write my principal leading articles at home, and not to call Mr. Perez in, when I wanted to put an end to the noise in the compositors' room.

"What is this, Mr. Perez?" said I, as I made my way hurriedly into the office one day, shortly after my installation, and seated myself at my editorial desk. A "proof," or first copy in print, of an article written the preceding evening lay before me, and there was something really distressing in seeing my well-turned sentences (as I considered them) upset and made nonsense of, by ignorant and unskilful compositors. It is true the *Observer* had pointed out, the evening before, some unfortunate mistake I had made in writing about something I did not understand; my temper was slightly ruffled—but there was really enough in the document on the desk to make any man, however equable his temper, annoyed and irritable. Hence my question. I had commenced a leading article thus:—

"When Æsop described the countryman praying to Jove to help him out of his difficulty—a difficulty which the suppliant easily extricated himself from subsequently, by putting his shoulder to the wheel—the fabulist was but suggesting a truth of universal application; a great and important truth, too often lost sight of. The coffee-planters, who hold such angry meetings at Kandy, who memorialize a Parliament that cares nothing for them, and are then angry at not being heard, forget, it is to be feared, this old fable, with its wise, practical application. Sympathizing, as we do, with the feelings produced by the injustice which has been done them," &c., &c.

Such were the sentences which I wrote: the printer's version of them was as follows:—

"Vihen 8soqs desunvi*d* the çum!vqum ?vaqung !o Foue !o helh hun ont o† tus biffunl!q —x diffunlhq mhicl the xupp*l*uonh uxily in!vua!ed humulf fu*m* xubseynmtly, ly p*u*ttiny tus s?onl*d*e* to the *m*lul. He †alm?xt mus lmt xuqqextmq, a tmnth of mnusal app!ica?nm—x qme! nud im&or!ant tunth tu o†!m lunt xqht of. &e coffee-ptanters mho hotb x*u*cb auqnj mutinys ot Kandy, mho numoria!ze a Pavliamuit thot cums mtbinj fm them, &, me thum auqrj at mt bmy he*a*nl, forje!. I is to lu jeareb, thm il*d* juble *w*it& iti mixe prac!icab appzcalim. 9ympattuzmj us me do mit2 !he f*u*lmjs probmud by the *m*justme whic† &ax bun dun thun," &c., &c.

"What is this, Mr. Perez?" I naturally asked, as I perused the above unintelligible document. Mr. Perez showed his teeth, according to his wont—as fine a set of white teeth, I will venture to assert, as any to be found out of Africa—and peering at the proof, shook his head reprovingly.

"Plenty bad work this," said he, at length; "that Hathacatarr doesn't know he's business

—idle man, too, plenty idle—pah! Singhalese; what you expect, saar? These black men have no mission, and so they don't fulfil none."

"Well, but," I replied, with all the quiet composure I could summon, "if Hathacatarr composes in this style, the sooner his place is better filled the better for all of us. Let him put up the large type advertisements, not my editorials, for the future."

"I am in the look-out for a good, earnest man, saar," was Mr. Perez' reply; "a Portuguese man that knows he's mission. I will let you know plenty soon, when I have catched him. That Mr. Fonseca" (the clerk) "hire Hathacatarr; but what he can know? Mr. Fonseca don't understand a galley from a printing-press." The concluding sentence was uttered in a low voice, for Mr. Fonseca was within hearing of loud conversation; Mr. Perez concluded with a subdued laugh, smothered in his throat, which showed the brilliant teeth more alarmingly than ever. "Send Hathacatarr to me," said I to him, as he retired, whilst I retained the proof.

Hathacatarr, a mild-looking Singhalese, of small size, with spectacles on nose, and a comb, of larger dimensions than usual, projecting four inches above his head, soon made his appearance, ready to enter upon a voluble explanation. "Is that your proof, Hathacatarr?" I asked, in Singhalese.

"Yees, zurr," he commenced, in reply, for he disdained the vernacular, and *would* speak English, though he could not understand all that was said to him in that language; "yees, zurr; him is mine. I tell every thing to you, zurr. Mr. Perez, zurr, he hate me all the same as one big snake. Why? because I tell him truth, I no tell lies. He make de boy Rickawille 'tribute (distribute*) all my type when I go home plenty early yesterday, with Mr. Fonseca's leave. Every body know, zurr, Rickawille not know him business yet. Him put *d*'s in the hole for *b*'s and *g*'s for *q*'s, and he make all tubsy-turby—I not know where get one letter when I want him. I put my finger in for one *a*, and I get one *x*; I want *t*, I get the note for tara-tara-mation (admiration). How I do well, zurr? You tell Mr. Perez let me 'tribute my

* To *distribute* the type, is to put each letter back into its own compartment in the compositor's tray, or "case," after it has been used.

type, no let de boy Rickawille touch my box, and I do plenty good."

Such were the difficulties of newspaper editing in Colombo at the time of which I write; every line had to be inspected by myself—advertisements, domestic occurrences, local reports, editorials, all—before the broad sheet was issued to the public eye. I had to see that the ship which indicated a shipping advertisement, (and served besides to fill up the advertisement columns)—the horse which pranced before the notice of a sale of Arabs, mules, or donkeys—the house which smoked, European like, above the few lines that indicated that a bungalow was to be let or sold, were all in their proper places, not turned upside down, or put in wrong places, a horse substituted, for instance, for a ship, or a house for a horse. Everything demanded the editor's eye —he was responsible for all—and it, therefore, may be easily conceived that his situation was by no means a sinecure.

The arrival and departure of the English mails were, like picking time on the coffee estates, the great seasons of bustle and activity in our little office.

The getting of the English papers on the arrival of the mail was by no means an easy matter. The clerks from the respective offices were first dispatched to the little post-office window, behind which the Post-Master-General himself laboured, like a little Hercules, at unwieldy bags of newspapers and letters; whilst his assistants, Europeans, native Portuguese and Singhalese, broke open boxes with praiseworthy diligence, and scattered their contents about the floor. Great was the commotion within, copious the perspiration, numerous the ejaculations—but far greater was the excitement, the commotion, the pushing and the crushing, the exclamation and the heat, without.

"I really cannot do more than I am doing, gentlemen," urged the post-master, his countenance burning in a fiery glow, that illumined his fine Roman nose like a coat of scarlet. "I really cannot do more than I am doing, gentlemen. Every one will get what he wants ultimately, if you have but a little patience, but things must take their ordinary course" —that ordinary course apparently being that all the letters and papers, as soon as they arrived, should be strewn about the floor and on the tables of the post-office in much-abused confusion. Outside the little window, anxious faces, with and without spectacles, peer eagerly into the *sanctum*, as if desirous of recognizing their property amid a thousand others. The aide-de-camp of the governor swears terribly because he is kept waiting for his own and the governor's letters and newspapers—the clerks from the various offices more mildly discuss the chances of a speedy departure in English, in Portuguese, and in Singhalese—the two newspaper editors, having hastened to the assistance of their clerks, drawn to the post-office by the delay, stand, most eager and most anxious, side by side, the *Observer* and the *Herald*, the *Herald* and the *Observer* in friendly rivalry, polite and affable to each other, strange though it may appear, yet each intensely desirous of receiving his papers and having his *Extraordinary* first out—joking the while, notwithstanding, at the scene and at the actors in it.

"Hot work," observes the *Observer*, as he casts an anxious glance into the mysterious chamber, vainly essaying to catch the post-master's eye, and with a glance assure him that old animosities, for the time being, are ended. "The newspapers certainly ought to be supplied first," replies the *Herald*, "because they are supplied *pro bono publico*."

"I really cannot do more than I am doing, gentlemen," replies the post-master, groaning. He is a public functionary peculiarly assailable by the press, and the *Herald* has been regarded for years as the government paper, on the strength of having once, in times gone by, borrowed a printing press from the government establishment. "The governor is waiting for his dispatches," growls the aide-de-camp, as he flattens his nose against the wooden frame of the open window, the words booming distinctly into the busy chamber. "No one is more anxious that the governor should have his dispatches at the earliest moment than I am, Mr. Tallboys," is the post-master's reply.

At length the desired newspapers are found; *Observer* and *Herald* are supplied simultaneously, that there may be no imputation of unfair play or of favouritism. With Chinese umbrellas (made of paper, and flat on the top, as figured on tea-chests) over their heads, the editors march through the sun to their respective offices, and then great is the excitement, and the activity of every individual in those offices. Mr. Perez has been ten times outside the verandah to see if Mr. Fonseca or myself be visible with the important papers. The *Monthly Times*—a summary of the European intelligence brought by the mail, and published in London for Indian subscribers—is at once opened. The "general summary" is cut up into convenient lengths for the compositors, and, in three minutes, Hathacatarr and his fellow-workmen are busily employed in putting the letters into words, the words into sentences, the sentences into columns, and the columns into the printing-press, whilst the editor runs hurriedly over another copy of the *Monthly Times*, to collect, as he calls it, the "cream" of the intelligence, and to give it, as a summary of his own, at the head of his *Extraordinary*, aware that in a few minutes long strips of almost unintelligible English will be crowding his desk awaiting correction, for he must examine every letter, inspect every figure, watch every comma, ere the hungry public can have this monthly feed of English news.

Mr. Perez, in his domain, exhorts his men to activity with many words, working the while himself without intermission. The honour of the *Herald* office is at stake, and Mr. Perez hates the *Observer* with a deadly hatred, so that he spares neither entreaty nor commendation, that the work may be done speedily and well. Even the Singhalese are praised by him for the nonce, and he is ready to declare that, so far as he can judge, Hathacatarr actually *has* discovered his mission, and is f'lfilling it. Nor is Mr. Fonseca idle—the covers of the newspapers to be posted are his charge, and he has them before him directed and pasted, ready for lapping around the expected *Extraordinary*—he is even ready to condescend to the working of the printing-press, rather than the sheet should be delayed, for he too has been for years in the *Herald* office, and its honour is dear to him.

Column after column is taken corrected, from the editor's desk to the compositor's room, to have the errors removed, and so the work grows under our hands into a goodly little sheet of six columns; we *have* aspired to eight, but it was under *very* favourable circumstances—these six columns containing the intelligence most desired in Ceylon, a brief summary of political news, a fuller digest of colonial matters or deliberations affecting the colonial interest generally, commercial items, particularly the prices of coffee, sugar, and cinnamon in the home market, and the extent of the sales effected, together with a list of the ships which had arrived in England from the island and those which had sailed for Ceylon. These, with an odd scrap of Indian news here and there, put in to fill up a corner or complete a column, and intended originally for our next regular issue of the *Herald*, complete the *Extraordinary*, which Mr. Fonseca distributes by messengers over Colombo, and by the post throughout the island. "Run over to the *Observer* office," shouts out Mr. Perez to one of his devils, "and see whether his *Extraordinary* is out, and what time he got done, if he is out." Away goes the boy, his ink-bespattered appearance telling of the printing-office in unmistakeable terms, and gets the desired information readily and truly, for courtesy prevails in both offices, and an emissary from either is well received in the camp of the enemy. The subordinates know that the editors shake hands when they meet —nay, that they dine with each other sometimes—and they, therefore, regard it as their duty to emulate this fraternal feeling.

The extra duty imposed upon the editor, however, by the arrival of the English mail did not end here. Leading articles were to be written on colonial topics of interest—speculations were to be indulged in of good or evil fortune, and hopes raised or warnings reiterated in consequence. Files of papers were to be searched for articles referred to in the *Monthly Times*, which merely gleaned the chief items of news for us, and directed us to the rest. Columns of the London daily papers were to be run carefully over with the fingers, pencil in hand, to extract a few lines from some debate, relative to Ceylon—how Mr. Stick had laid a petition from the coffee-planters upon the table of the house, and had then resumed his seat—how Mr. Stick had said nothing, or, if he did, how, what he said was inaudible in the reporters' gallery. Such a notice served for the foundation of an indignant comment, as to the way in which colonial affairs were neglected by the British parliament—a comment palatable to men, with irritated feelings, who had lost their fortunes in an artificial undertaking, fostered by one set of legal enactments, and overthrown by another.

Nor was the period of the departure of the English mail less bustling and noisy in our little office; we, too, had our *Overland Summary* to dispatch to subscribers in England, containing the editorials which we most prized—the local items considered of most importance—the commercial, the domestic, and the shipping news. A busy and a bustling time that in which this *Summary* was "got out;" for whilst, on the one hand, we did not wish "to go to press" a moment too soon, we must not, on the other, run a risk of losing the mail. This *Summary* was, for the most part, ordered by English residents in the island to be sent to their European friends—some minute-typed domestic occurrence or shipping announcement, intended to catch the eye of friends and relations left behind in the loved "home"—a few lines, to the rest of the world nothing, to the little circle for which they were intended of the utmost interest and importance. Not a paper published anywhere but contains many such notices, brief records of the joys and sorrows of a few, unheeded or unread by the many!

CHAPTER II.

THE EDITOR'S HOLIDAY.

My previous residence in the jungle had made me passionately fond of jungle sports. The chase of the elephant, the leopard, the elk, and the deer, were physical excitements craved earnestly for, amidst the mental wear and tear of editorial life; nor was I altogether excluded from such.

At the time of which I write, Captain Lister, of the Ceylon Rifles, was one of the finest sportsmen in the island; and having made acquaintance, nay, contracted a friendship with him, during my residence in the forest, I maintained that acquaintanceship and friendship uninterrupted during the period of my editorial labours. When a friend, whose discretion might be relied upon, could be procured for the purpose, and induced to look after the details of the office; when no English mail was expected to arrive or depart for some time—no stirring news anticipated; I would leave the requisite amount of leading articles in the hands of the aforesaid convenient friend, and start for the jungle, to enjoy a few days' sport with Captain Lister. The *Herald* was published on Tuesdays and Fridays, so that, starting early on a fine moonlight Tuesday night from Colombo on my own steed, with two fresh horses, hired or borrowed, at convenient stages on the road, and a pony awaiting me from the estate in Kandy, I could reach Ruminacudde by midday on Wednesday—not without laborious exertion, not without having undertaken and accomplished a long and harassing ride; but my apprenticeship in the jungle had fitted me for such work.

Casting, then, proofs and broadsheets, editorial squabbles, and complaining correspondents, to the winds on such occasions, I gave Uncle Toby (my black Arab) the rein, rode merrily through the intricate covered-ways and over the drawbridges of the German-looking old fort, leaving its frowning battlements behind me; and, ere the town subscribers of the *Herald* had received their copies of the paper, all steaming from the press and redolent of the office, its editor was miles away on the road to Kandy. Uncle Toby snorted approvingly as he felt that he might stretch out at his own convenient pace, a cloud of dust rising behind him at every footfall, to be silvered over by the moon's rays ere it fell to the earth again; and every native that we met, hurrying home to his palm-leaf hut, looking upon the horse as mad, and his rider still more so, as we scampered past them. The bounding elasticity of such exercise, when one was in light convenient jungle costume, the joyous animation of the tramping canter, the beautiful scenes that burst continually on the view—were all elements in one's condition at the moment that rendered it enviable. It is doubtful, I think, whether the most thrilling triumphs of civilized life yield more pure and unsullied enjoyment to the triumpher than such a ride to the active energetic youth, known to his horse and his horse to him, as he goes "tramp, tramp, along the ground."

Nor must the rest at the half-way inn be forgotten; the throwing one's self from the smoking steed; the stiff scrambling to the door; the answer of the expectant servant; the neat supper, appetizingly laid out in a room opening on the verandah, from which the moon's rays rush in like a flood of silver; the contemplative cigar, and much-relished glass of brandy and water, cold and refreshing, —with which the repast is ended—are all elements of joy, under such circumstances, which the memory in subsequent years will not let fade. But the fresh horse is already at the door, his trappings gleaming in the moonbeams, as the servant walks him up and down—he champing the bit the while, impatient to be off. An hour has already glided away since the inn was reached—an hour of the purest physical enjoyment, and leaping from the chair, the foot is in the stirrup in a moment, the saddle obtained; a kindly word, and to him of more value, a kindly rupee, thrown to the groom, and with firm hand and knee, the traveller is already wending his way in bounding semicircles up the hill's side, now lost in the shade of the overhanging trees, now glistening in the moonbeams, until, a bend in the road attained, the comfortable inn is lost to sight.

But is there no danger in such a moonlight ride—a ride at the very dead of night, through such wild districts?—asks some fair and interested reader. None to the bold rider, believe me, fair lady. The elephants will get out of the way the moment they hear you coming; they have no affection for horses. The hoofs of your steed talk roundly to the stones, waking the distant echoes; the serpents hear the sound, and will be gone. The wild leopard will seek no encounter with a brave horse and fearless rider, armed though they be with hard hoofs and a riding whip only. But there must be no hesitation, no brooding fears, no halting to look hither or thither, no seeing of eyes ahead glistening under a dark bush. Such eyes there may be, but you must dash on, never heeding. Their cowardly owner will slink, as befits him, into darkness, as you approach, leaving the field to light and you. Your horse may be timid; he must be urged on. He may refuse to advance—it is but a moment of doubt—the whip and the spur are cogent counsellors, and he must on. There is something fearful before him, to judge by his cocked ears, and elevated head, and snorting nose, but there are the whip and the spurs behind, which he dreads more, and there is a cheerful voice around him that encourages him, with its "Heigh, Toby! well, Robin! what's the matter now? On, boy, on!" He knows the sound well, and has confidence in it; his ears are already placed flat upon his neck; he *will* have a charge at it, snake or leopard, and the resolution is no sooner formed than the danger has vanished.

But the natives. Pooh! I had forgotten them. No Englishman anticipates harm from *them* for a moment. No Englishman above five feet high, who has an Englishman's heart between his ribs, and is not to be frightened at shadows!

I have ridden over this wild mountain's road repeatedly by moonlight—ridden continually, without a stoppage of more than an hour's duration,—sometimes from five in the evening till seven or eight o'clock the next morning, and never met with the slightest accident. "Tempting Providence" it may be, as you say, good old lady, and as more than one old woman, of either sex, has said before you; but, believe me, Providence aids those who thus tempt it, or rather boldly and honestly confide in the powers with which a man and a horse have been endowed doubtless for their mutual protection and advantage. I never met with an accident, I have said,—scarcely even with an approach to such. The nearest approach to an accident was the following:—

I had been riding by moonlight, as usual. I loved to feel the fresh cool air of a tropical night fanning my cheek and whispering of temperate climates. I loved to see the varied rays of the moon glancing on the thick foliage, and on the jutting rocks, throwing the dark shadows into the form of huge caverns and unearthly monsters. Indeed, it is only under such circumstances that the full beauty of the road from Colombo to Kandy can be realized, and its infinite variety of aspect discovered.

I had reached a rest-house, or government inn, near Kadduganava, being more than ordinarily weary on the occasion, for my horse from Ambepusse—the half-way house—had been a difficult one to manage; timid and fond of shying, he required the firmest management, the most determined exercise of authority, to prevent his turning round and retracing his steps. I threw myself into a chair to rest, delighted that I had got rid of my unpleasant steed, and that a fresh one was ready to carry me into Kandy. A bed stood in the room right in front of me—a large four-posted bed, without curtains or musquito net, without ornament or elegance of any kind—altogether as uncomfortable a looking object as one could well discover anywhere. It was nothing, in fact, but a large bedstead in the middle of the room, with a hard mattrass on it, over which was thrown a sheet that covered both mattrass and pillow. Tired and almost worn out as I was, however, I looked upon the bed as a luxury, and rising from my chair conveyed myself stiffly into the inner room, and threw myself into a horizontal attitude on the mattrass—my head resting, as usual, on the pillow, my spurs projecting below the mattrass, and my cigar, as usual also with coffee-planters, between my lips.

I had not been so lying for more than a minute, when I thought I felt the pillow particularly uncomfortable. Hard it was, of course—for that I was prepared; but for an uneasy oscillating motion which I thought I felt in it, I was not prepared. Deep in the midst of a thundering reply which I was contemplating to some article of the *Observer*, however, I did not heed the strange movement at first, merely pushing my head back more imperiously, and knocking the pillow impatiently, as it were, into its place.

The uneasy oscillating motion continued, however, nay, became still more perceptible. Strange, thought I, as I sat up and tossed the pillow over on the bed beside me, to discover the cause. The cause was apparent in a moment. Feeble as the light given by the oil lamp standing in the corner of the room was, I could plainly discern a dark lengthened object, curled up for the most part, but just beginning to untwist itself and raise its head—altogether as disgusting and slimy-looking a detestable reptile as one could well see anywhere, and if out of place anywhere, certainly out of place when under one's pillow! It was a snake, with a small deadly-looking head, two cold glassy eyes shining in vivid contrast to the dun brown body—a snake, gradually increasing in thickness from the head towards the centre of its body, and tapering off again towards its tail.

The forked tongue played incessantly, like the feelers of an insect, over the nose and upper jaw—the head was being elevated rapidly—not a moment was to be lost, for the first glance assured me it was a tic-polonga—one of the deadliest of serpents.

To leap from the bed with one bound into the middle of the room was the work of an instant. The stiffness I had felt on jumping from my horse had marvellously disappeared—I felt it no longer. The disturbed reptile, annoyed first at the unwonted pressure of my head, and afterwards still more annoyed at the removal of its warm and convenient covering, stood erect at the bed's head, half its length perpendicularly elevated, whilst the rest remained coiled upon the mattrass—the forked tongue playing more rapidly than ever—the diminutive, sharp-pointed head, oscillating gently backwards and forwards as if undecided as to what should be attacked—the cold glassy eyes peering after me, as I grasped a bar of wood with which the door was usually fastened within, calling loudly for my servant the while as I did so. But Nogo was busily engaged at the moment discussing a delicious meal of rice and curry, and found it convenient not to hear me.

I brought the bar down with all my force upon the venomous reptile, still standing in the attitude of attack as it had been. I brought the bar down, and left it there to see the effect of the blow, for to have elevated it again, without due caution, might have been dangerous, inasmuch as the snake might possibly have been raised with it, and have dropped upon my head—anything but a comfortable position for either of us.

The blow had inflicted much injury on the enemy, but he was not dead. His head now made its appearance between the wooden bars of the bed which served as a rail to support the pillows—the body, bruised and injured, was rapidly following. I seized the wooden bar again, and elevated it aloft ready to strike another blow, but found no opportunity.

Twisting and twining its body about between the rails, the reptile, bent on retreat, not on attack, made its way in a moment under the mattrass.

With the wooden bar still elevated, I meditated what was next to be done, standing near the door, and being ready to make my exit, in case the adversary charged. I stooped to have a look under the bed for him, but he was not to be seen. The big round drops were coursing each other down my cheeks with the excitement and the exercise.

"Let them kill their own snakes," said I, indignantly, throwing down the bar and shutting the door as I left the room—"why should I give myself any trouble about it? It's a Quixotic idea to suppose I am to kill all the snakes I see;" and so saying, I threw myself into the uneasy chair I had left to occupy the bed, and diligently proceeded to mop up the big round drops which were making their way down my neck.

"Mahathma," (Sir) said Nogo, coming in a few minutes after.

"Well?" said I, inquiringly.

"Did not Mahathma call?" asked the lazy

inquisitive fellow, his mouth still redolent of rice and fish curry, as he drew his once white sleeve across it.

"Did not Mahathma call?"

"I did," said I, "but that was some time ago, Nogo. I don't want you now."

The fellow's curiosity prompted his question, and I was determined to disappoint it, for, like all indolent do-nothings, Nogo was a very prey to petty curiosity. Having taken a survey of the room, and seeing that I had shut the bed-room door, Nogo retired, baffled, and, I have no doubt, annoyed at my incommunicativeness.

I rested an hour at the inn, as usual, sipping a little brandy and water, and enjoying a contemplative cigar, whilst I kept a sharp look-out in the neighbourhood of the closed door, lest my adversary should steal a march on me by making his way beneath it. The article intended to demolish the *Observer* was forgotten, or left half-finished, and to this day it probably floats in the limbo of half-developed schemes and unfinished projects, wherever that may be. If there be such a limbo, it must be a well-filled one, supposing that there be any bounds to it at all. There, doubtless, floats that half-concocted article, with those delicious air-castles, and châteaux en Espagne, which the dreamy and the imaginative love to build, and which are wafted off as soon as built to the aforesaid limbo.

Before I left the rest-house at Kadduganava, I opened the door of the bed-room cautiously. My adversary was still invisible. I called Nogo—this time he came at once, for the rice and curry had long been finished. He went boldly into the chamber—the tossed-over pillow and the disarranged bed and the wooden bar all arresting his attention at once, making him open both eyes and mouth to their utmost extent, anxious to hear the cause.

"Nogo," said I, "there is a tic-polonga in that bed."

"A tic-polonga!" cried Nogo, jumping rapidly back towards the door, and rubbing his leg as if he already felt the reptile winding round it. "A tic-polonga, Mahathma,—dead?"

"No, not dead," said I; "you had better tell the rest-house keeper, before we go."

So saying, I resumed my gloves, put my pith hat upon my head, and, making my way to the door, was, in a few minutes, on the road to Kandy, the tic-polonga forgotten, the beauty of the scene around alone thought of, as valley after valley opened up to view, until the river —the Mahavelle—was visible, winding, silvered with the moonbeams, round the mountain's base; its beautiful suspension-bridge of satin-wood* forming a picturesque object in the scene.

* Satin-wood, not sandal-wood, as I accidentally wrote it in "Forest Life."

CHAPTER III.

JUNGLE ACCIDENTS.

Arrived on one of these holiday trips at the estate near Ruminacadde, of which I was still part proprietor, I expected to find Captain Lister awaiting me. He had promised to be at the bungalow on Monday night or Tuesday morning at furthest, and this was Wednesday—mid-day on Wednesday, and he had not made his appearance, nor had Mr. Pinto heard anything of him. I was astonished at this, for Lister generally kept his sporting and dinner appointments, whatever others he might have neglected. I was too tired, however, to give myself much concern about the matter, and having enjoyed a substantial repast, I threw myself on a bed, and was soon fast asleep.

In the evening, Marandhan, a native chief

who had been an intimate friend of mine when I resided in the jungle, rode over to spend a few hours with me. Our friendship had continued unabated from the time that I first arrived in Ruminacadde. I felt more and more respect for my Kandian friend, the more intimately I had become acquainted with him, and few pleasures enjoyed in Ceylon were more pure and unalloyed than those happy conversations in which I listened eagerly to his impressions of men and things; impressions received from a point of view so different from that whence I regarded the same objects. He would point out the hollowness of much that appeared outwardly honest and upright, but only so appeared because conventionalism had clothed it in its own robes, hiding the inward deformity with an external coating of proprieties that concealed, but could not remove, the heart-rottenness within.

He was a faithful counsellor too! that rarest and most invaluable of acquisitions. When other "friends" approved of all I had said, and assured me the *Observer* was quite wrong, Marandhan would often convince me that ignorance alone prevented my seeing the object in its true light; that the *Observer* was but denouncing abuses actually existing; that the remarks of the *Herald*, however right and true, abstractedly considered, were not quite applicable to the circumstances of the case; that, in fact, the government required rough handling to prevent excessive supineness and superciliousness; that a case must necessarily be overstated by those who feel an injury or endure an injustice, and that they are not to be blamed for the strength of their language under such circumstances, as long as facts are not distorted or misstated.

True, at the time, I regarded such lectures as the result of a radical bias, but I felt that they were valuable notwithstanding, as showing the impressions made upon an honest, truthful, ardent soul, who desired only the welfare of his country in all candid sincerity.

Next morning, Thursday, I strolled over the estate with Mr. Pinto, our superintendent, combining business and pleasure by inspecting the premises and popping at the birds which presented themselves as we proceeded, wondering all the while where Lister was, and why

I had neither heard nor seen anything of him. When the dinner hour drew near, however, whilst I was sitting in the verandah that overlooked the road to the bungalow, inspecting some accounts, I saw, to my great satisfaction, the portly figure of the mighty hunter making its way on his good steed *Robin* up the hill, both horse and rider travel-stained and weary-looking. "If you have a spark of friendship for me, my friend," said he, as he drew near, "let not dinner be delayed a moment. It's near the time, is it not?"

It was some time since I had seen Captain Lister, but it was evident he was still the same—dinner and elephants his prevailing tastes, the great objects of his attention. The shining glow which suffused his countenance was with him but an everyday affair: a glow to be seen there, whether he was scouring the forests for the haunts of its wild denizens, or reposing in quiet at home experimentalizing in sauces. He lived in a perpetual thaw—the oiliest of men. His light thin hair hung as of old, in a straight lock over either ear, giving, with the almost imperceptible whisker, the appearance of extreme juvenility to a frame which in other respects spoke roundly of man's prime, and of a rapid advance towards "the sere and yellow leaf" of age.

In the course of the twenty years he had lived in Ceylon, he had brought down more than five hundred elephants,* and was fond of declaring that, owing to the tough beef and scraggy mutton of the island, he had not enjoyed in twenty years half that number of good dinners. Were it not for the sauces he had invented, his impression was, that his life would be unendurable.

When dinner had been concluded, and cool claret had warmed his heart a little, bringing forth its better feelings, and driving annoyance and chagrin into the back-ground, he set himself to give me an account of his adventures, with his usual honest vivacity and truthfulness:—

"I had been down to Giggagigge looking after some stores the general had ordered into

* To the uninitiated this may appear like exaggeration. It is not so. Major Rogers, of the Ceylon Rifles, in the course of his residence in the island, shot upwards of twelve hundred; he was the prince of elephant-hunters.

the interior," he began, "when I determined to meet you here for a week's shooting, as I could easily have a few days to myself in riding about the country. I ought to have been here on Monday; and this, if I do not mistake, is Thursday; the Tuesday and Wednesday have been spent as civilized man never spent a Tuesday and Wednesday before, and, as I humbly pray, I never may again. Thinking I should certainly be here on Monday night at furthest, and knowing you had sent word to Pinto to prepare for me, I laid in no great stock of anything for the journey, but merely put up half-a-dozen of beer, a bottle of claret, and a cold tongue for the day's provision. I never could take to that brandy and water some men are so fond of; it wants the soothing, fruity flavour of claret altogether; but then, as you know, I was never an epicure, so that my simplicity of taste need not astonish you, though you smile at it. Besides, water is a dangerous beverage in Ceylon, where so much that is unwholesome is to be met with; no man ought to tempt his fate by drinking it in any shape. Were I commander-in-chief, I should order a supply of beer to be provided for all marching regiments and every officer on detachment duty. I speak of the tropics only, of course—in cold and temperate climates, in Canada and the Cape, the water is excellent. If you newspaper editors would but leave squabbling with each other, and take up measures of social and political importance, some good might be done; but it's no use talking to you about it, I know; anything is considered good enough, now-a-days, for the soldier; the time was, when he had the best of everything.

"With a couple of coolies, my groom and faithful old Tom carrying a brace of rifles, I set out from Giggagigge, intending to take a snack in the middle of the day, when Robin was being rubbed down, and an occasional bottle of beer when I felt thirsty. Tom—don't you know Tom?—my Singhalese valet, that knows the 'sign' of an elephant as well as I do, and will tell you his height, age, and sex from a few yards' trace. His name was Tomalitiwagamahe; but I found that rather long, and he now answers to Tom, and likes it.

"I rode leisurely on, skirting the Knuckles,*

* A chain of hills in the neighbourhood of Kandy,

that Tom might keep up with me, expecting to meet with something on the way, and intending, if possible, to greet you with a haunch of venison on your arrival. But we must all submit to fate. By nine o'clock the sun was getting troublesome; and as we were in a nice shady place, I thought a little breakfast would be refreshing. Collins had brought up some fresh prawns the day before, from Colombo, and as I knew his cook would spoil them, and as he had overslept himself as usual, I took them with me, telling Tom to get the curry and rice ready, and to cool a bottle of beer, while I strolled into the jungle to look for something worthy of a shot. No jungle-cock, however, was to be met with, and not caring for anything else, I pocketed my disappointment, and returned to look for breakfast. On a nice little green mound, under a mangoe-tree, I sat down to await the curry and rice, a slice of tongue, and a bottle of beer.

"You know the long faces these horrid niggers put on them when they have made

so called by the planters of the neighbourhood. "A Knuckles brick" is Anglo-Ceylonese for a first-rate planter of the "fast" school.

you particularly uncomfortable by their stupidity. I saw at once, when Tom put the rice and curry appetizingly before me, that there was something wrong.

"'What's the matter?' I asked.

"'Master tell the butler at Giggagigge, to put up some spoons?' he asked, in reply.

"'I told him to put up all that was necessary. Any kind of one will do,' said I, benevolently extending my hand towards him, as the grateful flavour of the fresh prawn curry was borne full into my face by the morning breeze.

"'One spoon not got, sir,' was the reply.

"'Then what the ——' I was going to swear at him, but checking myself, and remembering that at best we are all but vanity, as somebody says, I merely asked him quietly how I was to eat the curry and rice!

"'Master not know?' he asked, scratching his woolly head, as the best of these savages will do when at a loss for an idea.

"'Give me a fork,' said I.

"He had but one, a two-pronged fork, unfortunately. I tried it in desperation; but to eat my rice and curry with that was to lose the finest part of the dish—the rich sauce and gravy which the prawns flavoured so well. Tom saw that I was gradually getting angry, for it was really enough to disturb the patience of a saint; and, jumping up as if a bright idea had just struck him, he returned, a moment or two afterwards, with the brass lid of my shaving-box, bright and clean. Men talk of there being few trials now-a-days in living in a tropical country like Ceylon. Fancy eating prawn curry with the lid of a shaving-box. Is that no trial? The very remembrance makes me almost sick. I must wash the thoughts of it down with the claret, if you'll get another bottle open, for this is empty. It has been too long at your end of the table to allow of its being otherwise.

"Breakfast done, Tom told me by way of consolation, after the mishaps of the meal, that a herd of elephants had passed the adjoining cottage, where he had cooked the curry, the night previously; and further, that they could not be far off, as they had evidently been going very slowly. I was delighted at the idea of a little sport after my misfortunes: I sent him and the coolies and the groom off before me as beaters, whilst Robin enjoyed a quiet graze near the cottage. The jungle grass was high and wiry, the bushes thick, and the pathway not very well defined—scarcely a path at all, indeed; so that I cannot say the tramp was a comfortable one. The hope of knocking a tusker over, however, will make a man go through much in the way of fatigue, so I trudged patiently on, keeping a sharp look-out and my gun ready. From the top of the tree into which one of the coolies had climbed, he sang out that he saw the herd, about twelve in number, a short distance to our left, so I turned that way, leaving the path, and making in the direction indicated. The short distance proved a difficult one to get over, such was the thick undergrowth of the forest. It was getting towards mid-day, I was astonished to find, before the vanguard informed us that they saw the herd in the jungle.

"I now prepared for operations. Taking Tom with me, I advanced near the herd, careful to keep the wind blowing from them to me, and sending off the groom and coolies to some distance in the opposite direction, so that by shouting, yelling, roaring, screaming, and all the other noises usual on the occasion, as well as by waving their long white wands, they might prevent the herd breaking off that way when I had succeeded in bringing one or two down. These arrangements hastily completed I crept stealthily round, in the fullest expectation of excellent sport. But what's that somebody says about disappointments? something about somebody baulking the best-laid plains, 'rough hew them how we may;' that's all I remember of it, but it's very apt, if I could only recollect the whole of it.

"The elephants, when I got near them, were playing in a sort of muddy pool in the jungle, the effluvium from which was by no means of the pleasantest. Not one of them had his head turned straight towards me, and as they were playing I could not get a fair chance, so I was obliged to creep further round; Tom and I still keeping behind the thick bushes and shrubs. Whether they heard us or not I cannot tell, but certain it is, the leader of them, a black-looking tusker, took a trunkful of the half-water, half mud, that was round him and discharged it right upon us with a mathematical accuracy that would have made him a lion in

Cambridge. We were bespattered amazingly, notwithstanding the thick bushes in front of us, and of all the horrible complications of vile smells that the most lively imagination ever conjured up, that which then covered us all over like a cloak, as Sancho said about sleep, was the most horrible and the most vile; I wanted to be revenged, but after this little *jeu-d'esprit*, the black fellow's trunk went incessantly for a few minutes, over his forehead, plastering it with mud and filth, and *into* the trunk I had no desire to fire.

"At length he put his proboscis down again to take up a fresh supply of the filthy lotion, and whilst he was doing so, I sent a ball into his forehead; an ounce of zinc was never sent more truly into an elephant's brain I felt convinced; yet, half imbedded as he was in the filthy marsh, it did not produce its ordinary effect, and I was deceived. He made a plunge to the right—a convulsive plunge—whilst the rest of the herd dispersed right and left, as if a mine had sprung up in their midst. Too impetuous, and afraid the ball had not told, I made a leap after the black monster, and sank knee-deep in as vile and disgusting a thick slough as could be found in or out of Ceylon; whilst, just as I got there, imbedded firm and fast, and sinking with accelerated velocity amid half-rotten creepers, and slimy black mud, down went the huge monster of an elephant within ten yards of me, down with a tremendous splash head foremost into a still softer place. Faugh! The recollection is horrible, it will take a tumbler of claret to clear my throat.

"Eyes, mouth, nose, and ears were drenched with the abominable slush, whilst I stood transfixed, imbedded, bemired, half dead, the gigantic monster in his dying struggles so bespattering and befouling me, that one might almost suppose his object was to make me a mountain of mud. To fire at him again with his tail towards me would have been wanton unmeaning cruelty, no fatal discharge was to be sent into him in that direction, whilst Tom had disappeared at the first rush of the herd, to look for the other coolies, and aid them in beating back the runaways.

"It's very easy to ask me why I did not get out, but it wasn't so easily done. Had I been a spare man like you, I should have sunk for ever in that ocean of abominations; my obesity, as you were once pleased to call it, was my salvation. At length my adversary, every whisk of whose tail sent a drop or two into my face, sank over on his side, motionless, dead; my whole thoughts were now occupied in considering how I should get out. Fortunately a fallen tree, extending from the firm bank into the middle of the slough, lay at no great distance; indeed, it was to jump upon it, in the hope of getting another shot at my foe, that I had made the *faux pas* which imbedded me. By herculean exertions I dragged myself to the fallen trunk, each leg sinking to the knee, and further, as the other was raised; and so half-floundering, half-wading through the mud and slime, I seized the stem, was upon it in a moment, and the next instant stood upon the firm bank beneath a *suria* tree. Nothing could be pleasanter than the feeling that I had found secure footing at last—I stamped and stamped again, delighted to find that I *could* stamp without sinking.

"My attention was then naturally drawn to the fallen foe who lay on his left side in the very middle of the quagmire, his tusks more than half imbedded, and the ample rotundity of his huge body standing prominently out of the slough like an old hut black with age. I had not the slightest intention of attempting to get out to him. I had had enough of the marsh, and my condition, as I then stood looking at him, hands, face, breast, body and legs coated with slimy filth, feelingly reminded me what the consequences of a second immersion would probably be; not even the thirty pounds at which I roughly valued his tusks, supposing them to be sound and good, could have induced me to tempt the slough of despond again 'You cheat me once, more fool you,' said the Highlander, 'you cheat me twice, more fool me;' and in my mind, there was much practical wisdom in Sawney's observation.

"There was nothing for it but to wait till I could get the aid of the coolies, and as I began to seek for them, I thought it strange that neither their cries nor the loud vociferations of Tom were at all audible. As to the herd, it had long been gone in various directions, nothing more to be heard or seen of it from where I stood. I resolved therefore to make my way to the cottage near which I had taken my breakfast, and in the neighbourhood of which Robin was still doubtless enjoying a quiet graze; but to find my way through the pathless forest was no joke. I searched for our trail of the morning, but soon lost it, in consequence of the elephant tracks which passed and repassed it. I stood still, quite at fault at length, and shouted as loudly as I could,—a few birds, terrified by the unwonted sounds, rose heavily from the trees, flapped their wings lazily, screamed, and disappeared; the echoes of the forest took up my shouts and repeated them again and again, more and more faintly, until at length they died away in the distance, and all was still again.

"I went on, determined to find some tree which would afford me a view of the country around; for, much as I hate climbing, I have often been obliged to have recourse to it. But no such tree was to be seen, none that afforded the slightest chance of an extensive prospect, so thick and burly was the foliage, so little open space was anywhere to be discovered.

"That forest appeared to me interminable as I trudged ever on and on in it, hour after hour, and monotonous as interminable. Not an animal was to be met with; my shouts, loud and long drawn, scared them from my path, save a few birds that screamed from the trees above as I drew near; vast stems, hollowed by time, threw out gigantic branches here and there, not far from the ground, causing me to stoop constantly as I made my way on, I knew not where; younger trees, with stout, well-knit trunks, telling of strength and durability, rose straight as pillars on every side, before and behind; no difference anywhere—trees, trees, trees, on the right hand and on the left, in the front and in the rear, and all so like each other, it was marvellous. It was as if magic were acting around me; and although I was constantly pushing on, it was only apparently to find myself at the end of each half-hour exactly in the place I had started from at its commencement.

"Yet it was not the huge hollowed trunks, nor the straight stems of the younger giants, nor the branches of either, that formed the greatest impediments to my advance. It was the thick brushwood, the interlacing creepers twining and intertwining themselves round everything, and stretching their long thin arms on every side looking for support; it was the long wiry grass too, with its saw-like edges, hurting the hands and the face as it touched them, that formed the chief difficulties of my progress. What hours those were! what hours of weary exertion, almost hopeless; of exhaustion, of gloomy anticipation, of real misery, and above all, and worse than all, of burning thirst! Externally I was a moving cake of mud and hardened slime, whilst through my clothes my body steamed like a dish of hot soup—internally dry, parched, thirst-consumed, altogether as miserable a specimen of humanity enjoying itself, as any race-course in England ever presented. The idea of passing the night in the jungle, was in itself sufficiently unpleasant; but the idea of passing a day and night without food, was infinitely more gloomy. I had brought but one bottle of beer with me from the morning's bivouac, and that had been finished before I reached the elephants, so that the prospect which was gradually opening before me,—however dense the jungle,—as I made my way on, hour after hour, was a dinner of foul water, and a bed on a branch of a tree, with a serpent or a leopard, perhaps, next door, that is, in the next tree.

"It is a long lane that has no end—a remark

strictly applicable to my then condition. As I walked on, keeping my gun under my arm, and a bright look out on every side, I came at length upon a path, a human path; I had met elephant tracks enough before, and you may fancy the delight with which I saw evidences of human feet on the dried leaves, and brown grass beneath me. It was not the path we had travelled in the morning, *that* I saw at a glance; but still it was a human path, and must therefore, as I concluded, lead somewhere. I followed it joyfully, and at length a little cottage opened to my view, coyly peeping through the palm trees that surrounded it, and which formed, as it were, land-marks of humanity.

"A few children were the first to recognize me; and having never seen a civilized man, bemired or unbemired, before, they screamed and shouted at the utmost pitch of their voices, immediately on perceiving me. Had my face retained its usual colour, I should have said, judging from the fright they exhibited, that they took me for one of those unnatural spirits of the nether world which their priests delineate on the walls of their temples, which ought to be black, but which by some strange mistake they always paint white.

"One does not like to be screamed and shouted at by children, and run away from, as though he were a wild beast; and although I was approaching the house in an excellent humour, delighted at finding a house at all, I felt my temper a little ruffled at the dismay exhibited by the children. The father advanced however, and with many salaams, expressed his willingness to be of any service he could to me. His professions and his civility chased away the chagrin which the conduct of his children had roused, and I spoke kindly to him in my best Singhalese.

"I went into the cottage and they brought me a native bed to sit upon, one of those execrable machines with coir-rope tied from side to side of the frame, and supported on four sticks at the corners. I sat down with pleasure, but the coir-rope on which I was seated—and which, hard and open-spaced as it was, was a delightful seat after the fatigues of my journey—gave way shortly after I had placed myself comfortably upon it, so that I was obliged to perch, bird fashion, upon the round stick which formed one of the sides—a stick about as thick as the round part of the stock of a gun.

There was nothing else to sit upon, so I was e'en obliged to be content; but I groaned as I thought of the tongue and beer that Tom had at the other cottage for me, and the remains of that delicious prawn curry too. I got some water, however, and there, in the presence of my host, his wife, his two grown-up daughters, and a host of naked little savages, I made my toilette in the best way I could. It was not my fault if they were lost to every sense of decency, and chose to inspect the process, nodding and grinning the while to each other without intermission.

"After my exertions and fatigue, it was but natural that I should feel hungry, and I consequently looked for something to eat; my inquiries on this head elicited the fact that rice and plantain-curry,* coffee and plantains, comprised the entire list of edibles in the house. Of the rice and curry my host assured me he had some already cooked of an exquisite flavour; and that it would take but a moment to heat it. I asked to see it. He produced a dirty brown earthenware pot, in which the appetizing

* The plaintain of the East, is the banana of the West, Indies.

banquet, as he seemed to consider it, was contained. His thumb was stuck into the midst of the rice, as he held the pot for my inspection. I shook my head, muttering a faint 'na, na;' he was astonished, his eye-brows gradually threatened the precincts of his hair, his mouth distended, it was evidently inexplicable to him that any man should be hungry and not eat what he had to present, so grateful and savoury a meal.

"At length, to render it more inviting, he thrust his left hand into the pot, opening his fingers, and so stirring up the mess, as one might run his fingers through his hair, exclaiming as he did so, 'Look, how nice it is, only cooked this morning—hungry, and can't eat *that!*' The means he took to render the dish more enticing but completed my disgust. It was some time before I succeeded in convincing him that it was no use to tempt me further. I then requested him to go out and look for my horse and servants, making him understand, after infinite talking, that I had a horse and servants near a cottage somewhere in the jungle, and telling him at the same time to let his wife or daughters prepare a little coffee for me, I intending to eat plantains with it.

"The man went out as I desired, but evening was already drawing near, and he did not feel disposed to wander far from his own abode, so that he soon returned, stating that neither horse nor servant, neither the cottage nor Tom was to be found. In the mean time I was enjoying my primitive meal of cold plaintains, and hot coffee; the plaintains were good enough, just ripe, rich, luscious, and sweet, and after dinner would have done admirably well to flavour a glass of claret; but the coffee! such coffee! ground into coarse lumps, blackened and burnt in the roasting, it had been boiled with the water as it was, no straining used, all the black abominations floating about in the thick, dark soup-like mess; floating about, and adhering too to the sides of the dish —and then the dish itself! it is wonderful how I ever got through that meal; the dish was of the common brown mud-like earthenware, its rim more than half an inch thick, without glazing of any kind, or even smoothness. From *such* a dish I had to drink *such* coffee! may I never have again to endure such a misfortune; may I never again have to live so like a savage as I did that night.

"The native bed, on which I had been first seated, had given way, as I told you, in the middle; that is, the coir ropes which formed its top, had broken as I sat on them. To remedy this, as I saw I must pass the night where I was, I tied a rope firmly backwards and forwards from side to side, from end to end, and on this rope so extended I had to lie all night. Sitting upon it was far from pleasant, lying was perfect torture, but I could not make up my mind to repose on the earthen floor as the family around me did, not knowing what insects and reptiles I might be plagued with during the night; misery acquaints a man with strange bedfellows, for even as it was, I did not wholly escape the attacks of ants, bugs, fleas, ticks and spiders; all these I discovered —how many more there were, invisible in the gloom of the flickering lamp, which I insisted should burn all night, I do not know.

"I spent that night in turning from side to side, from back to front,—at one time gazing at the palm-leaf ceiling above, black with soot and dirt, on which lizards and spiders were crawling about, at another inspecting the other inmates of the house. It was impossible to tell the moment at which one of the reptiles above might drop upon me, so I took care to keep my mouth shut. The man and his wife slept on my right, their mat stretched simply on the earthen floor, and there they snored in concert. The two grown-up daughters were similarly stretched on my left, on a mat almost worn out, their scanty drapery just covering their knees, whilst as delicately shaped feet and ancles reposed, unconscious of covering, upon the floor, as ever ascended the great staircase of Buckingham Palace, or the Tuileries. The little ones were crowded into a corner not far off, lying like so many young pigs, one with his hand on the breast of another, the other with his feet across the body of a third, mutually giving and receiving warmth, for they had no clothing or covering of any kind; nature, Sir, pure, simple, unadulterated, unsophisticated nature interesting to behold! A few simple cooking utensils reposed here and there upon the cottage floor in the most admired confusion. A heap of cocoa-nuts enveloped in their coir-husks was piled in one of the corners, whilst numerous branches of plaintains, hung from the roof above.

"Such was the scene around me that miserably long gloomy night! I had plenty of time to survey it; there is no fear of my forgetting it for years. The combined torture of the heat and the hard ropes on which I lay prevented sleep. Had I been as spare a man as you, I verily believe I should have been cut in two that night, or rather in four, for whilst one rope was insinuating itself into my shoulder and upper arm, as I turned, another was equally galling on my loins; a third threatened my thighs with amputation before morning, and a fourth alternately cut into the calf of my leg and my ancle as I changed my position, extending or drawing up my foot. It is a fine thing, however, to be able to bear the slings or arrows of outrageous fortune well, as somebody says somewhere. I have much to be grateful for in not being a grumbler.

"Next morning, as soon as day-light dawned, I sent off my host to make a fresh search in the jungle, whilst I tried to fortify myself against further troubles and misfortunes by a second edition of the execrable coffee and plantains. I was hungry, of course, but I thought it my duty to sustain my strength, in order that I might be the better able to endure; and, therefore, I ate and drank on principle—for is not man 'born to trouble as the sparks fly upward?' as the Apostle says; and why should we repine?

"I determined, in case Tom and the coolies should not be found before mid-day, to start for Giggagigge on foot—my host informing me it was about twelve miles off—for I concluded that Tom would lead my escort back there if he could not find me, and I hoped we might meet upon the road. Hour after hour passed away in almost intolerable anxiety. I sent out every one likely to be of the slightest use, not venturing forth myself, however, lest I should lose my way again in the jungle. At length, as I was making up my mind to try the road to Giggagigge, under the escort of my host's eldest daughter, I heard Tom's welcome voice in the jungle, approaching the house, led by the head of the reputable family with whom I had bivouacked the previous night.

"'Hallo!' I shouted, gladly.

"'Here, saar,' was Tom's reply, still invisible.

"'Have you got the tongue, and the claret, and the beer?' I asked, listening eagerly for the answer.

"'One bottle beer got, saar,' was Tom's reply.

"Even that was better than nothing; so, seizing it as Tom approached, I knocked off the neck, and drank it all foaming from the bottle. It was almost luke-warm; but how delicious it was, notwithstanding! And there stood my brave old Robin, glad to see his master again—it was truly a joyous *réunion.*

"I was astonished to find that I was now six miles from the little cottage near which I had taken breakfast the previous morning, and six miles, too, in the wrong direction, that is, lying far out of my route to Ruminacadde. When I got back to my previous morning's quarters, I found Tom had made comfortable arrangements for me to pass the night there. Sending off the coolies and groom for the tusks of the elephant I had shot, I made a delicious meal of the tongue, the remainder of the famous curry, the claret, and two bottles of beer—consuming, indeed, all the remainder of my provisions, for I intended to reach this early next day (yesterday).

"I had had no sleep the night before, so that, in my new quarters, I slept like a top, never opening my eyes till it was past seven o'clock—an hour one would consider early enough in England, but for a man travelling in a tropical forest, two hours too late at least. I had scarcely made my dispositions for the morning, determining to make one clean sweep of it without delay or interruption, regardless of sun or heat—determined, I say, to reach Ruminacadde without turning to the right hand or to the left—without delaying unnecessarily a moment; but you remember the old proverb about man supposing and God disposing. My evil star was still in the ascendant, and I was destined to more trials. They, doubtless, have their use, these trials; but, like many other useful medicines, are nauseous and unpleasant exceedingly.

"I set off with the intention of diligently eschewing elephants, deer, jungle-fowl, everything that could divert me from the road, impelled the rather thereto by the hunger and thirst which began to assail me, and which, bad anywhere, are doubly so in the tropics. About eleven, the thirst was unbearable, so I dismounted to get a draught of clear water at a spring on the hill's side, over which I was riding. Constitutionally, I dislike water as a drink, regarding it—I mean such as one gets in Ceylon—as being far from wholesome. There was still a glass or two of claret left in the bottle, so I filled it, to give the water a flavour, and then drank the contents. That finished, I strolled up to the top of the hill, trying to persuade myself that I did so to inspect the scenery, but really because I heard some elephant-calls coming from that quarter. We are such frail creatures at best! I only intended to have a look at them, but, when I saw them, I asked myself why my misfortunes of the previous day should not be revenged? How did I know but it was the very same herd that had been playing in the slough of abominations, of which my clothes still retained the odour.

"Thus it was that I reasoned myself into taking advantage of a favourable wind, making a detour round the hill's-side, loading my rifles with zinc, and telling Tom to keep up, whilst I made my way towards the herd. The road led us further round than I anticipated, and the herd seemed still at a distance, when one of them made his appearance suddenly on our right. I was not prepared for this; for, knowing that Robin was not to be depended upon, I had intended dismounting before I came up with them. Never had a horse a greater dread of elephants than he has—a fact scarcely to be wondered at, indeed, for he was, on more than one occasion, very near losing his life from them. No sooner, therefore, did he see the huge beast making his way towards us, and suddenly appearing in a sort of clearing to our right, than he threw up his heels briskly into the air, turned sharply round, and left me sitting on the ground. With the exception of a bruise a little—ahem—to the side of my hip, I was not hurt. Tom was near me. I jumped up at once. The elephant had apparently been as much scared by our apparition as Robin by his, and turning tail, was off in a moment, trumpeting forth his fears loudly to the others. Tom and I pursued, for our blood was up; and we thought neither of horse nor of coolies. I could not get a fair forehead aim at the monster, so I fired as he was abreast of me, hoping to penetrate to the heart behind the shoulder-blade as he stepped out; but it is not an easy shot that; and the want of breakfast, I suppose, had made my hand unsteady. I failed to bring him down, or even badly to disable him; and the rest of the herd, alarmed by his loud trumpeting and the report, were flying in all directions through the jungle.

"We pursued them, our blood roused with the sport, for a considerable time, but without success. I fired another long shot, which did not tell, and then gave up the chase as a bad job. Now, for the first time, I began to think of Robin. Tom knew as little of his whereabouts as I did. I hate walking in the jungle, as you know, and I had no intention whatever of losing my horse. When we had rejoined the coolies, one of them, who had been deputed to climb the hill and look after us, informed me that he had seen Robin scampering back in the direction we had come. I felt tired, hungry, thirsty, vexed, annoyed, and dispirited. There was nothing to be done, however, but to send the groom and a coolie back after Robin, when we had established ourselves in a native hut hard by.

"From one o'clock on that luckless day to five, did I sit in that miserable hut drawing figures on the floor with my ramrod. At five Tom brought me some rice and a vegetable curry he had succeeded, after infinite trouble, in cooking. It was palatable, but there was no beer, no claret, no brandy—nothing but that eternal water to wash it down. By way of supper, he prepared some rice-cakes and coffee for me, and I partook of the meal gratefully, remembering that we are but dust and ashes after all. It was not till it was dark that the groom returned with Robin.

"To have pursued my journey at that hour through the forest would have been madness. Tom made me as comfortable as possible during the night, and next morning I set off for Ruminacadde, after a breakfast of rice cakes, and coffee. What a breakfast for a man of my dimensions, and accustomed to the exercise I take. Rice cakes and coffee! and *such* coffee; Well, well, I know it is not for nothing that trials are sent, so I try to be grateful," concluded Lister, as he tossed off a final glass of claret.

We soon after separated for the night, I to

indulge in visions of sport to be enjoyed with my portly friend, before duty called me back to Colombo, he to refresh himself after his persecutions by a sound and protracted sleep.

CHAPTER IV.

NO PARAPET.

The centre of Ceylon is occupied by a rugged mountain steep, surrounded by a low-belt of sandy coast that slopes evenly down to the sea. On the east and south this rugged knot of high land, with its picturesque valleys and forests, table-lands and pointed hills, approaches nearer to the ocean than on the north and west. The south-eastern portion of the elevated district is occupied by the most extensive table-land in the island, immediately by the side of which rises the highest mountain in Ceylon, between eight and nine thousand feet in elevation.

During the long centuries of native rule, when Ceylon was independent, this south-eastern district was the fertile source of insurrections and revolutions; every disappointed minister fled to Rohona, as it was then called, and there he was sure to find congenial spirits, ready and able to help him in opposing constituted authority. Newera Ellia, or the city of Ellia, is the name which, in later years, has been given to the extensive table-land that occupies a large portion of this south-eastern district—a plain between five and six thousand feet above the level of the sea, and from ten to twelve miles in circumference. It forms at present the sanitarium of Ceylon. The Anglo-Indian or the Anglo-Ceylonese, worn out and debilitated by long residence amid the heat of the low-lands, finds a refuge from that heat at Newera Ellia; finds a bracing atmosphere that reminds him of his home in the far-off north-west so long forsaken. In the middle of the day, during a large portion of the year, even at this altitude, the sun shines in tropical majesty, rendering it unpleasant, if not dangerous, for the invalid to brave his beams, by walking; but the mornings, and evenings, and nights, are deliciously cool, the air often dry and frosty, with that clear, bracing purity so enjoyable on a frosty morning, during clear weather, in England. At night, sometimes, during the winter, actual frost *does* cover the ground, and is to be seen from bed-room windows in the morning, and a thin coating of ice is to be found in the pools and ponds of the large plains.

The untravelled can scarcely fancy the delight with which the worn-out Anglo-Indian sees such things. He peeps forth from his cozy bed-room, and sees the grass white with hoar frost, and he thinks of England, of boyhood, of home, of father, mother, sister, brother, of ties and affections long since severed, rent asunder by time or death, but the remembrance of which is very dear to him. The white coverings of the fields, the crisp tread of the road as he walks along it, the thin, crackling ice, as he tries its strength with his stick, all remind him of far other scenes and of a far distant land, scenes that never can again recur, a land that never can be again to him what it has been.

Memory hallows the recollection, however, and wreck though he be of what he was, debilitated, worn out, enfeebled, with diseased liver and a more diseased mind, he drops a tear upon the crackling ice as he touches it with his walking-stick, a tear consecrated by love, hallowed by fond memories, sufficient to prove he is not all changed, sufficient to prove an English heart still animates and warms his bosom; an English heart, capable of high and holy feelings, that may not have been awakened for years, and which he himself has fancied, perhaps, have been long since dead.

To attain to this temperate table-land of Newera Ellia, is by no means an easy matter. The journey to it leads through a rugged mountain pass, in which a beautiful waterfall gladdens the landscape and endangers the journey—the pass of Rambodde. At the foot of the hill, where the waterfall raves and foams perpetually, stands a rest house or inn, in which the traveller may refresh himself before he commences the ascent of the mountain. He then crosses the brawling, boiling stream fresh from its precipitous descent, by means of a bridge, that, to nervous eyes, is by nomeans safe. No parapet serves as a protection to the traveller, should his horse prove restive, for the timid animal cocks his ears at the scathing flood that rages beneath him, that whirls its white masses of foam from eddy to eddy, and dashes them against rocks and into ugly crevices, to remain there till wanted to be played with again.

Nor is the danger only imaginary. During my residence in Ceylon, Lieutenant Barry, of the Rifles, when crossing this bridge, on his way to Newera Ellia, rode a spirited Arab he had brought up from Colombo—by no means a horse for jungle travelling, too fiery, too timid, too skittish, and too mercurial. Doubtless thinking of pleasant things, fearing no danger, Barry was carried jauntily along by his steed, the rider firm in his seat, having a quick eye, a steady hand, and a muscular leg; the horse fresh and playful, disposed to show himself off, and to have as much fun as possible.

They stood upon the unparapeted wooden bridge—the huge mountain on the left, with its black and white boiling stream in its recesses—a frightful chasm on the right full of raging waters and projecting rocks, with here and there a stunted shrub, all deep, deep below, fearful to look at. They stood upon the bridge, and the jaunty Arab caught a glimpse of a huge white mass of foam, perhaps, whirling rapidly round on the stream to his left, and coming towards him—caught a glimpse of *something* that terrified him unquestionably and started—started with a thrill of terror. Barry pressed the spur gently to his side, and spoke an encouraging word; the horse felt the spur, and heeded not the word—he reared, trying to turn from what had affrighted him—his hind foot trembled for a moment on the edge of the unparapeted bridge, and but for a moment.

Barry saw inevitable fate staring him in the face, and tried to throw himself off, on the near side, but it was too late. One wild semicircle in the air, one snort of terror from the horse, one cry of despair from the rider, and both were lost in the fearful chasm below. There was a faint splash, and a hard succession of thumps borne by the air from the boiling abyss, as the two were hurled from rock to rock, and then all was as usual again; the stream boiling as before; the echoes of the valley sounding with its commotion; the bridge quivering; the rocks bleak, black, stern, and immovable; the vegetation as of old; and a dead man and a dead horse lying far away in some deep recesses below. Barry's groom was a short distance behind him, and had seen the whole catastrophe.

The perils of a journey to Newera Ellia were then by no means imaginary—far other than imaginary truly.

Nor even when the fatal bridge has been passed, and the ascent commenced, does the traveller feel sure that he has left all danger behind. By no means. The road runs zigzag up the mountain's side, steep, precipitous, angular, with the sharpest cuttings and the most sudden transitions from left to right, and from right to left. Views constantly present themselves of the sublimest character, views of wide valleys, and encircling mountains in the distance, as well as of deep and dangerous declivities on every side, looking down into awful chasms, black and fearful, in which the eye seeks vainly for some object on which to rest, tree, or shrub, or rock, or rivulet, for all is a dim, indistinct haze, fearful to contemplate in its magnitude and depth—fearful, as one thinks of the probable consequences of a fall, and shudders at the thought.

So monotonous is the angular z-like ascent of the mountain at Rambodde, so numerous are the turns, the sharp angles, at which the road runs in straight lines, first to one side and then to another, the traveller gaining a little upon the hill at each turn, that more than one tourist has fancied there was no end at all to the ascent, and that he must have long passed the diverging point where the road runs off on the hill's summits to Newera Ellia. The despairing looks thrown upwards by such voyagers, as turn after turn is passed, are ludicrous amazingly—despairing looks at ever the same mass of jungle vegetation, laurels, myrtles, and other evergreens, which abound at these heights, mingled with stunted tropical bushes, and half-green plants of more temperate regions. The traveller, however, innocent of botanical information, sees no difference at all in the vegetation as he casts his despairing glances upwards—to him it is ever the same, whether round the base, in the middle, or at the summit—and he begins to doubt whether he is at all in the right way, or whether so interminable a road can lead anywhere but to the clouds.

Pleasure and business combined, not ill-health, took me to Newera Ellia. I enjoyed its delightful temperature and strength-inspiring breezes all the more keenly because I was in perfect health, and therefore able more perfectly to enjoy both. Its English-looking cottages, with their chimneys smoking à la Londres, were sufficient in themselves to rouse a thousand hallowed associations.

I met here, unexpectedly, at the little inn which hospitably receives forlorn travellers, a Colombo friend of the name of Katchit. Mr. Katchit was a politician of that old school so beautifully described by Addison in one of the Spectators : " He looked extremely thin in a dearth of news." Newspapers were the only literature he indulged in. Politics were the perpetual fount whence he drew mental draughts of nectar to cheer his soul—the ambrosia on which he silently fed—as he wandered through the groves of cocoa-nut trees by the sea-shore, or amidst the mightier vegetation of the forests in the interior.

Of all quidnuncs I knew, Katchit was one of the most insatiable ; ever on the alert for what was novel, and regarding all other gratifications as infinitely inferior to the hearing and telling of some new thing. My acquaintance with him hitherto had been limited to an occasional conversation in the Colombo Library, or a chat upon the steps of his office in the fort. He had been a successful merchant in Colombo for years, and, if report spoke truly, had amassed a large fortune. He had left the island a short time before, intending to return and settle permanently in England; but finding himself a mere nobody there, and a little great man in Colombo, he preferred returning to his old haunts and resuming his old ways. On the evils of free trade he was eloquent. Seeing the evil it had produced in Ceylon, he could not persuade himself it could anywhere else be advantageous, and he was fond of prophesying ruin and the decadence of the British Empire as its result.

Having thus assumed a decided attitude in the field of English politics, every mail afforded precisely such food as he desired, wherewith to feed his mind. He pored over the columns of the *Morning Herald* in fond admiration, and lost no opportunity of having a hard rap — the harder the better — at the mighty thunderer. I never heard, however, that the one paper was a whit the better, or the other a whit the worse, for his adulation or contempt.

We were, of course, all Protectionists in Ceylon, naturally and inevitably so. Katchit, therefore, had no great quarrel to maintain with either of the local papers, although as to the particular means by which the Ceylon planters might, ultimately, succeed in reversing the policy of the British Parliament (!) and in obtaining what they believed to be only justice, he might occasionally differ from either of the editors.

Some article on the subject, more fiery than usual in the *Ceylon Herald*, had opened his heart to me, and he had lately contributed several letters and leaders for its columns, so that, when we met at Newera Ellia, it was with the cordiality of old friends accidentally thrown together in a crowd of strangers. There was so much that was original about the man, that I felt pleased at becoming more intimate with him, particularly as no one gave better dinners, or was more careful as to the quality of the champagne he put upon his table.

"Do you want to make your fortune?" he asked me abruptly one day, when we were seated together by a blazing wood fire in Newera Ellia, discussing at the same time, some excellent claret he had brought up from Colombo, and the last speech of Sir Robert Peel brought out by the Overland Mail. "Do you want to make your fortune?" was his question.

"Does an Alderman love turtle?" was my reply.

"You do then," said he; "I am glad of it. Now listen to me. The only way to bring the British public to its senses anent the matter of Protection and Free Trade, is to publish a popular work—a novel, suppose—in favour of the former and against the latter."

"An excellent project," said I, "there is but one thing wanting, and that is the work itself. Its publication in a proper form to attract public attention may be a difficulty, but until the work itself is forthcoming, it would be folly to discuss that point."

"Quite true," was his reply, as he drew his chair nearer; "I am glad to see you taking up the matter in so business-like a way. The work is written,—nearly ready, sir, at this moment for publication."

"Indeed!" said I, seeing how the wind lay; "indeed?"

"My intention was to have offered it to the *Observer*, but as I see you are taking up the matter of Free Trade roundly now, and not merely nibbling at it, I have determined on letting it appear in the *Herald.*"

The mystery is out, thought I, scarcely able to suppress a smile at the idea. "Do you think then," I asked, "that its publication in the *Ceylon Herald* will excite so much attention as to bring the British public to its senses?"

"Listen to me," said he, dogmatically, clasping his right knee, after his custom, in both his hands; "When it has been published in the *Herald*, chapter by chapter—it contains eighty-nine chapters, and you publish one hundred and four *Heralds* a year, so that it may easily be completed within the year—it will excite *some* attention, I flatter myself. People in India will talk about it, and write about it. Distance lends enchantment to the view, and when the public in England first hear of it, as coming from Ceylon, their curiosity will be excited, and I shall have an edition of eight or ten thousand copies ready for sale at a mere trifle each; no three-volumed affair, at a guinea and a half, but a well-printed book of six or seven hundred pages all for half-a-crown, or less. I want no profit—none, sir, none, not a farthing. My supposition is based on the work exciting attention in India, but that is a certainty, for I have contributed to more papers than the *Herald*, I assure you, so that you see the whole matter is in a nutshell."

"Which you can open when you please," I added.

"Which I can open when I please, to continue the figure, as you say—ha! ha!"

The project did not appear a very feasible one to me at the moment, and the more I reflected on it afterwards, the more I became convinced of its utter absurdity; but Katchit had set his heart upon it, and an evening was appointed when I was to dine with him and hear a portion of the great work read which was to change the destiny of Britain.

CHAPTER V.

THE REVOLUTIONARY NOVEL.

"Now, what shall it be?" said he, when every thing had been prepared for the lecture, and he was opening a huge pile of MS., formidably tied up with red tape. "I have been working to-day at the conclusion, in which, of course, everybody gets killed or married. Shall I read you the opening chapter?"

"By no means," was my reply. "I have an insuperable dislike to opening chapters. But you forget I don't know the title of the book yet."

"It's only a name," said he—" '*Horatio Clomstock, or the Soldier of Fortune*'—the great art of the thing is, you see, that, being the autobiography of a soldier, no one will expect to find anything about politics in it; and then, my hero being in a regiment of the line, I am able to take him all over the world, and to describe the Cape, Canton, Ceylon, Calcutta, Canada. The work contains, sir, ludicrous, pathetic, sentimental, philosophical, sporting, and political chapters."

"Excellent!" said I. "Then you conduct him to Ceylon?"

"Yes; and he becomes acquainted with coffee-planters, merchants, and a host of people, all which permits the introduction of commercial topics beautifully; that's the great art of the work," continued Katchit, rubbing his head with his handkerchief, for he was gradually working himself up to excitement.

"And you have sporting scenes, too?" I asked.

"Certainly," said he, with enthusiasm; "admirable sporting scenes. I had Major Rogers dining with me half-a-dozen times, just to get elephant stories out of him for *Horatio Clomstock*. Little did he know what I was pumping him for—ha! ha!"—and, so saying, Katchit mopped his forehead and bald head again.

"I love sport," said I; "let us have a sporting chapter."

"Very well, sir; a sporting scene let it be," replied my host, turning over the masses of manuscript — "Chapter forty-fifth — *The Elephant Hunt*—listen—

"'Midst the monotony of garrison life in a distant colony, such as Ceylon, it may be fancied with what ardour we heard of the elephant hunts, the pig-sticking, the deer-stalking, and the bear-shooting of the interior. With the exception of an occasional ball at Government House, and a dull, formal dinner-party at the house of some Civil Servant or merchant, there was little at Colombo to reconcile a man of active habits to the vegetation of the Fort. A ride in the morning, billiards before lunch, a stroll into the library after it, and a ride again in the evening, formed the usual routine of the day, enlivened once a-year by an exceedingly poor attempt at races, and occasionally by a row between the Governor and some of the big-wigs of civilians, invariably ending in the discomfiture of the latter. The little that I had already seen of the interior rendered my curiosity but the greater to plunge into the excitement of its sports, accompanied by some of those connoisseurs in hunting who abound in that favoured island."

"A connoisseur in hunting," said I, "is a strange phrase."

"A perfectly legitimate one, sir. Don't interrupt me," replied Katchit, rubbing his head again, and proceeding hastily—

"'An opportunity to see some of the wildest districts, and engage in some of the wildest sports the country afforded, at length presented itself, in an invitation which I got to join a party, to be headed by Mr. Boyd, a coffee-planter, and a veteran sportsman. Major Stretton of our corps, Captain Growler of the Ceylon Rifles, Mr. Sturt of the Civil Service, and myself, were to join Boyd in the neighbourhood of Kandy; and he engaged to take us through his own estate to a district in the south-east, where game was abundant, and had been for some time undisturbed. I accepted the invitation with alacrity, and never did I prepare for a journey in which I promised myself more unalloyed enjoyment than on this occasion.

"'Boyd was, what every Englishman ought to be, a model of a man—tall, broad-chested, athletic, and powerful, with a fine open countenance and intelligent expression, that bespoke the man of honour and probity, of independence and resolution—in fact, the English gentleman.' "

"Do you think that won't tell?" asked the reader, when he had got so far, and then, without waiting for a reply, continued:—

" 'Major Stretton had been but once in the field before, but had, on that occasion, proved himself fitted for an elephant hunter, by his calm intrepidity and quick resolution when in danger; without the great physical advantages of Boyd he had strength enough for all ordinary purposes, and was a first-rate horseman. The remaining two of our party are now no more, and are not likely to be recognized under the assumed names I have given them, save by their most intimate friends.

" 'Growler was the impersonation of *bonhomie*; joyous, mirthful and witty in no ordinary degree. He was not the man, however, that could vegetate for years without change or excitement, upon his dinner and his wine, contented with the dull routine of garrison duty and garrison pleasure. Action was necessary to *him* as excitement to the gambler, and it was only when worn out by action or satisfied by danger and escape, that he could resign himself with real zest to the pleasures of the table. He had now been fifteen years in the island, and his appeaıance spoke well for the *cuisine* of the Rifle mess, and the staples of the Ceylon market.

"'I was astonished when I first saw him, and was informed he was one of the most successful hunters in the island; astonished, not that he was altogether unwieldy in form, but that he should form such a contrast with Sturt and the other noted sportsmen. They were spare and sinewy, with the bloodless countenance and quick eye that denote the nervous temperament. He, on the contrary, rotund and happy, had a merry laugh and a gay appearance, that banished gravity almost immediately on his entrance. Yet when aiming at an elephant, I have seen that man of fun and drollery stand with rifle presented, a very statue in his immobility; with feet nearly closed, body perfectly erect, head slightly advanced, and eye of singular lustre, he would stand, covering his victim as he approached, and to the eye of the spectator appearing not even to breathe until the deadly rifle had rung forth, and, confident in his own powers, he dropped the but-end of the weapon on the ground to contemplate the effect of his fire.' "

"Why, that's a description of my friend Lister," said I.

"Ha! you recognize it at once—good," replied Katchit.

" 'Sturt had been——' "

"But why do you call him Growler, and say he is dead now?" I asked.

"Growler, sir, is a good name," was his reply, "for a man that's always grumbling; and I say he's dead, of course, because he's alive. It would never do to let people suppose I was painting living characters."

"Then all the people you say are dead are still alive," I urged; "and those you say nothing about are dead, I suppose, or imaginary."

"Precisely so," replied my host, impatiently, and giving a testy rub to his forehead, "precisely so. Let me go on."

" 'Sturt had been Growler's pupil, was still young, and presented in every respect physically an extraordinary contrast to his former *protégé*. He was a man of infinite jest and fun, of that dry, sarcastic kind, which makes one wince while he laughs. The total want of *vraisemblance* between Growler and Sturt had drawn them only the more closely together—' "

"Why do you put in so many French words?" I asked. "You have used half-a-dozen already, and *vraisemblance* does not mean—"

"Every body uses French words in novels," he remarked interrupting me, "I know what I'm about. Don't interrupt me this way."

"'Had drawn them only the more closely together, each enjoying with the greatest possible good humour the sallies and stories of the other.

"'Being well supplied with horses, we determined on riding leisurely to Kandy, and resting there for a few days preparatory to starting with Boyd. That ride was one of the happiest of my life. On an excellent Arab, and travelling over a very well-kept road, surrounded with the most lovely of nature's scenes, all the more lovely from their variety, and accompanied by the gayest of companions, what could earth give more? Some may fancy that a scamper over a country with a fair lady by one's side to make love to, is decidedly more interesting and more joyous than such a ride as I then enjoyed. They will talk of the deep feeling, the admiration excited by a fine form in the most graceful of attitudes, the love perhaps, and sweet converse, which beguiles the roads. Good! I do not deny the happiness of such a position, but I maintain that to the man of action, the rude mountain road, the bounding steed, the boon companions, and the rough refreshment, after a life of monotonous luxury or ease, are infinitely more grateful than even the blandishments of the fair sex, winning, captivating, soul-stirring though they be. The man of sentiment views the matter in a different light perhaps. I speak of what I think the man of action most esteems.' "

"Why, Horatio Clomstock is quite a misogynist," said I, half aloud.

"O don't be bothering me," was Katchit's reply,—"O don't be bothering me. Misogolist! What's *that?*"

And then, without waiting for an answer, he continued to read:—

" 'The transition from the low sandy belt which encircles the mountain-zone of Ceylon, to the rugged and precipitous interior is one of the most pleasing characteristics of a scenery, ever more varied and delightful as the traveller recedes further from the shore. At first, for thirty miles from Colombo, the road runs through a low level district, enriched indeed with the luxuriant vegetation of the tropics, but tame and monotonous when compared with the scenery of the mountains.

"'The first aspect of these mountains as the traveller approaches them, is exhilarating in the extreme. Fatigued with the heat and monotony of the low lands, he gazes upon the rugged cliffs, the high-soaring foliage, and the cloud-capt summits that rise before him into the heavens, feeling in anticipation the elasticity of spirits, the bounding sprightliness with which the cool, delightful breezes of these altitudes will inspire him as he ascends. The spur applied more peremptorily than before, infuses something of his own kindling energy into his horse, and he dashes onwards along the road hewn through the solid granite in the side of the hill which rises precipitously on his left, whilst on his right the descending rock stretches far down to the regions he has left; the mighty pillar of that mighty temple of nature's rearing, destined to last for countless ages, called into existence long ere man made his appearance upon his present stage of existence, and doubtless intended long to outlast him and his puny works.'"

"Do you know that the last remark is scarcely orthodox?" I observed.

Katchit turned his eyes impatiently on me for a moment, looking over his spectacles, and then continued:—

"'Here the wooden bridge thrown over the mountain torrent, shakes beneath the sturdy tread of the small but noble Arab, whilst the rushing stream dashes down from rock to rock beneath it precipitously, seeking the quiet and luxury of the plain below, just as the sinewy youth spends his energy and strength in constant conflict with the world to reach the haven of peace and comfort in old age. There the path rushes in between lofty trees, that appear to grow from the solid rock on either side as strong, and sturdy, and immoveable as that rock itself, the growth of ages, the proud monuments of what unassisted vegetation can accomplish, likely to remain there till the puny destroyer, man, comes with his hankering after gold, and cuts, and hews, and fells, the noble trees, and burns them at last, to make way for his paltry but more useful coffee shrub.

"'Deeper and deeper into the forest on either side runs the mountain path upon the summit of the hill, until the dark foliage meeting above the head of the wanderer, shuts out, except in broken glimpses, the brightness of the sky, and throws a dark, black shade, even in tropical noonday, upon the road beneath. On, still further upon the various way, and we meet a vast sturdy mass of rock rising right in the path of the engineer who formed the road; there was no going above, below, or round it; it could not be removed. Yes, it must be so; he dives right into it, and the perforated rock yields, in an ample tunnel, hanging strangely over the almost perpendicular side of the mountain. a passage by which man can make his way through the eternal hills.'"

"Bravo, Clomstock!" I exclaimed; but Katchit heeded me not, proceeding uninterruptedly and hurriedly with his reading.

"'It was on such a ride as this,' said Growler, as we proceeded, 'that I first found out that

Sturt had the materials of a good sportsman in him. He came out here some seven years ago, the greenest of all green griffs—knew nothing, positively nothing of the world, and fancied himself perfect in everything; he had a letter for me from an old friend; and to keep him from the gaming-table at Colombo, I asked him to accompany me in a ride to Rambodde, some forty miles south-east of Kandy, where I promised he should see, if not enjoy, some good sporting, for R—— and B—— (noted names amongst the Anglo-Singhalese) were to meet me.

"'During our ride to Rambodde, I saw that, however Sturt's education had been hitherto neglected, he was quite capable of becoming almost anything he liked, and was evidently never intended by nature to vegetate through life as a bookworm. Chilled at first by the cold sarcasm with which he spoke of everything he did not understand, I soon found that his eye kindled and cheek brightened, in the true English style, at the narrative of danger and excitement, and that there was all that relish of the mountain and of the jungle which bespeaks the true mountaineer sportsman. He had assiduously practised with the rifle ever since his arrival, and during the voyage, and was not a bad shot (at a target) when I first took him up the country.

"'I did not much count upon this latter accomplishment, being perfectly aware how often the excellent shot at the target becomes the most wandering on the field, more dangerous often to the companions than to the adversary of the young sportsman.'"

"But where are the sporting scenes, and the jokes, you promised?" I asked.

"My God, sir!" replied Katchit; "am I not coming to them?"

"'We had a noble gathering,' continued Growler, 'and some excellent sport at Rambodde, although our happiness on the occasion was somewhat marred by the death of a griff whom B—— had brought with him, and who, insisting on taking care of himself and following his own views, went out one morning before we were ready, rode off in the direction of a herd, of whose position we had intelligence on the previous evening, was charged by their leader on his wounding one of them, and having fired upon him unsuccessfully, was caught by the enraged tusker, as he stumbled over some parasitic plant that was creeping to an adjoining tree, tossed into the air, trampled, and left a corpse.

" 'Such, at least, was the story of his servant, who, I suspect, saw nothing of the encounter; certain it is, however, that we found the poor lad, for he was not quite twenty, mangled and dead when we reached the spot. A melancholy catastrophe, indeed, but such accidents *will* happen under the most favourable circumstances, and no man who values his life much, that is, extravagantly, ought to risk elephant-shooting. However, that circumstance took place after the initiation of Sturt into the mysteries of the hunt, not before, so that at the time of which I was about to tell you we were all in the best possible spirits, and quite prepared to appreciate a joke.' "

"Rather a stiff joke that," I ventured to observe.

"*That* wasn't the joke," said Katchit, contemptuously; "*that* was'n't the joke; we're coming to it."

"Oh, I see," said I, apologetically, and Katchit continued—

" 'To the east of Rambodde there is a gentle elevation that rises from the valley, lying behind one of the mountains which forms the pass, at a distance of four or five miles, by the bridle path, from the station. This path is of the most rugged description, even for a mountainous district, and one who ventures to ride over it, must be sure of his own seat and his horse's steadiness, ere he trusts himself upon the verge of a ravine, into the far depths of which a body of water precipitates itself from the adjoining hill, plunging, foaming, boiling in its mad course from rock to rock, and scattering the spray far over the path to which I allude, in its onward course, with nothing between him and the yawning chasm beneath, but the three feet of projecting rock or soil on which his horse with difficulty finds a footing.

" 'By this path we wended our way early one fine morning in the direction stated, having heard the previous day that a herd of deer which had been grazing there a short time before, had given place to the lordlier elephant, of which there could not be less than from thirty to fifty scattered over the hill. It was then with a very lively anticipation of excellent sport, that we journeyed over the dangerous road by the side of the ravine, each one, doubtless, planning in his own breast the means by which he could contrive to bring down more than his neighbour. Some three or four miles beyond the hill upon which we understood the elephants to be, a surveyor and a party, belonging to the superintendent-of-roads' department, were engaged in constructing a road through the valley leading, I believe, to Allbagge. Elephants had been numerous in the district, and had greatly impeded the operations of the surveyor, so that B—— informed us we should be aiding government, and improving the country by knocking as many of them on the head as possible.

" 'On emerging from the narrow valley into which the ravine I have described led us,' continued Growler, 'we saw a wide extended amphitheatre, stretching far away for miles on all sides surrounded by lofty mountains. In the centre, with a gentle swell, rose the hill upon which the herd had rested and were then resting. 'Take it for all in all,' it was one of the finest spots I have ever seen for an elephant-hunt.' "

" 'Take it for all and all,' " I exclaimed, " excuse me, but is that intended for a quotation?"

" Of course it is—it's from Shakspeare; is it possible you don't remember where? I forget who, is describing somebody," answered Katchit, impatiently.

" Hamlet, describing his father," I replied, " says, 'Take him for all in all, we shall not look upon his like again.' "

" Ay, that's it, to be sure," said Katchit, composing himself to continue his reading.

" But you have it—'Take *it* for all in all;' *that's* not what Shakespeare wrote," I urged.

" Well, it's very easy to take out the inverted commas," testily answered my host; " nothing can be easier. I'll proceed with Growler's story now, if you'll let me."

I said not a word more, and the reading continued as before.

" 'Our dispositions were soon made,—long ere our arrival the beaters (men who drive the elephants in the desired direction) had been despatched to the other side of the hill, to drive the herd towards us, whilst, on the two flanks, strong parties had been posted to prevent escape that way. By the shrill trumpetings of our huge foes, we perceived that they had been already disturbed and were coming towards us, their forms hid in the tall grass and taller trees with which the hill, nearly to its summit, was clothed. We speedily dismounted, and were soon ready for the fray.

" ' I had, as usual, my single-barrelled rifle, carefully loaded, in my hand, and my trusty old servant with a double-barrel (not a fowling-piece, a rifle,—I never trust a fowling-piece amongst elephants) close behind me. I told Sturt to keep near me, whilst the rest separated to convenient distances, and we commenced slowly ascending the hill. It was some time before I heard the leader of the enemy loudly indicating his whereabouts to the others, but, unfortunately, he was too far to my left for me to hope that I should meet him.

" ' In his progress towards us, I distinctly perceived, from his movements, that he was making towards *my* side of the hill, and waited with breathless impatience, but he turned again, and, in a few minutes, I heard R——'s rifle (I could distinguish it from a hundred) popping at him, and down he went with a tremendous crash amongst the dried grass and dead wood beneath the trees. R—— has such a combination of luck and skill in his composition, that he invariably bears off the most honours, although many men shoot better.

" 'Keeping together, Sturt and I made our way with difficulty up the hill, the shouts of the beaters far in advance informing us that the death of the leader had momentarily turned the herd. On they came again, and here and there through the forest could be heard the crushing of brambles, the trumpeting of the elephant, and an occasional roar, as some lusty young monster tried his strength against a tree. The distinctness with which we heard the tread of the advancing animals, made me fancy we were in the direct line of the thickest of the squadron, and I anticipated glorious sport. Nearer and nearer came the rushing, crushing sound of the foe, and at length a huge female, accompanied by her two young ones, filled up the gap in front of us, a gap formed by a tree that had been overthrown in some recent gale.

" 'Now for it,' said I to Sturt, 'leave me the mother, you take the young one on the right—wait—not yet—now—fire!'

" 'I had fired just as the mother, apparently aware of her danger, had made a headlong rush forward, with curled trunk and elevated tail. She fell just as she had cleared half the distance between us, and I was obliged to leap to the side, to prevent being entangled in a sapling which she had brought down in her fall. Sturt had fired at the same time at the largest of the youngsters, but found a second edition of the dose necessary to quiet him. The other had rushed on with his mother, and now stood beside me with his trunk leaning over her, apparently disposed to fondle her, and evidently disturbed by her sudden fall.

" 'I could not muster up cruelty enough to put an end to the life of the little monster, it seemed so innocent and so quiet. It offered no resistance, no opposition, but, as it stood over its dead mother, I could fancy that I heard a groan rushing from its young heart, as it turned its eyes first upon Sturt and then upon myself. An exclamation from our attendants drew our attention, both at the same instant, to an enormous male and a tusker, that now rushed wildly towards our little group.

" 'I had scarcely time to seize my double-barrelled rifle from my Singhalese attendant, ere he, with Singhalese agility, had disappeared in a tree, not having yet finished the loading of my discharged weapon. Before I could get it to my shoulder, Sturt had fired, but again unsuccessfully, nor could I get such a fair aim at the monster's forehead as I wished. However, he was now very near me, and fire I must, and did, shouting out to Sturt to get behind the large tree on his right. My fire did not bring down the animal at once, and I had only time to slip behind a tree to the left, when he stood where I had stood the moment before.

" 'His attention was for an instant directed towards the mother, and his advance impeded by the young one, who wished to fondle him, when he turned with a loud snort of rage upon myself. I was waiting for him, and as he wheeled his unwieldy carcase round, the end of my rifle was within reach of his trunk. Its contents were soon lodged in his brain. Sturt had fired at the same moment, apparently looking upon my position as a dangerous one, and as the animal received both balls he fell, hurting the young one in his fall, who uttered a shrill cry of pain as he descended.

" 'It was now, when Sturt believed all danger over, that we were really most in danger, for I heard the advancing cries of the beaters again, and the loud shots and shouts in the jungle around, and knew not the moment at which another might be upon us. My servant, with my trusty single barrel, was with me in an instant, and I felt relieved, telling Sturt to look to himself, and lose no time in getting his weapons reloaded.

" 'That done, I felt easy, and contemplated leisurely the strange scene, strange not so much to me as to my companions around me. The male and female had fallen within six feet of each other, and lay motionless side by side, their huge rotundities as high as the top of my little hunting cap Some paces in advance lay the muscular youngster who, had he lived, would doubtless have emulated his more bulky parents in size. Around us stretched the dark forest, with its lights and shadows in strong contrast to each other, our swarthy attendants fit actors in such a scene.

" 'In giving directions about marking the spot so that our prey might be subsequently found with ease, I suddenly missed Sturt from my side. He had gone off to the left, apparently discontented with his own bad luck and my success (for I was a superior shot *then* to him). I was sorry for this, and feared the consequences; but, after shouting lustily, gave up the search, certain that if he did not wish to return, my search would be unavailing. I continued my progress up the hill, fell in with R—— later in the day, and had excellent sport, having laid seven or nine dead (I forget which) before I made my way to the *rendezvous* where we were to règale ourselves with lunch. It was not for some days subsequently that I heard a connected recital of Sturt's adventures and their *dénouement*.' "

"More French words," I exclaimed; "why, you have got on admirably well without them so far. That spirited encounter with the herd is told all in English."

"You like that tale of Growler's," said he, calming down, for the reading made him amazingly excited. "I thought you would; but you must hear what became of Sturt; it's very ludicrous;" and so he proceeded with that apparently interminable chapter.

Whether it was the claret, however, or the unaccustomed blaze of the fire in front of me, or "Horatio Clomstock," I know not, but I soon found myself vigorously nodding at the fire-place. I had been up to the summit of one of the loftiest peaks in the neighbourhood of Newera Ellia that day, so that the fatigue, too, may have had much to do with it. Certain it is, however, that I retained no distinct idea of how Growler's story ended, nor did I ever arrive at the sporting adventures of Horatio Clomstock himself. Katchit saw me nodding, and became indignant. He put down the manuscript, and, looking at me over his spectacles with a severe look, ceased reading. The interruption roused me, and I started up.

"Ha! ha! admirably described, and very

ludicrous," said I, anxious to soothe his ruffled feelings.

"It was, without exception, the most pathetic description in the whole book," he replied severely.

"But I thought you said Sturt's adventures ended ludicrously," I explained.

"So they do, further on, but I have not come to that yet," was Katchit's reply.

A coaxing word or two induced him to continue his fruitless labour. I tried to listen and to keep awake; I rubbed my eyes, crossed my legs, pulled my fingers, but all to no purpose. The blaze of the fire was too powerful for eyes long unaccustomed to contemplate a fire at all. I was soon fast asleep, and before I awoke again, Katchit had tied up his manuscript and put it away, nor could any subsequent entreaties of mine, in which, indeed, I was not very earnest, induce him to reproduce it.

He still occasionally wrote a letter for the *Herald* after this; still occasionally urged some topic in an article intended for a leader; still occasionally conversed with me in the library or on the steps of his office; but our intimacy was at an end from that day forth, and of "Horatio Clomstock" I neither heard nor saw more—*requiescat in pace*.

I left Ceylon for Calcutta soon afterwards, and, for all I know, "Horatio Clomstock" may be now appearing in the *Colombo Observer*

CHAPTER VI.

THE ABODE OF DEATH.

CALCUTTA cannot fail to strike the European or American traveller as a city most remarkable and unique in its appearance. It is built upon the level bank of the Hooghly, on the alluvial deposits brought down from the hills by the Ganges and its tributaries—these deposits now forming an extensive region of many hundred square miles in extent, and of the most astonishing fertility, from the richness and depth of the vegetable mould. As the traveller steams or sails from the low, marshy banks of the mouth of the Hooghly, the "Sand-heads," as they are appropriately called, he is astonished to see ever the same monotonous level plain, stretching out on either hand without a hill or a distant chain of mountains anywhere visible to give variety to the prospect.

Near the mouth of the river, the accumulations of mud and sand brought down by it are, of course, the most recent—a vast work-shop of nature, where dry land is being formed by the mighty river, for the future abode of man. Low-lying, marshy districts are there, of great extent, called the *Sunderbunds*, and covered with a dense tropical jungle, in which death lurks, in many shapes, waiting for his prey. The vast tropical plants, with their rank odour and noisome exhalations, but decay to form manure for others, equally rank, equally noisome, equally huge and thick. To penetrate some of these recesses—to make one's way through the dense aquatic plants and creepers, over the marshy land—would be certain death, from the foul gases generated by the decaying vegetables. *Miasma* lurks under every creeper, and broods in every bush—*miasma* of the most fatal character.

These *Sunderbunds* have a melancholy interest of their own, as the birth-place of cholera. Amidst their slimy soil and rank jungle that fatal scourge was born, which has swept, like a destroying angel, round and round the world since. Numerous as have been the victims of cholera—manifold his conquests—he is not yet much more than thirty years of age. Verily he casts a Cæsar and a Napoleon far into the shade—thousands died that they might be great; millions have probably died that cholera might be feared. People will, doubtless, by-and-by, begin to prepare for his visits, for cholera, like other conquerors, lives and grows great on the vices and evil habits, the passions and bad blood, of nations.

The traveller, as he coasts those death-brooding shores, shudders at the impenetrable jungle—dank, dark, slimy, and foul in its horrible recesses—he shudders to think of being cast into its midst, as he pictures to himself the horrible creepers twining round him, the deadly smell overpowering him, the large, damp leaves of the semi-aquatic plants brushing against his face—he shudders when he remembers that he is in the very abode of cholera, whence the mighty scourge was begotten and brought forth, and where it is still, doubtless, lurking, unseen, greedy of corpses. But he shudders at far more than this—horrible as all this is. In such places the tiger and the serpent find congenial abodes—minor ministers of death—the humble, visible, and grosser auxiliaries of the great invisible pestilence that sits throned in the jungle.

There is, perhaps, no district upon earth on which a greater variety of deadly and poisonous snakes is to be found—none, certainly, where larger and more ferocious tigers may be met with than in these *Sunderbunds*. The Ganges makes its way to the sea through them by a hundred winding channels, offshoots from the great main stream. By these channels the river steamers of Bengal are obliged sometimes to navigate in getting to or from the Ganges—sometimes, nay, generally, in the dry season, when the Hooghly does not afford water enough in some parts of its wide, sandy bed, for their passage.

At night, these river steamers are obliged to moor, wherever they may be, as the navigation is fraught with too many dangers to admit of their proceeding in the darkness. If possible, they will not moor in some of these narrow but deep gullies, with the thick jungle waving forebodingly on either side of them—if possible, they will not; but this cannot always be avoided; and if fate brings them into the middle of one of these long channels as the sun goes down, there they must remain till he rises again, unless the friendly moon is almost at the full.

Let the passengers then beware of deadly *miasma.* Fever and ague lurk in every whiff of the night air, as it is borne to them from the jungle around. Let them shut their cabins close, to keep the death-dealing vapour out—close as they can—and if the occupant rejoices in a pair of whiskers—I must not say in a beard, for Englishmen have no beards—let him smoke a cigar within the narrow confines of his cabin. He cannot do better, believe me, madam; and should you ever be in a like position, I should advise you to get your husband to smoke two or three cigars before he and you go to bed that night—tobacco smoke is better than malaria—innocuous nausea than deadly jungle fever. But I spoke of your husband, did I, madam? I beg your pardon. I forgot you had none. You still rejoice in the euphonious appellation of Miss: well, then, if you can't get any one to smoke in your cabin before you go to bed—in India, people are not particular, you know—do it yourself.

But it was not of the deadly dews and foul exhalations of these districts I intended to speak, in getting the steamer to an anchor, in the centre of one of these narrow water-courses. The jungle is on either side—thick, dark, and dank—almost touching the paddle-boxes as the steamer stands still in the black stream, which rushes on blubberingly from stem to stern. The anchor has been dropped—the engine fires extinguished—lights gradually put out—the officers and the passengers in their cabins are vigorously smoking, with closed doors and windows, notwithstanding the heat. Peep in, and you see Lieutenant Soosty of the B. N. I., reclining on his couch, with the preserving weed in his mouth—one leg thrown over the side of the berth, the toes dangling within an inch of the floor, the other elevated aloft, as he plants it against the bulk-head or partition at his feet; two feet higher, and it would touch the ceiling. A glass of brandy and water is on the box by his side, within easy reach, and a book in his hand, over which he yawns amazingly.

Of his dress the less said the better; it must be remembered that it is excessively hot, and he therefore may be excused. He is lucky indeed that he does not require a mosquito-net, which would but increase the heat; but it is a common joke in Soosty's corps, the "Kuzits-ze-kinkas," that no mosquito had ever yet succeeded in piercing the fatty envelope in which Soosty is encased.

"What, you would peep in at another cabin? would you? Why, that's a married couple's—come away, sir, at once—do you suppose this villanous heat attacks the male sex only?" Away! away! Ah! here's the Captain Sahib's. Yes, I permit you, take a peep. See how the swarthy sailor is almost lost in the cloud he blows from that dingy pipe. Believe me, sir, that fellow knows what he is about; he is evidently preparing for his night's repose. In two minutes more he will be under that mosquito-net fast asleep, with no more clothing on him than Adam had in Paradise. He will not lose his time like Soosty, for he must be up with the first faint dawn of day." Such is the little comedy enacting below—on deck, a tragedy.

A solitary native seaman, the watch, stands at the helm, for the current is strong, and the helm must be attended to, though the vessel is at anchor. See, he is lashing it with a rope, and now sits down, crouching on the quarter-deck, to enjoy his hubble-bubble, or native pipe. The jungle is on his left, thick and threatening, whilst the steamer's stern floats merrily towards it. The bank is nearly on a level with the steamer's deck, and two fierce eyes are glaring through the darkness on the unconscious native sailor as he inhales and expires the grateful smoke, not merely taking it into his mouth as occidentals do, but into his lungs. Two fierce eyes glaring on him ferociously, and not six feet distant. Crouched on the bank under the thick jungle is a tiger, crouched cat-like, the eyes alone showing life, even the tail uneasily quiet. That tiger has marked his prey, and will have it. The vessel's stern floats near the bank; the man still smokes heedless of danger; the tiger still crouches greedy, anxious, and determined. There is a cry—a loud, piercing cry—of anguish and despair on that steamer's deck—a rustling in the thick jungle by the side—cries fainter and fainter heard through the rustling, and all is quiet again on the shore.

On the steamer, however, all is commotion; the watch is gone, he has disappeared; a gout of blood, near the rudder, alone shows where he was. The truth flashes upon them at once. "Baug! baug!" shout the natives; "A tiger!" whisper the Europeans. This is no imaginary case; such things have happened more than once on the river steamers going through these narrow streams of the *Sunderbunds*. Such things, and even, indeed, more horrible—

An indigo planter, in an unwieldy boat, was moving slowly and laboriously along. The thick vegetation overhung the stream, the banks gradually narrowed, approaching each other, leaving but room for the broad unsightly vessel to make its way through. There was but the faintest possible breath of wind, and that breath altogether favourable. The few men who guided the craft and acted as sailors in this nondescript ship, were seated in the fore part, eating their usual daily meal.

A servant of the planter's was seated at the rudder, crouching down on his heels, after the manner of Bengalese. The indigo planter himself was being fanned below in his cabin, sheltered from the burning heat above, languid and slumbering.

He was awoke from his slumbers by the noise of bare feet on the quarter-deck over his head; he thought he heard a strange gurgling sound, preceded by a half-expressed cry of alarm, and interrupted by a hideous crunching that made him shudder. He started from his couch, and went cautiously forth, merely putting his head above, and that slowly and warily, to see what was the matter. A tiger had leaped from the bank upon the servant, had caught him at once by the throat, and was now drinking the life-blood of him, as it welled from the severed arteries and veins of the neck.

Starvation had evidently impelled the beast to this bold measure, for his gaunt frame was angular from want. He saw the planter's head and the forms moving about in the fore part of the vessel roused by the unwonted event, and he growled fiercely as he saw them;

growled as a cat would do threateningly when disturbed in enjoying a feast of a rat.

The planter's gun was unloaded; he had been shooting at birds that morning, and overcome by the heat, had thrown it from him empty as he entered his cabin. He proceeded forthwith to load it, but before he again reached the deck, the tiger and his prey had gone. Doubtless scared by the human forms and by the cries of the men in the bows, the hungry beast had grasped the man in his ample jaws and leaped on the bank again, there, in the midst of the jungle, to devour at his leisure the choice morsel. Such are the stories with which the captain of your steamer will enliven the voyage through these jungle wilds, and there is ample testimony in India to confirm many such.

It is not only the *Sunderbunds*, however, that present the extraordinarily level appearance already noticed, as the visitor enters the Hooghly, and steams or sails to Calcutta. When *they* have been passed, the same flat surface continues to present itself on either side, until the picturesque villas of Garden Reach and the old-looking gothic pile of the

Bishop's College on the opposite bank, inform the traveller of his approach to the city of palaces. And truly the specimens of Anglo-Bengalese houses which he sees on his right, make him already suspect that Calcutta is not called a city of palaces wrongfully, for the villas that line Garden Reach are, for the most part, if not beautiful, at least imposing, their white walls and pillars forming an agreeable contrast with the green lawns and shrubberies that stretch from them down to the river's bank.

So far all is elegant, nay, picturesque. But India is a land of contrasts, and although so far all is well, it will not do to look deeper into the adjuncts of these merchant-princes' houses. On the bank of the stream, by the very side of the well-kept lawn, all is filth and slime, as the river retires from it with the ebbing tide, worse than filth and slime but too often. From the deck of the vessel may be discerned a bleached corpse perhaps lying on the bank, the crows or the vultures making their morning meal on it, the air giving unmistakeable warning of its condition.

Dwellers on the banks of the Hooghly are obliged to keep a watch for such nuisances, and a gardener goes down daily to see if any corpse rests within his master's boundaries, and if so, to push it off the bank again into the river. If it be on the bank of the next garden, although only a few feet from his master's paling, that matters not to him, he has nothing to do with such an "unmannerly corpse," and leaves it to be pushed off by some one else—it is not *his* business.

CHAPTER VII.

CALCUTTA AND ITS VEHICLES.

THE view of Calcutta itself, as the traveller rounds the reach, and sweeps past Fort William towards the dense mass of houses, is not very imposing, from the level character of the surface, and the distance from the shore of the principal buildings. Past Fort William, I say, but the reader must not, therefore, picture to himself a building like the Tower of London, of stone or brick and mortar, with turrets, embattlements, archways, and gloomy courts. Fort William was built in far other times than the Tower of London—in times when men had discovered that wide ditches and broad earth-mounds were stronger defences than stone walls. All that the visitor sees from the river is the green glacis and a few frowning cannon at the embrasures—a broad dry ditch, generally coated richly with green—a draw-bridge, a gate-way, and a sentinel. Within the broad earth-works, which are encased in walls, are numerous barracks and officers' quarters—a picturesque church and green esplanades.

The various *ghauts* or landing-places on the river's bank, attract the observer's notice as he approaches the town, becoming more numerous as he advances. They consist, for the most part, of steps leading down to the water's edge, and terminating above in a paved platform, over which a roof, supported on many pillars, is sometimes reared. On *many* pillars, I say, for in some they are so numerous that as the visitor stands amid them, he naturally asks himself whether it is not a pillar-nursery that surrounds him, the stone plants waiting transplantation to their allotted stations.

In these, as in every foreign station where John Bull reigns, the traveller is made painfully conscious that *taste* is by no means that quality of the mind which the aforesaid John most strikingly displays. Instead of picturesque cupolas, and strange Hindu columns, which would have well become these landing-places, and made them points of attraction for the eye in the surrounding scenery, we have orthodox Grecian pillars, supporting orthodox Grecian entablatures. John Bull has evidently heard and believes that Grecian art is beautiful and refined—that its proportions are exquisite, and its structures architectural models. All which is true enough. But it does not hence follow, as honest John evidently supposes, that every other species of art must be necessarily grotesque and ugly, or that Grecian buildings are suited for all places and all periods. A Gothic cathedral impresses the visitor with an awe-stricken reverence that a St. Peter's or a St. Paul's, with all its vastness and outward sublimity, altogether fails to produce. And so of other places and other purposes. The best type of Hindu column—and there *are* Hindu columns by no means contemptible—supporting the peculiar dome or a series of domes, in which Hindu architecture delights, would have been the appropriate margin to the sacred waters of the

Ganges—the appropriate portal, to the traveller, of the wonderful city behind. A Grecian column by his side, as he steps ashore from the native boat—a Grecian roof above, are equally out of place and incongruous.

But, alas! it is not in this instance alone that John Bull displays his dogged stolidity, and imperturbable blindness to the fit and the appropriate. When he gets hold of an idea he does not easily let it go, and it takes a long time before he will resign it. He turns it over and ruminates upon it, he catches it, at one side and at another, inspecting it from every point of view; he thrusts it in every body's way, and in every man's face, and will not be content till he has thoroughly wearied out himself and all the world with it. A hungry dog, with an unmanageable bone, is but a feeble emblem of the way in which honest John twists and turns around his idea —now catching it at one end and shaking it heartily thence, now grasping it at the other, straining the while to the utmost to make the most of it, and growling if any one else but looks at his idea for the time being. Let him alone, he will strip it bare, I warrant you, before he has done. It *was* architecture, it *is* drawing, it *will be* music. See if he does not astonish humanity before he concludes!

Crouched down by the feet of the pillars supporting these severe Grecian roofs over the landing-places, not lounging against them as Europeans would do, may be seen crowds of palanquin-carriers—some seated on their heels, a favourite attitude, smoking a noisy pipe with water gurgling in it, as the smoke is drawn through; others extended at full length in the shade, dozing. A single cloth round the loins constitutes their entire bodily clothing, whilst another, of ampler dimensions, is perhaps tied round their heads. The palanquin, a huge box with sliding doors at the sides, and a pole projecting from either end, stands on the ground, at some distance, also in the shade. The men are waiting for hire, for numerous boats are constantly plying backwards and forwards between the shore and the shipping, and men of business, or ship officers, or even English sailors, may like to be carried into the town.

The weight of the palanquin is by no means inconsiderable, and with a man of more than ordinary dimensions within, the four slight Hindus have enough to do to stagger along, groaning the while vehemently, as the strange conveyance rises and falls with their half-trotting step. Hard work truly, beneath such a sun as that of Calcutta, and the streams which glisten on their backs, making their way between the shoulder-blades, attest that it *is* truly hard work—the guttural "hee-haw! hee-haw!" which bursts almost involuntarily from their throats, and the oily exudation which covers them soon after this labour has commenced, attesting its severity. They do not live long, these men—seldom attaining to forty years of age—but no class can be more jovial and less care-worn. The lazzaroni of Naples are grave in comparison. Their lives are spent in laughing, sleeping, and eating, and when they have laughed, slept, and eaten, they are ready to laugh, to sleep, to eat again.

Even in the midst of their severe labour, when steaming like London horses in a severe frost, or after a heavy fall of snow making the roads slippery—even when so steaming, with the thermometer at 150 degrees as they stand or progress full in the mid-day sun's beams, even then they will chat and joke

—joke on the weight of the passenger within, and on the probable quantity of rice and curry it takes to satisfy *him*. Careless, happy wretches! to whom civilization would add much misery and many wants, to whom education would be a doubtful blessing, if not altogether an evil.

They like the sailors, for Jack is liberal, and has no objection to "shy them a copper," as he passes to and fro, when in a good humour —their dark countenance beaming with delight, and their white teeth exhibited (whilst they seize the money) to great advantage by a broad grin. In Calcutta, however, Jack often exhibits himself in new characters—driving up and down the Strand, amid the fashionables of the town, in a hired buggy, which he "steers" through the crowd of carriages as best he may—finding, for the most part, little difficulty in so "steering," for native coachmen and gentlemen, anxious to avoid an entire break-up of their vehicles, give Jack a wide berth.

Jack is laughed at, of course, for the blunders he makes in trying to accommodate himself to the new world of the east,—and the mistakes he makes, and the new methods he adopts, render it far from wonderful that he should be laughed at.

"Palkee, sahib, palkee," shouts a native, offering a palanquin to a sailor who is mounting the steps of the ghaut with his box on his shoulder.

Jack has been paid off, and has plenty of money in his pocket. He looks doubtingly at the palanquin. In a moment it is hoisted on the shoulders of the bearers awaiting Jack's arrival. The embarrassed sailor comes up to the side; an officious native—one of the carriers—puts his hand on the trunk. Jack has carried it easily enough on his shoulder from the boat up, but the slighter Hindoo would find it beyond his powers.

"Ah!" says Jack, "is that it? Very good! Put the traps into the box, and I'll walk on by the side."

And so he does: the trunk is placed carefully within the palanquin, by Jack's assistance, the doors shut on either side, and, grinning at the novel burden, the bearers trot on with their usual "Hee-haw! hee-haw!"—whilst

Jack walks briskly by the side to keep up with them.

It is not very far—half a mile at the utmost—to the Bow Bazar, where sailors "most do congregate," in Calcutta, and there Jack finds himself, as he says, brought to an anchor, in one of the lodging-houses for sailors, with which the Bow Bazar abounds. The trunk is taken from its hiding-place, and Jack marches in with it, after paying the bearers liberally, mopping his face the while, for they have gone rapidly over the ground.

"I'd as soon have had a man to carry the traps, and have walked on quietly by his side," says Jack to his new landlord, "an it wasn't for the honour of the thing."

The palkee-bearers, as the carriers of the palanquin are usually called by Europeans, form a very strange class of the lower orders of native society in Calcutta. They congregate in stations allotted to them, with their odd vehicles, or where they consider themselves most likely to be speedily hired. The palanquins are placed, the one behind the other, in a long line, like cabs on a stand in London, whilst, of the four men attached to each, three are invariably smoking, or sleeping, or eating—one being on the alert for a fare.

"Palkee-ee-ee!" shouts a servant from some house in the neighbourhood; the sleepers are aroused—the smokers alert. All is bustle, and hurry, and excitement to be the first.

Two men seize the nearest conveyance, and stagger on with it towards the door, their long cloths hanging from their heads in great confusion. Half-a-dozen palanquins are being so carried towards the door, when only one is wanting: but see!—one has its full complement of four men, and comes bounding along. It passes its competitors—reaches the door first—is deposited on the threshold, and great is the laughter, vehement the gesticulation of the successful bearers as they take up their station in anticipation of their fare, anxiously looking into the house or court-yard, however, to see the size of the intended passenger, for the laugh will be against them if they get a robust lady or gentleman of fifteen stone weight. A lady or gentleman!—for even in Calcutta there are *both* ladies and gentlemen of fifteen stone.

Where a man or woman of preposterous dimensions is known to reside in a certain house, and is in the habit of going out in palanquins, there is by no means a race to *that* house, when the well-known shout of "Palkee-ee-ee!" issues from the gate—the race is rather the other way, in truth. Should the formidable passengers however, issue boldly from the house, and walk towards the standing, the commotion is great. In hot haste the palanquins are borne round the corner, or along the road, or into the first gateway—anywhere, in fact, but towards the mountain of flesh that wishes to be quietly reclining within; and great indeed is the laughter if one be caught, and forced to receive the enormous freight. Great the laughter amongst the others who have escaped, for, to the unfortunate bearers of that particular palanquin, it is far other than a laughing matter.

But the palanquin is but one form of the various vehicles in which the citizens of Calcutta make their way under a tropical sun hither and thither, and a form that has long been becoming quite unfashionable. There are modes of conveyance both above and below it, however, in the social scale. It is not fashionable, it is true; rather the reverse in these days, indeed. But there is the *karanchee*—a vehicle as ugly and uncouth as its name—which ranks far lower. The karanchee is to be found in all places where natives abound. Its low fares suit the pockets of those who are too well off to walk, but too poor to afford themselves the luxury of a palanquin.

It consists of a large, old-fashioned carriage, badly balanced on springs, which lift it high above the wheels. The wheels themselves are high too, so that one would almost be disposed to fancy that ladders would be requisite to ascend. The karanchee is generally hired by a party who club their *pice** for the purpose—four inside, perhaps, and two or four seated on the top—all chatting and laughing vehemently. It is an airy vehicle: there are no glasses, no venetians, so that elbows, arms, and heads may be observed stuck out on every side as it advances; the elbows, arms, and heads, for the most part bare, of native clerks in the government and mercantile offices.

In front of this vehicle, attached to the long pole by which it is pulled along, are two animals, entitled, by courtesy, to the name of

* Small coins like farthings.

ponies—ponies, innocent of the curry-comb or the scrubbing-brush, in all the unsightliness of untrimmed hair and matted filth; too often, also, in all the repulsiveness of unhealed sores. A more than half-naked savage seated at their tails—not on any coachman's seat, or in a comfortable "box" prepared for the purpose, but simply anywhere as he may find convenient—is the steersman of this strange vehicle. Uttering unearthly shouts, he flourishes a long cane or slender bamboo, which he brings into feeling contact continually with the hind quarters and sides of the "ponies." Their tails are twitched uneasily hither and thither, the pole moves convulsively from side to side, the wheels squeak, the springs creak, the panels clatter, the natives shout, and they are off—ponies, pole, karanchee, Jehu, outsiders and insiders, all off—rushing along at no mean pace, the long cane still flourishing, the Jehu still shouting in an unearthly manner, the pole still jerking from side to side, the wheels still squeaking, the springs creaking, the panels clattering, and the natives laughing—noises which continue without abatement till the goal has been attained, and the freight deposited.

Whether Karanchees ever walk, I cannot of myself undertake decisively to say. I only lived a few years in Calcutta, not sufficient to decide that point; but, as far as my experience went, I should say they do not. They seem to be always dashing about in a wild, half-savage kind of way, man or boy and "ponies," equally excited and untamed-looking, whilst the combination of noises they emit in rolling along is really wonderful. I have often stood still to analyze these noises, but never succeeded. It was impossible to distinguish the creaking of the springs from the squeaking of the wheels—impossible to separate the sharp, angular clatter of the panels from the no less sharp and angular vociferations of the driver, as the half-naked individual perched on the end of the pole must, I suppose, be called.

But these are but two of the vehicles that abound in such numbers and in such amazing varietyin Calcutta—only two, the palanquinand the karanchee; why, if I go over the others at the same length, my chapter on Calcutta and its vehicles will be swelled into a volume, and *de re vehiculari*, which means good madam "of the karanchee," &c., become a very portly chapter in itself of that volume. No, no, I must cut it shorter than that. Even in the karanchee we have not got to the lowest degree of the social scale of Calcutta vehicles. I cannot stop to describe them, but the ekka and the bullock hackery are decidedly lower; whilst the reader's patience would be worn out, did I do more than enumerate the palanquin carriage, the office jaun, the brownberry, the American spider, the brougham, and the barouche, in which Europeans and the more wealthy natives make their way from place to place.

CHAPTER VIII.

MEN AND MANNERS IN THE CITY OF PALACES.

Calcutta, like most other oriental towns, contains two quarters—the well-built, cleanly-kept, broad-streeted European quarter, and the ill-built, filthy, narrow-passaged native town. Even the palaces of the native princes, many of them magnificent in outward show, and built, of course, for the most part, in imitation of the Parthenon, or, at all events, with Grecian porticos, must be approached through long filthy streets, so narrow, that between the ditches on both sides, it is only by assiduous care and watchful edging that two carriages can be induced to pass each other, without one or both finding their way into the open drains on either side.

In these native palaces we see the effect of John Bull's one idea on art, thrust everywhere but where it ought to be. He has assiduously taught his Hindoo fellow-subjects that Grecian art is sublime and perfect, and therefore, argues logical John, for he does not stick at consequences, every other kind of art must be ridiculous and imperfect. Anxious to be in the *mode*, and to accommodate himself to circumstances, the native prince orders a front to his house, something like one of the wings of the British Museum, and when he has paid his ten or twelve thousand pounds for it, hates it and praises it amazingly. There may be a high wall within thirty yards of it right in front, or thousands of miserable mud huts, thatched with leaves, in its immediate vicinity, but it is Grecian, and that suffices; John Bull says it is all right, and that is enough.

The Governor-General's palace is Grecian too; the Town-Hall, the churches, the bank, all Grecian. He is certainly in the *mode*, and if not contented, he will pretend to be so. A Hindoo structure, sobered by the withdrawal of a few extravagancies, would have been far more picturesque, and to him infinitely more convenient, but John Bull would not have it so. Amid the narrow streets of the native quarter of Calcutta, are situated the principal bazars. Like many other Eastern words, the word bazar has been adopted into our language, to mean, however, a very different object from the original. A genuine Eastern bazar differs even more from its European imitation than the turban which Dowager Lady Littlewit wore at the rout the other night from the turban of an orthodox Mussulman.

In Calcutta, a bazar is simply a collection of shops, generally in a narrow street, and for the most part of shops containing similar articles, the one to the other. Thus, in one bazar, the prudent housewife, who shuns the exorbitant prices of the European shopkeepers, will purchase linen, silk, woollen cloth; in another, her supplies of tea, sugar, spices; in a third, her furnitnre or ornaments for her rooms, and so on. A lane full of small shops, with open fronts, where the shopmen sit extolling their wares and inviting the passers-by to make a trial of them, is, in fact, a native bazar.

The shops appear small, from the confined frontage, but enter one of them, and you discover, as in some of the dingy shops of Wardour Street, in London, room after room behind, filled with goods. You go up stairs and down stairs, to the right hand and to the left, goods, goods, goods, still goods, and a native sycophant your mentor, who is ready to take his oath on the "Gunga-pawnee" (Ganges water),* that the worst article in his shop is the best of its kind. To get you in is the sole object of the man seated in the shop window. His eloquence is made use of as a decoy. "You not go that man's shop, sare," he shouts, when he sees you irresolute as to which you will enter, calculating by your flushed cheek that you are a new-comer, and therefore to be addressed in English; "you not go that man's shop, sare; that man plenty bad man; him d—— cheat! You go that shop, you get plenty cheat. Ebery ting plenty good this shop, sare; you come in here, sare. Me show you what you want, ma'am; silk, satins, ribbons, ebery ting got you want."

When he has succeeded in enticing you to

* The Hindoos are sworn by the water of the Ganges, as the Christians on the Bible, and the Muhammadans on the Koran.

enter, he coolly hands over you and the lady to other men within, whilst he takes his place at the door to laugh and chat with the "plenty bad man" opposite, the "d—— cheat," whom he abused so roundly a minute before. The compliments were returned, of course, for every one of the six shopmen in your vicinity were vociferating exactly the same words, making altogether a Babel from which you were glad to escape by rushing into any shop.

Of native articles, the best may be obtained in these native bazars, but of European by no means the best; rather, indeed, as a general rule, the inferior goods, made, not to give satisfaction or be economical to the purchaser, but to sell at a cheap rate. In the shops of the Europeans, generally speaking, really good articles are sold, but at enormous prices. Take tea as a sample; in Calcutta there is no duty on that import, the freight from China is by no means a matter of importance, yet tea in an European shop in Calcutta is absolutely dearer than in the first London-houses.

The European confectioners' coffee-houses are the great resorts of the idle Anglo-Indians during the heat of the day. They are situated in the neighbourhood of Government House, as the Governor-General's palace is called, and are kept as cool as possible; within, marble floors and tables, and perpetual breezes, caused by constantly swinging fans, forming a delightful contrast to the red-brick dust, the painful glow and intense heat without. Ices and sherry-cobblers are the articles most in demand in the day-time in these establishments; all kinds of American drinks are to be had at all times, and the quantity of ice used in the concoction of the majority of such drinks, renders them great favourites in India.

The familiar faces of the principal London periodicals meet our eyes upon every table and in every recess, mingled with Indian newspapers of various names and as various type and appearance. *Punch*, here as elsewhere, an universal favourite, the best thumbed, coffee-bespattered paper of the whole, known as well to the Hindoo servants as to the Anglo-Indian visitors. "Punch, Saheb," mutters the obsequious Bengallee, as he puts the well-known paper under the visitor's eyes—"Two sherry cobblers—dota—atcha, Saheb," two sherry-cobblers,—two—very well, sir; and whilst the visitors divide *Punch* or the *Hurkaru*, the *Times* or the *Purnochundodroy* between them, the waiter flies off to supply their wants.

Even in the busiest thoroughfares of Calcutta, where bullock-hackeries, and karanchees and office jauns most do creak, there is an air of languor and of subdued indifference about the scene—a total want of that earnestness which characterizes the busy scenes of the west. Time is little valued in the east generally, and not more in Calcutta than elsewhere. A London policeman, traversing a quiet street when on his beat, saunters along imperturbably enough, but a Calcutta policeman creeps through the busiest thoroughfares still more slowly, and with far less appearance of energy. The labourers carrying a heavy parcel or a bale of merchandize—the drivers urging on some contumacious bullock—the mechanics plying their vocation, all do so in Calcutta with the smallest possible amount of energy and exertion necessary to ensure the desired result. If they cannot succeed, the resource is easily procurable—a seat upon their heels, and a pipe. They have no idea of putting themselves out about the matter, or allowing themselves to be annoyed—not they. They sit quietly down by the road-side and produce the never-failing hubble-bubble, with which they beguile the time till fate relents, till assistance is procured, till the bullock becomes less obdurate, or till it becomes too late to prosecute the task for *that* day, trusting to the chapter of accidents for the morrow.

In cases in which the Englishman would be striving, steaming, struggling, perspiring at every pore, and rapidly losing his temper, perhaps, the Bengallee is perfectly composed. *He* sees no reason why he should at all annoy himself, and, as to struggling out of the difficulty, he would as soon think of placing himself voluntarily in a lunatic asylum.

"What does it matter, Saheb, as long as we're happy?" he will ask you, if you want to know why he does not make a strenuous effort to arouse himself.

"They are going a great deal too fast," said the complacent Bengallese, when they first saw railway carriages flying over the road—"a great deal too fast—all the people will be killed."

That was the only idea the novel scene

aroused in *their* minds, with all its astonishing display of force and power.

This air of languor, of indisposition to exertion, pervades the entire community, and is, doubtless, to a great extent, the product of the climate in which they have been born and reared. Sharp enough in business details, full of intellectual vigour, when their minds have been trained by cultivation, fond of physical or mental stimuli according to their tastes or dispositions, and eager in the pursuit of physical gratification, there is yet this air of indescribable languor about all alike—the rajah and his slave, the student and his servant, the merchant and his clerk, the mechanic and his family—the spirit of the tropics has put his hand heavily upon them, and marked them as his own.

Few cities present a more heterogeneous mass of inhabitants than Calcutta. To say nothing of the pale-faced Anglo-Indian, who reclines, in a state of incipient liquefaction, in his carriage, and his congeners, the small sprinkling of Germans, French, and Americans, that become like him, liver-diseased and irritable as years roll round—to say nothing of the Portuguese descendants, or the vast variety of mixed descent, Eurasians as they are sometimes called, a word intended to combine their European and Asiatic descent in one appellation—

To say nothing of these, who may be looked upon as exotics, there is a vast variety of Orientals to whom the climate is congenial, who suffer little inconvenience, comparatively speaking, from the heat, and who are as various in their dress and appearance as in their origin. Turks, with their massive turbans and wide trousers, move majestically along, the most self-satisfied of men. Arabs, with loose drapery floating about them, their unaccustomed walk telling of the well-used saddle, and of their better acquaintance with the horses' legs than with their own. They, too, partake of the self-satisfied character of the proud Turk, despising the infidels as heartily, feeling quite as conscious of their favoured origin, and of the inferior descent of the rest of mankind.

The Persian, with his high conical cap and slit sleeves, his loose robe fluttering in the air as he stalks along, is no less proud, no less conceited inwardly, but hides the feeling, confines it to himself, knows, indeed, that a Paradise is awaiting him, to which neither the pale-faced Englishman, nor the yellow Chinese; neither the inelegant Hindu, nor the revengeful Burmese can at all aspire—he *knows* this, to him it is a conviction which could only be plucked out of him by dragging out his heart itself; but he sees, therefore, no reason why he should exhibit the feeling *now*, or, sure of his advantage hereafter, assume an earthly superiority at present. His high conical cap makes him tower above the crowd, as he passes along somewhat majestically. He pities the Englishman, despises the Hindu, hates the Turk, hates, because they are of rival creeds, or, rather, of two rival branches of the same creed, and he does not, therefore, feel so strong an antipathy to the miserable infidel, who has no chance of salvation, as he does to the degenerate heretic, who will not seek it exactly in *his* way—precisely as the bigoted Protestant, who is full of the controversial mania, feels more toleration for the Jew, the Turk, or the Infidel, than for the Roman Catholic, and,—for things must be squared—precisely as the bigoted Roman Catholic would rather embrace a Budhist or an African fetish-worshipper, than a heretic.

The Muhammadan of India is a totally different being from his co-religionists of Turkey, Arabia, and Persia. With him the contest is between infidelity and Muhammadism, not between rival sects of the latter alone. He cares little for that particular party of his faith to which he may belong, whether a Sheeah or a Soonie—little, comparatively speaking only—bu tis as eager in the maintenance of his faith as a whole, as any Mussulman in Europe or Asia. In outward appearance, he presents but a slight contrast to the native Hindu. The large turban of the Turk or the Arab he is altogether without, wearing a small white scull-cap instead, on his shaven crown, an article of dress too closely resembling a clipped night-cap to look either picturesque or imposing.

He is generally distinguished by his ample girdle—a vast mass of cloth, in fact, wrapped round and round his waist, containing his accounts, his writing utensils, his sweetmeat-box, and often his stock-in-trade, too, if that stock consist of jewellery, or small ornaments.

He is an indefatigable trader, going about from house to house, with hired servants of his own carrying trunks, in which a miscellaneous assemblage of cottons, linens and silks, tapes, bobbins and pins, shawls, laces and muslins will be extricated from each other in a moment, and displayed, in tempting novelty, before the languid *Mem-saheb*, as he calls the European lady. She is too indolent to go to the bazar or to the European shops for what she wants, or she finds it inconvenient to go, for her shopping involves the preparation of a carriage, dressing, the attendance of servants, and a large amount of trouble. She need not stir. She will not go to the shop—the shop will come to her. The box-man, once squatted on the floor of the apartment, in the midst of his wares, his wily porters, generally Africans, dismissed to sleep in the verandah, exhibits novelty after novelty in tempting succession—a dress-piece, or a new lace, or a handsome shawl, or a brooch, or a ring. She must be hard indeed to please, if he has not something to please her—his boxes once deposited on the threshold, his goods once spread in most admired confusion about the floor, and he is sure of a sale.

Some "charming pattern" attracts the eye of the fair dame herself, some "love of a dress" enchants her slim daughter, who looks at the goods with "most hungry eyes," and after an hour spent in a strange conversation, half English, half Hindostanne, the Mussulman pockets his rupees, packs up his boxes, and prepares for departure, well-satisfied with the result of his morning's work. The ebony porters—brawny fellows, the very *caryatides* of male African humanity—place the huge trunks upon their heads, and slowly depart in Indian file; the Mussulman salesman, with many salaams to the fair purchasers, bringing up the rear, as he counts his gains mentally.

The extent to which this method of traffic is carried on in Calcutta is amazing, and not by any means patronized by Europeans alone. There are probably from fifteen to twenty thousand men so employed in the City of Palaces in fine weather; during the rainy seaso n the traffic is, of course, nearly suspended.

The Parsees form another and a most interesting class of the native community. The descendants of the fire-worshippers of Persia, who were driven from their native land by ruthless Moslemism, they retain pertinaciously to this hour the faith of their forefathers. An enlightened, interesting race notwithstanding—enlightened, inasmuch as they seek with avidity the illumination of the west; interesting, like the Jew, as a persecuted race. As much attached to their prophet, Zoroaster, as the Jew to Moses—money-making their employment—an employment in which they are wonderfully successful. "As rich as a Parsee," is almost proverbial in the East. Their mercantile houses are spread over the Indian Ocean in all its hives of commerce—from Australia to Arabia—from China to the Mauritius—their head-quarters at Bombay, however, where they abound in the greatest numbers.

In Calcutta we shall find the richer Parsees, as elsewhere, at the head of great mercantile firms, known honourably for good faith and honesty; their homes perfect palaces in luxury and magnificence, combining, not ungracefully, the superior taste and elegance of western ornament with the sensual comforts of the east. The poorer classes amongst them—for even amongst the Parsees there are *some* poor—work in ivory, in fancy woods, in metals, manufacturing elegant boxes, beautifully inlaid with all manner of ornaments too, and costly drinking-cups.

The appearance of the Parsee in the street indicates his success in the world; his self-reliance, his consciousness of being not of the crowd, but of a peculiar sacred class, very far removed from that crowd. The peculiar hat, covered with brown or purple figured silk, slopes back in a graceful semicircle from the forehead to the back of the head; his white tunic, neatly buttoned over his breast, fits tightly to the figure, and reaches nearly to the knees; his wide pantaloons, and shoes with curled toes, all combine to give him a strange appearance, even amid the groups of strangely-dressed Orientals in the street. His elevated head and large beaming eyes—his erect figure and portly person—all combine to impress the beholder favourably.

The Parsee passes the poor uneducated Hindoo, or drudging Indian Mussulman, with a somewhat supercilious smile. For *them* he has no respect. Both have persecuted him and his race cruelly in times past, and he has his revenge by pitying them now. They had their day, when he could but look forward to the future—to the future Paradise of the true believer, feeling sure that the time would come when *they* would be miserably damned, and when *he* would be for ever happy—but now things are changed. He still looks forward to that bright future, whether as confidently as before, I cannot decide; but the present has its bright side—illumination, cultivation, prosperity and ease for *him;* ignorance, want, drudgery for *them*—"revenge complete."

The inelegant figure of the yellow Chinese, with his ungraceful, loose shirt, and wide, ill-fitting pantaloons, is seen frequently, too, gliding about in these streets. A totally different being from the Muhammadan or the Parsee—different many ways. Business is the sole absorbing thought of *his* mind; and truly to look at him, with his odd, conical cap, and his ugly blouse, one feels certain that he has not sacrificed to the Graces, whatever may be the chief moving springs of his existence. A persevering, plodding, active workman, however, proving by his industry and his skill that if he is not so sure as the Mussulman or the Parsee of Paradise hereafter, he is surer of the necessity of attending to his business in this world. His expertness is proved by the fact, that if a Chinese carpenter, or a Chinese shoemaker, or a Chinese porter can be obtained, no Hindoo or Mussulman has a chance of employment. So that, with all his want of grace externally, there is a something hidden in the uncouth frame which makes the Chinaman take his place easily at the head of Orientals for dexterity and skill. The Parsee may perhaps compete with him, but, if so, the Parsee alone.

Having thus introduced the reader to the chief varieties of the genus *homo* to be found in Calcutta, it is but right that I should now allow him a little breathing time. As to buildings, there is not much that is necessary to be said here of *them*. Take *one* European house, and multiply it indefinitely, and you have the European quarter of Calcutta: take a sample or two of native hovels and native palaces, and multiply them indefinitely, and you have the native quarter. One bazar is a picture of all the bazars: one square, with its Grecian lines of architecture, broken by green venetians, a picture of all the squares: one tank, with its green margin and encircling rails, with its dusky watermen filling their pig-skins called "mussucks," to carry the water to the houses, a picture of every tank. The varieties of the human animal are the true curiosities of the town, and of these I have endeavoured to give you, good reader, a picture, however imperfect it may be.

CHAPTER IX.

HOW IT STRIKES A STRANGER.

"You will come to church with us to-day?" said the fair Miss Ducklet to me, one Sunday in May, a week or two after my arrival in Calcutta. We were literally melting on two opposite sofas at the time, looking out upon the wide level plain surrounding Fort-William—the *maidaun*, as it is called there. A Hindoo was vigorously pulling to and fro the large fan suspended from the ceiling, in the vain attempt to keep the air of the room in an endurable condition. The heat was astonishing—"*bohuth gurm*"—very hot—were the words upon every one's lips.

"*Bohuth gurm,*" said the servant, as he mopped himself with his scanty habiliments, untying the corner of his turban for that purpose.

"*Bohuth gurm,*" responded the Saheb, as he looked ferociously at the dusky automaton-looking native that was pulling the fan, and desired him to pull harder. Even Miss Ducklet, who was an iron-nerved young lady of the tragic order, that allowed nothing to ruffle or inconvenience her, and would never confess herself disconcerted or put out; even *she* did once deign to admit that it was "a remarkably hot season;" adding, however, by way of corollary, that she "had known many hotter."

But, in fact, there never was a May yet in Calcutta, since the black-hole business, that was not solemnly denounced by plethoric, apoplectic-looking gentlemen, in short jackets and tight whites, as *the hottest—the very hottest*—season they had known. The oldest inhabitant—that respectable individual so invariably appealed to on all points of meteorological science—positively did not remember a hotter season; so the newspapers said, and, of course, they know everything, and, equally of course, all they say must be true.

We were reclining, I said, on two couches, both commanding a view of the level plain without, stretching away to the Fort, I in a condition of incipient liquefaction, and finding it utterly impossible to do anything but mop, and mop, and mop again, as stream after stream kept coursing down my neck, Miss Ducklet enjoying the soothing influence of the breeze created by the punkah, as it gracefully waved her black curls about, and agitated pleasingly her muslin drapery.

Without, on the road that separated us from the brown grass on the maidaun, a native cart, drawn by two diminutive bullocks, occasionally creaked along, its driver sitting carelessly on the pole to which the bullocks were attached, using their tails, as the rudder of a ship is used, to guide the machine in the required direction. But it was only now and then that even he could muster up energy, amid the sweltering heat, to grasp the tails and shout out maledictions upon the mothers, sisters, grandmothers, and female relationship generally, of the innocent bullocks. For the most part, he resigned himself to an agreeable doze, out of which the bullocks would by no means have taken him by any violence of theirs, did not a deeper rut than usual start him now and then from his propriety, and make him grasp violently the rudder-like tails anew. On the dried-up, brown, crisp grass beyond, an occasional Muhammadan was to be seen at devotion, his little carpet spread out neatly before him, and his mouth constantly brought into contact with it as he stooped to kiss.

To the Anglo-Indian the sight is too common to cause a single turn of an eye, but to the reflective man of any race or clime, it is suggestive of many things. Faith is to be seen in its highest exercise in that man's unflinching eye and steady gaze; faith of the most exalted character, and hundreds of thousands of his co-religionists in India and elsewhere have similar faith, a faith that nothing can shake, which can make them endure anything, practise any amount of self-denial, do anything for their religion. Ludicrous, you say; yes, to us, the position is ludicrous; we are not accustomed to see the portion of our frame on which we sit elevated high into the air, whilst the face and feet are both upon the ground. It *has* its ludicrous aspect, too, like most other things, but it has also its deep sig nificancy, its high and holy meaning notwithstanding.

Blind, infatuated, bigoted, ignorant, unenlightened, superstitious that man may be, and probably is,—his whole duty, perhaps, consisting in shouldering a palanquin day by day, and carrying his fellow mortals in that vehicle for four pence a day or less,—but he has within him, too, a living principle that makes him see a far-off paradise to which *he* can aspire; a living principle, not a dead effete one, infecting the whole mind with its own corruption, but one that would make him dare and endure anything, rather than yield it up. You might tear his heart all bleeding from his body, but you could not make him give up that sturdy faith of his. Is it not, then, a living faith? and does not the man who is capable of retaining such, demand your sympathy and admiration?

A young officer in Bengal, not very long ago, saw only the ludicrous side of this exhibition, and as he passed a Mussulman sepoy who was praying to God and to Muhammad after his own fashion, he struck him a smart blow with his cane on the protruded portion of his person. The insult was not for him but for his religion, doubtless thought the sepoy, and grasping his bayonet, which lay beside him, he plunged it into the grinning Englishman—plunged it a foot deep into his body, and the young officer died. And the Mussulman? Why, the Mussulman, of course, was condemned to death by the *lex talionis* of Christian judges—could you doubt it?—He was hung by the neck until he died; "and the Lord have mercy on your soul," said the judge to him, as he passed the sentence.

But I am wandering from the plain, and the window, and the two couches, and the fair occupant of one of them.

"You will come to church with us to-day?" she asked.

"I will," said I.

I had never yet been in a Calcutta church, and I was anxious to see whether the listlessness of Anglo-Indian existence pervaded their worship as well as their daily life. No one who goes to India can help noting the religious enthusiasm of the Hindoos or Muhammadans; no one who has been in Ceylon, the want of religious enthusiasm amongst the Budhistic and Christian community. To thousands, I doubt not, in these days, it makes little difference whether the Almighty is worshipped by those around after the manner of the Roman Catholic, of the Lutheran, of the Presbyterian, of the Methodist, or of the Churchman, so that he *is* worshipped; and indeed it is a noble thing to see enthusiasm in worship of any kind. You go into a Roman Catholic chapel on the continent, and you see a man acting on a raised platform, and little boys waving censers, and men and women—four-fifths women and one-fifth men,—kneeling at the backs of the high chairs, and crossing, and sprinkling a little holy water on, themselves as they come in and go out, but there is no heart in it all—it is all form, vain, ostentatious, theatrical display. Not quite all, perhaps, but very nearly all.

You see a church full of people in England, and a popular preacher is to perform. Some are dozing, others admiring and being admired, others yawning, the majority apparently looking upon all preliminary to the sermon as a bore. The popular preacher never reads the prayers, he reserves himself for the pulpit, and when he gets up there, there is a little display of enthusiasm, but not much. These are not sights that can refresh the heart of man, or make him feel that religion is a want and a necessity, a great living eternal truth. Enthusiastic Puseyism has its noble aspects as well as enthusiastic Methodism; but better, a thousand times better, this earnest conviction of any kind, than the apathetic indifference and want of all faith too common now-a-days.

The Hindoo and the Mussulman seem for the most part at the present day, the most earnest worshippers, the Budhist and the Christian are alike indifferent. The one goes into his church or chapel to yawn and doze, the other into his temple to chew betel and expectorate, whilst they both equally pretend to be listening to what they will languidly assert to be the words of life. The Hindoo, however, who devotes his arm to a deity of his or others' imagination, and keeps that arm aloft hour after hour, and day after day, and week after week, until it can no longer be taken down, until it remains ever aloft, stiff, wasting, useless, and withering, that man must see far other things in his religion than mere senseless forms, and unmeaning acts of worship. To him religion must be a living reality, an active, yeast-like principle pervading the dull, inert mass of humanity. And to the Muhammedans, likewise. Think of the endurance necessary in India to keep intact the fast of the Ramazan; think of the poor labouring wretches that have been broiling all day long under a tropical sun, every particle of moisture in them exuding with heat and labour, and yet from sunrise to sunset they refrain from drinking a single drop of water. Yes, and rather than break that rigid fast, worn out with exhaustion, with thirst, with direst feverish, parching thirst,—they will lie down under a tree or in a verandah, and *die*—yes, die, rather than break the fast.

Such things happen every year in India, nay, hundreds of cases of such every year; and surely the faith that can make a man yield up his body to a lingering, torturing death, rather than break one of its commands, must be a living, working faith, and by no means a dead principle.

"This heat is almost unendurable," said I, as I got into the carriage into which I had already handed Mrs. and Miss Ducklet, in order to accompany them to church.

"What's that you said?" said Mr. Ducklet, a short, testy, round, puffing specimen of the Anglo-Indian species.

"I said this heat was almost unendurable," said I, raising my voice, for Mr. Ducklet was slightly deaf.

"A fine dry heat," he growled out in reply, "do nobody any harm—very healthy weather —pooh! pooh! griffins are always complaining."

"Griffin or no griffin," said I, "the thermometer at ninety-four degrees in the coolest room in the house is no joke; and besides, the newspapers, *Englishman*, *Hurkaru*, and *Star*, have all declared that it is one of the hottest seasons known for a long time."

"What's that you say?" asked my amiable companion again.

I repeated my observation in a louder key.

"The newspapers say so, do they?" asked Mr. Ducklet; "then that's the very reason why I would not believe it to be the case."

"Not even when the thermometer confirms their observation?" I screamed.

"What's that?—no, not even the thermometer," replied Mr. Ducklet; "there's not a thermometer in all Calcutta that tells the truth."

"Then, perhaps, you think that this is cool, agreeable, pleasant weather?" said I, as I endeavoured to stanch one tide that was pouring down between my whiskers and my ears, and another that went drop, drop, drop, from chin to breast.

"What's that you—a fine dry heat, very healthy weather," muttered Ducklet, as he lay back, exhausted, in the carriage, and fanned himself gently.

There was an end of the colloquy, and I did not rouse the ire of the rabid Anglo-Indian by saying another word about the heat.

"You have never yet been to a church in India?" said Miss Ducklet.

"No!" said I, "you are aware I only stopped in Madras three days, and last Sunday I was driven off by Mr. Sutra to see his country-house up the river."

"True," said she, "you will be delighted with Mr. Lollipops, such a dear, sweet, nice man he is, and his sermons I assure you are powerful, although as simple as the language of a babe."

"Indeed," said I. I could not well say much more.

"Yes," she continued, "he is foolishly blamed by many for being so simple, but surely without cause. It is exquisite to hear the sublimest truths in his mouth becoming food for the tenderest believers—the faintest-hearted beginners."

"Is it possible?" I asked, not knowing very well indeed what to reply under such circumstances.

"O, Julia is quite enthusiastic in Mr. Lollipop's praise," said the mamma; "she thinks that there never was such a man before."

"Mr. Lollipops is to be envied," said I, solemnly.

Miss Ducklet smiled, her mamma looked grave, and old Ducklet starting out of a doze into which he had been just gliding off, cried out, "What's that you say?"

Following in the wake of many other similar vehicles, we at length entered the enclosure round the church, and in due time were deposited upon the steps leading into the sacred edifice. Before I had time to offer my arm to Miss Ducklet, her mamma had taken it, and conducted me majestically up the aisle, Mr. Ducklet following with the fair Julia. It was evident that Mrs. D. had no idea of allowing her daughter to be walked off with by a man whose lacs of rupees were yet to be made, and whose monthly income was of an extremely attenuated character. She was too prudent for that!

Now the Ducklets were people of consideration in Calcutta. By the exercise of a vigorous constitution Ducklet *père* had lived up to a high position in the service, that is, had outlived numerous competitors, and was in a fair way, if he survived, to become, in a few years more, a Member of Council. As we brushed up the body of the church therefore, Mrs. Ducklet held her head higher as we occasionally heard a whisper from admiring lips of—"The Ducklets!" This felicity was denied to the old gentleman himself, but mother and daughter equally enjoyed it, and as they swept up to their pew in the best position the church afforded, and, like a box at the Opera, therefore all the more expensive, their forms became more and more erect, until it was impossible for the human frame to attain greater rigidity. A few nods of recognition were exchanged with the people in the vicinity, and at length we found ourselves seated on the coolest soft cushions that could be invented. How it had come to pass I could not discover, but I found myself in a corner by the side of Mrs. Ducklet, who had her husband next to her, and beyond him, at the extreme end of the seat, was situated the enchanting Julia.

There was a moment of repose, during which we endeavoured to recover our breath after the exertion of making our way on foot up the church, and of tumbling over hassocks and footstools to get into our places, and then mother and daughter simultaneously precipitated themselves upon two hassocks in front of them—the movement was rapid but graceful, and nothing could be more elegant than the ribands and the white muslin of the young lady fluttering beneath the punkah, as she bowed her head easily over the velvet-covered prayer-book she had first deposited on the ledge in front of her. Mr. Ducklet retained his seat, and, as I was rapidly melting, I followed his example.

The scene presented by the interior of the church was a strange one. In all directions the large fans, called punkahs, were hanging by ropes from the lofty roof, and were pulled vigorously to and fro by natives who attended church for that purpose. With the turbans on, and bare feet—*their* symbols of respect—they moved noiselessly over the vacant spaces by the sides of the rows of pews, each holding the end of a rope in his hand, and as the large canvas fan fixed on a wooden frame swung from him he followed it a few steps, and then, with a vigorous tug and a few steps backward, brought it back again to the side. A long line of natives so employed stretched down either side of the sacred edifice, whilst similar functionaries lined the galleries above, all busily and noiselessly plying their vocation, their ordinary every-day vocation on this day of rest, in the very House of God. It looked strange, but, as Mr. Lollipops assured me subsequently at dinner one day, it was absolutely necessary; the heat would be otherwise intolerable, and people would not go to church;

and besides, they were heathens, those punkah-pullers, and might possibly be improved by some word in season by their attendance—which, as I found they were ignorant of English, did not subsequently appear to me to be very probable, although at the time I had nothing to say against it.

Leaving the morality of the question aside, however, for the present, let me describe what was actually the case. Backwards and forwards swung the heavy-looking punkahs, backwards and forwards walked the noiseless natives pulling them, without intermission and without variation. A similar fan moved over the head of the junior chaplain in the reading desk, as he read the prayers, another over the venerable Mr. Lollipops at the communion table, who was wisely reserving himself there, in the coolest portion of the church, for the pulpit. For a moment the heads of the junior chaplain and his clerk were apparent as they made their way monotonously through the appointed prayers, and then they were lost to view in the broad fan that came sweeping along with its fresh current of air, hiding clergyman and clerk, reading-desk and pulpit, at once from the view. The congregation was accustomed to it, the ministers were accustomed to it, and to them it was the usual aspect of the church in the hot season—nothing new or strange about it.

To me it was altogether novel, and what with watching the sudden appearances and disappearances of the chaplain's head, and the angry looks cast by indignant elderly gentlemen, yes, even by Ducklet himself, at the unfortunate punkah-pullers when they relaxed in the slightest degree from the orthodox strength and vigour with which the punkah *should* be pulled, I found it utterly impossible to give my usual attention to the service.

The circumstances were so novel, I might well be excused. Immediately in front of me sat the celebrated Dr. Mouthit, a medical man of small dimensions and large pretensions, and well known from Puttledangah to Cassiabegaun. His shining black hair just appeared above the rail in front of me, as he maintained his seat of imperturbable gravity, a gravity suited to the place, but caused by his own sense of his own vast importance, notwithstanding his personal insignificance. Some one has said that the true ruler is the man of a great idea. Dr. Mouthit was then a venerable ruler, for he had, as *Punch* said long ago of Disraeli, a great idea of himself. It was amusing to see even this man roused to irate displays by the overpowering heat. When the dingy air-disturber's movements became slower and more feeble, until the heat seemed to descend, and, like Sancho's sleep, cover a man all over like a cloak, then would Dr. Mouthit wax wroth, and with the sternest possible expression of countenance turn slowly round upon the culprit.

The moment their eyes met the effect was electric—the punkah jerked back or was pulled forward with an energy that sent the leaves of the prayer-book fluttering hither and thither at any but the right places, and lifted up the heavy load of caloric that was gradually settling down upon one's head and shoulders. The worthy doctor's head, however, was not immediately restored to its wonted calm dignity and attitude of repose. For a full minute the awful gaze that had worked such wonders was continued, and then, as on a pivot, the face revolved into its usual position, and the look of supreme self-satisfaction and conscious dignity was resumed.

I could not help thinking sometimes, and the thought added to the ludicrous aspect of the entire scene, that "darky" was playing tricks upon the magnificent doctor, tricks of which I by no means approved, for two reasons; the first was that they were unsuitable to the place and the occasion; the second, that I was a victim of these experiments as well as the supreme Mouthit. It struck me that "darky" was a quiz, and that to excite and arouse the little doctor's wrath he voluntarily relaxed his efforts occasionally, and permitted the punkah to subside into easy-going monotonous vibrations; if so, he really deserved the awful frowns with which the usually imperturbable face of the doctor reproved his ill-timed trickery.

It was too hot to kneel I found,—judging by what I saw around me, in the hot season,—and, indeed, at all seasons in Calcutta, people dispense with kneeling altogether in churches. Standing is a relief after a long interval of listless sitting repose, and stand they will accordingly, but, with the exception of a few enthusiastic ladies like Mrs. and Miss Ducklet, who like to obtain a reputation for sanctity, and to keep it when obtained, none knelt.

I could not help observing everything that went on around me; the circumstances were so strange, every-thing about the church wore so entirely new an aspect, that it would have been impossible for the most fervent piety at once to have settled down into its wonted spirit of devotion.

CHAPTER X.

THE FASHIONABLE CHURCH IN CALCUTTA.

On looking round the church I was astonished to find that the men who were labouring at the punkahs were the only natives in it! After the glowing accounts I had read in England and Ceylon of the success of missionary exertions in India, I was naturally astonished at this, and looked and looked again, in the vain hope of discovering some quarter of the church set apart for neophytes and proselytes. No, there was no such thing. I was in a fashionable church, and were native converts encouraged to attend it, it would no longer be a fashionable one.

I found on enquiry that there *were* churches which the native converts attended, but they were those which the European community did *not* attend. There might be a community of feeling between English and Indian Christians, but there was no community of seats and sittings and churches. Even those who were warmest in praise of missionary exertions were sometimes also warmest in deprecating the idea of mixing Europeans and Hindoos in places of worship—"It would be putting the natives on a footing of equality with us at once," observed one fair enthusiast; "And Christianity does not do so," I remarked. "Yes, in religious privileges, it does, but not in material matters," was the reply; "there must be due subordination and proper distinctions made on earth."

It is the very principle which has driven the poor so much from the Church of England in its native home. The well-dressed "respectability" of England can find pews and seats ready for them, where they may meet other well-dressed respectabilities like themselves, but the poor man finds no such welcome; his worn or torn coat is a sufficient reason for thrusting him into remote corners and inconvenient seats where he can probably hear nothing, or else is made a gazing-stock for his well-dressed neighbours; and finding that the House of God is no home for him, he turns on his way, determined that he shall intrude no more. The very poor, at the present day, too often have *not* the gospel preached to them by the Church at least in England—let the Church look to it ere it be too late.

At length, Mr. Lollipops mounted the pulpit stairs, and, with a bland, benignant aspect, surveyed the congregation beneath him in all the meekness of clerical inspection. He would have been a well-looking man had he allowed nature to make him so, but he would not, and the large cheeks and chin which she would have covered with black shining curls were left in as naked ugliness as the razor could accomplish. He was one of those extraordinary products of this extraordinary age who united the ideas of sanctity and shaven faces, of wickedness and beards, forgetting that the Divine master whom he professed to follow, and the early fathers whom he professed to imitate, shaved off neither beard nor moustache. Plastered down carefully on either side of his face were black locks, which nature had intended to be waving and beautiful in form, not stiff in ugly rigidity and waxy immobility. But these well-combed ornaments, these shining plastered black hairs that exhibited so well the phrenological development of the saint-like Lollipops, were other symbols of piety and meekness, or, at least, were intended as such, and by numerous ladies of his congregation were so regarded. Such men would leave soldiers alone the attributes of humanity, sinking themselves and others into a state of mawkish insipidity and affected sentimentalism, which would have all the characteristics of female weakness without its charms.

Miss Ducklet was quite right in saying that the sentiments of Mr. Lollipops were like those of a babe in simplicity. He was one of those men who, without being fluent, insist on preaching extempore. He explained to us that light and darkness were opposed to each other, that the one was considered the contrary to the other—that "the glorious light of the sun illumined the earth in the day time," and that "in its absence the darkness of night brooded over the face of nature;" that "these phenomena were constant and incessant, unvarying and invariable, whatever might be the wishes or desires of men." He was proceeding to enforce, elaborately, the novel truth, that darkness was symbolical of evil, light of good, when my attention was diverted from him by a low smothered sound,—like bare wet feet pattering over a slippery pavement,—which was evidently in my immediate vicinity.

I looked round, but could see no signs of animation save in the indefatigable punkah-pullers, who still plied unremittingly their monotonous labour. The congregation was reclining easily in the pews, the majority of the eyes closed in order to shut out that very light the preacher was describing and illustrating "so simply and so powerfully," as Miss Ducklet afterwards described it, when a repetition of the sound caused me to turn my head once more in search of it. I found out the cause at once.

A rustling of stiff muslins and ribands in

my immediate vicinity convinced me that Mrs Ducklet's elbow was making its way forcibly into her husband's side to prevent another similar explosion; audibly had Ducklet snored twice, the second time louder than the first, and the cavernous rattlings and rumblings which preceded a third ebullition were already commencing, when Mrs. Ducklet's elbow was thus brought into rapid collision with the old gentleman's ribs. Not before it was time, however, for other heads as well as mine had turned to find out the cause, their owners discovering it readily, however, as if they were not altogether unaccustomed to it. Even Mr. Lollipops himself had looked down at the noisy delinquent reproachfully and yet mildly—reproachfully, as his meek eyes reposed for a moment on the offending nose of the innocent Ducklet, which was elevated higher than any other portion of his head; mildly, as they met those of the still more innocent Julia, who was drinking in his words with all the fervour of female devotion, and who had left the correction of the culprit to her mamma.

Mrs. Ducklet's elbow, I said, came rapidly

into collision with the old gentleman's ribs—I had no doubt of it—I felt it plainly, seated as I was at the other side of her. The rumblings and rattlings of the offending nasal organ ceased at once, and, turning towards his better-half abruptly, Mr. Ducklet sharply asked, "What are you about?"

"Hush!" said the lady, fixing her eyes on the preacher—"you have been snoring."

"What's that you say?" asked Ducklet, louder than was consistent with the place and time.

"You were snoring—snoring," said Mrs. Ducklet, tartly, in his ear, and shaking herself testily into an attitude of attention again.

"I wasn't snoring," said Ducklet, pertinaciously—"I wasn't snoring—you shouldn't poke a man in that sort of style."

"You *were* snoring," repeated the fair dame, still keeping her eyes fixed on the reverend orator.

"What's that you say?" asked her husband again.

"You *were* snoring—snoring awfully," reiterated Mrs. Ducklet; "you disturbed everybody."

"What's that? I wasn't snoring, and if I do snore, I'll thank you not to poke me that way again," said the offended husband, wiping his spectacles at the same time, and putting them on, to look angrily at Mr. Lollipops.

But Mr. Lollipops was a meek man, and would by no means return such a stare, or indeed notice it at all, acting in this matter as prudence and common sense dictated, for Ducklet every one expected would one day be a Member of Council, and it was useless to stand on bad terms with him. Indignantly kicking over a hassock that lay in front of him, pushing a little from side to side, thereby disturbing both his neighbours, and twitching his spectacles testily upon his nose, Ducklet settled down again into an attitude of attention, satisfied apparently at length with the annoyance he had given his wife and daughter for the rude assault he had endured.

"Yes, my friends," continued Mr. Lollipops, "the Christian should be a burning and a shining light, particularly in a pagan land. He should illuminate the darkness around, as a lighted candle introduced into a dark chamber sheds a flood of light into the remotest corners. Let us ask ourselves the question, Do we indeed shine? you ask yourselves the question each one, Does he shine? and I will similarly interrogate myself, Do I shine? There must not only be the appearance of shining, there must be the reality; without that reality we are not what we ought to be."

In this strain the reverend gentleman was proceeding in his shining discourse, and I have endeavoured in both instances to give as nearly as possible the very words he used, for they are engraven on my memory, when another rumbling foreboded a determined snore on Ducklet's part, and brought Mrs. Ducklet's elbow and foot both into play, to prevent it. Poor woman! she was to be pitied, and the consciousness that she was to be so pitied, sat upon her countenance and illuminated it. 'Look at me, martyr-like, enduring all these sufferings from a bear of a husband, uncomplainingly, unrepiningly, losing the discourse of the good Mr. Lollipops, and having my temper tried so severely, yet without a murmur!' Such was the translation of her pursed-up mouth, her quickly-moving eye, and her air of would-be stoical endurance.

"You're beginning to snore again," said she in her husband's ear.

I could not tell whether the sentiment of disturbed devotion or pleasure at being enabled to punish the delinquent prevailed in the words, but certainly both were to be found there.

"Bah! nonsense!" replied the offending Ducklet, "there must be some mistake about it; but it appears to me that Lollipops will never be done to day."

Miss Ducklet and her mammasimultaneously turned a look of horror on the culprit, and then resumed their attitude of attention.

"He! he!" quietly laughed Ducklet to himself, as he observed it, and, taking his spectacles off his nose, he looked hard at the punkah puller, who noticed the glance, pulling all the harder in consequence; and then, replacing his glasses, the great man once more prepared to turn his attention to the preacher and listen to the discourse.

It was certainly a long sermon, there could be no doubt of that; and, as far as I could discover, the greater part of it consisted in a constant reiteration of the figurative meanings of light and darkness, which he had so fully explained at the beginning, and of the exhortation to put the question searchingly home each one to himself, Do I shine? One would almost fancy the reverend orator was conjugating the verb "shine" interrogatively? Do I shine? Dost thou shine? Does he shine? Do we shine? Do ye shine? Do they shine?

Some years have rolled away since that discourse was delivered, but the portions which were at the moment impressed upon my memory have never left it. If Mr. Lollipops had condescended to write his sermons, they would doubtless have been very different; as it was, they consisted solely of repetitions and truisms of the tritest possible character. Before the conclusion of the sermon, the church reminded me of Hogarth's picture of the Sleeping Congregation; one striking difference, however, there was—in Hogarth's picture the clerk, at least, is wide awake; in the fashionable Calcutta Church the clerk was fast asleep. All around were to be seen closed eyes and heads leaning back as softly as hard rails and wooden ledges would permit; here and there an energetic snorer, who had threatened to disturb the slumberers in his vicinity, had been rudely called to order and awaked, but those whose nasal organs did not similarly offend, were allowed to sleep on and take their rest.

It was truly a lamentable, and, at the same time, a strange sight. The vast majority of those for whom the sermon was intended, and who could have understood all of it that was at all intelligible, were fast asleep; whilst those who knew nothing of the language, and who could not therefore profit by it in the least, were actively and wakefully employed in adding to the comfort of the sleepers. As the clergyman closed the large Bible and squared it before him, a signal that his remarks were at length coming to a conclusion, there was a general rustling amongst the congregation, that indicated preparation for the *finále*.

Altogether, a more truly melancholy spectacle than this outrageous burlesque of devotion, it would not have been easy to parallel elsewhere. To judge by the fashionable Calcutta Church, religion was a mere ceremonial mockery—an ingenious contrivance for passing away one day in the week in strange contrast with the others. There were doubtless there, as elsewhere, pious men and pious women, but they were singularly the exception. Drowsy discourses, ill-prepared, or not prepared at all, and drowsy congregations who listened to little of them, the rule—neither an energetic preacher, nor a wakeful audience, was to be found in the fashionable church in the City of Palaces at that time.

It is in no spirit of hostility to individuals that I make these assertions, and, if I have described what many would have concealed, it is rather with the object of drawing attention to the fact amongst those who have it in their power to remedy this lamentable state of things than merely to point a moral, or adorn a tale. There is not much to boast of, it is true, in the fashionable churches of London, with regard to energy and earnestness; but the earnestness displayed there, little as it is, is absolute enthusiasm when compared with the total want of heart in the best finished and most comfortable churches in the City of Palaces.

To proceed, however, with my description.

Mr. Lollipops' Bible was closed—a general buzz of preparation for departure pervaded the congregation—active ladies who had slept comfortably with one eye partially open, proceeded to urge their children and spouses to wakefulness and alertness by kicks, pushes and nudges—oily gentlemen, who had been dreaming of inflicting summary vengeance on offending punkah-pullers, rubbed their heads energetically with their handkerchiefs, and then slightly fanned themselves in the hope of aiding the punkah—little boys and girls screwed their knuckles into their eyes and rubbed them until they peeped out red, bleared and angry-looking at the treatment—while fast young men, who had come to church to please their uncles or their innamorátas, seized their hats, and brushed from them imaginary particles of dust; thereby displaying at one and the same time, their new hats or staff caps, their elegant handkerchiefs and their "superb" rings. So great a sensation did the closing of the clergyman's Bible cause in that fashionable church.

"I never could discover," remarked a facetious friend to me, subsequently, "why Mr. Lollipops ever left off talking, there being neither beginning, middle, nor end to his discourses, properly speaking."

"When one has preached a congregation asleep, the only way to awake them is by stopping," I replied.

"Yes," said he, "that accounts for it in the hot weather, but leaves the mystery unsolved as far as the cold season is concerned."

In the verandah without the church, where the carriages were awaited and called for with much noise, reminding one forcibly of the large staircase at the Italian Opera in London, some of the ladies praised the simplicity and beauty of Mr. Lollipops' sermon, whilst the gentlemen speculated on the arrival of the next mail, and conjectured the condition of European politics, which it would disclose. At length we found ourselves boxed up as before in Ducklet's luxurious carriage, every one in excellent spirits—Ducklet himself evidently refreshed by his nap, and anticipating joyously the delicacies of the luncheon, which in Calcutta has grown into a normal meal of the most formidable dimensions and length. Towards evening we rode out upon the Strand by the river's bank

—a drive and promenade where the European population of Calcutta endeavour to get a little fresh air in the short interval which elapses between the intense heat of the day and the approach of darkness.

CHAPTER XI.

THE EVENING DRIVE.

The display of carriages and saddle-horses which nightly traverse the Strand and the Course in Calcutta in fine weather, would surprise even the cockney fresh from the glories of Hyde Park and Rotten Row. The expense of keeping a vehicle in Calcutta being comparatively insignificant, every family, in even middling circumstances, has its carriage, with either one or two horses, the proportion of really elegant vehicles being greater than elsewhere. In too many cases, I believe, the anxiety to make a proper display upon the Strand is carried to a ridiculous extent. Parsimony is equally practised at home, for instance, by Mr. and Mrs. Smudge, who came out lately from England, and by Mr. and Mrs. De Souza, whose swarthy little ones proclaim their country, to enable them to drive their elegant barouches with a coachman and two livery servants behind.

To this foolish display the small cost of keeping servants tends to lead many who would otherwise avoid it. For each horse a *syce* or groom is employed, at the rate of eight or ten shillings a month, wages on which he feeds himself and his family, smokes constantly, and is all day lounging about his master's stables, if not actually employed in working. A few more shillings provides for him a neat white or red cotton dress, with a sash and turban displaying the colours of his master's livery; and it is really astonishing to see how much show can thus be made at a very trifling outlay. Hence it is, that behind Mr. and Mrs. Smudge's, and Mr. and Mrs. De Souza's barouches, we see two idle *loons* with blackish brown faces, arrayed in clean apparel, and displaying the red and yellow of their liveries to the best advantage; hence the uniformity apparent between the coachman on the box and the servants behind, which gives a stranger the idea of a really well appointed and elegant establishment.

But the horses?—ah, we must not be too critical upon the horses in these cases. The barouche glitters, it is true, in all the glory of newly-applied varnish, laid on, indeed, by Messrs. Smudge and De Souza themselves, or by their servants under their special supervision and direction; but, on the horses, we really must not be too critical. The chestnut one on the off-side, which conveys Mr. Smudge or Mr. De Souza to office every morning, is rather thin, it is true, and does not look particularly likely to run away either now or at any future time; his companion, a black-a-moor, with a shaggy coat, is a vicious specimen of horse-flesh, that obstinately refuses to go in single harness, and can only be coaxed along by having the chestnut Rozinante to play with and attempt to bite as he proceeds, the said unfortunate Rozinante pulling him and the barouche, and the five Smudges or six De Souzas with three servants along—no wonder he is not fat.

Did you but see the knowing cuts that ferocious-looking coachman, with his wiry moustache, gives the pair as he gets to the end of the drive and is about turning—did you but see how he takes care to avoid thrashing them when really good equipages are in the neighbourhood, and how *brawly* he lays it on when they have passed—upon the black-a-moor for impeding the chestnut—upon the chestnut for not drawing on the black-a-moor faster—you would say the man had a discretion and a carefulness of his master's reputation which were highly commendable.

The horsemen and horsewomen, too, present contrasts as striking as the carriages. The noblest Arabs and the swiftest Australians may—or rather, might *then*—be seen bestrode and managed by some of the best horsemen in the world; I say "might then," for in the altered condition of affairs, it will probably be some time before Australian horses are again brought to the Calcutta market. Accustomed continually to horse exercise, sometimes of the most violent and dangerous description, as in pig-sticking, the Anglo-Indian is probably one of the best horsemen in the world—the true Anglo-Indian—he who has spent fifteen or twenty years in the country, and who, instead of sinking down into a debauchery that unfits him for all manly exercise, or gross gluttony, has retained some of his English energy amidst the suffocating heats of the tropics.

Not by any means that all the horsemen whom one sees on the Calcutta Course or Strand are of this character, far from it. Mr. Grildam, for instance, who has lately arrived to be an assistant (there are no "clerks" in the mercantile houses in Calcutta) in the house of Mota, Soostey, and Co., and who regularly takes his vespernal ride upon the Strand, has not yet arrived at such perfection in horsemanship as to feel at all easy or secure in his new seat, notwithstanding the experience of horseflesh he acquired in the Battersea Fields on Sundays. He is tortured by those unsteady ears of the animal, which no soothing on his part can keep quiet; he watches them with all the diligence of an aural anatomical student as they now bend forwards, and Grildam prepares for an agonizing shy by grasping the mane with his fingers and the saddle with his knees, smiling the while, or attempting to smile.

Cruel horse!—it was a false alarm, and the

indignant Grildam is trying to forgive and forget, when the ruthless ears are pricked up at the clattering rumbling of an old vehicle coming up behind. Grildam throws his head anxiously round, wishing devoutly that these very old carriages were consigned to the kitchen fires, and bestowing anything but a blessing, in concise but emphatic English, on their occupants. His steed trots a few paces as the vehicle comes nearer, sending Grildam thereby up and down, much after the manner of the shuttlecock that children knock into the air and hit falling to "keep it up;" it is precisely thus that Grildam is kept up, constantly coming down on exactly the same spot as that from which he ascended, and pulling hard, but not *too* hard—he knows better than that—upon the reins.

The big, round drops that course after each other down Grildam's cheeks, are evidence at once of the sufferings he endures, and of the heat of the climate. But the lumbering carriage, with its rattling, disjointed roll, has passed by, and for a moment Grildam feels what it is to be a horseman; feels, indeed, an honest pride at his success, firmly convinced that he has just emerged from a frightful contest with the animal, and has completely conquered him. He has no doubt that others are admiring him as well as himself, and throwing himself jauntily forwards, he proceeds to get his handkerchief from his pocket to wipe his face withal after the conflict.

He does not give up his inspection of the ears, however—such carelessness would be dangerous; and just as he has succeeded in abstracting his handkerchief from his pocket, he sees them laid almost flat down upon the animal's neck, pointing ominously towards him, as if to tell of kicking, rearing, plunging, and curvetting to come. There is not an instant to be lost; and thrusting the handkerchief anywhere, Grildam devotedly prepares for another encounter, thinking to himself what an abominable horse, whilst he soothingly mutters, "poor fellow! poor fellow!" He would pat his neck if he dared, but the experiment might be perilous; he therefore contents himself with the "poor fellow! poor fellow!"

His horse has an antipathy to flies, and one of them having settled on his side, he has thrown back his ears, and lashed it off with his tail; but how was Grildam to know that was all? He had often heard that a horse's ears were the index to his mind, and every change of them brought some corresponding fear into his own imagination. It is no wonder, therefore, that he should be constantly alarmed, particularly after having had two tumbles from the "eminently quiet animal" his friend Sukchilly had sold him. He has been recommended horse-exercise, however, and with John Bull pertinacity, he *will* persevere until he succeeds in sitting a horse with tolerable comfort, although why he should learn to ride, or rather to walk his horse on the Strand or Course, instead of going to a less frequented part of the large plain round the Fort, is a matter of taste which Grildam alone can decide.

At present it is quite evident the horse is the master, and knows it well, with all a horse's instinctive sagacity; but "the time *will* come," as Grildam has been known grimly to declare, "when he will smart for it." The reckless, break-neck way in which men will ride up behind him and pass him at a hand gallop, has often called forth Grildam's mute but not less hearty condemnation. From afar he hears the horrid sound, and has two or three times mustered up courage enough to take a glimpse at the dare-devil who is about to torture him, but he finds that the glance round is useless, so keeping a tight grip with hand, and knee, and foot, he watches the ears intently, and prepares for disaster.

Like an avalanche crashing down upon the doomed village at the base of the mountain, on comes the clattering trooper at a pace that makes Grildam feel as if just pulled from the bath, the horse's hoofs madly plunging over the well-kept road or grass, and, as Grildam too well knows, steering directly for *him*. His impression is, indeed, that any wild horseman in Calcutta would willingly go out of his way a mile or two to have the pleasure of madly cantering up and passing him at the least possible distance, and at this conclusion he believes he has arrived, by the soundest principles of inductive reasoning.

On, like a hurricane, rushes the furious equestrian, and Grildam's horse, anxious to be off too, pulls hard at the rein, and tries to break into the mildest possible canter, but his master is firm, and will not yield an inch, so after a useless bobbing up and down of some minutes' duration, during which Grildam feels as if his head and his body were playing at "hide and go seek" with each other, the contest ends, and our hero breathes freely once more, that is, as freely as a man under such circumstances can be expected to breathe.

Here, again, I recognized the great Mouthit, enjoying himself in all the glories of a military coat and staff cap. In the church he had been the personification of all that assumed dignity and pompous importance, which are ridiculous in any one, but particularly so in the hero of five feet nothing. On the Strand he was the personification of affected, foolish, and middle-aged foppery. The livery of the servants proclaims his barouche to be one hired from the first livery stables of the town, and therefore known to be expensive. He likes that; his own barouche is *nominally* constantly under repair, and so he is obliged to send to "Gorah, Wallah, and Co." for "one of their machines;" but as his official duties necessitate the frequent hiring of vehicles from them at John Company's expense, he doubtless has an account with them.

Mouthit, as I have intimated, is a true Calcutta star—a great little man there of the first importance. He does not see himself how Calcutta could get on without him. He, Frederick Mouthit, is secretary to at least half-a-dozen committees; the Baboo Goluck Chunder Testimonial Committee; the Sir Smith Pelham Fund; the Consumption Hospital Committee; the Pharmaceutical College Board; the Council of Sanitary Improvement, and a host of others, besides holding *six* staff appointments, all, as the play-bills say, "too numerous to mention."

He is a useful man, then, somebody suggests; notoriety, sir, is what he wants, and he gets it. He lives up to his own small ideal, and realizes it. Not that he does the work of any one of these committees; he will attend them as long as Members of Council, and Judges, and Governors attend, but no longer; the work is done by European or native assistants, not by him. Indeed, it would be impossible for him to do it, for has he not in the press the great Bengali anatomical work, which is to immortalize him, and of which "Fasciculus Fifteen" has just appeared? Not that he understands a word of Bengali, he has no time for that. Government pays him for the work, and he pays others for the Bengali and the plates, and the work is issued with *his* name and titles in full on the title-page. *That* is what he wants—the title-page is his object. Notoriety honestly if you can, but notoriety at any price, is his motto. He has the tact to sail with the wind, and he is a successful man, as charlatans and humbugs often are. He can lick the hand of the man high in office whose patronage he wants, and he can stamp and swear indignantly at the quiet remonstrance of the drudge for whom he has no further use, and so, trimming his sails to the wind, he gets swimmingly along, a wonderful man, as hundreds are ready to affirm.

There is scarcely a colony in which some Mouthit or other is not to be found upon a larger or smaller scale. Calcutta, however, is an extensive place, and the inlet to a continent, so there is room in it for a more gigantic specimen of the genus humbug than elsewhere. He is seen through, of course, by hundreds; but amid the constant whirl of Calcutta life, the coming and going which form the bulk of Anglo-Indian society, a man who has wormed himself, corkscrew fashion or otherwise, into half-a-dozen good berths, is sure to find support.

The men at the head of society have no time to investigate character or merits: they find a man regarded by their predecessors as active and able, quite willing to do their faintest bidding quietly, and it is enough. They will find no opposition in that quarter, let their measures be never so absurd—no hint of any such thing—but, on the contrary, all servility, all obedience, and it is enough for them—they ask no more.

These convictions as to Mouthit's real character were, of course, the growth of some years' subsequent experience. On the Sunday of which I write, I knew nothing of him, for, celebrated as he was from one end of Calcutta to the other, his fame had not reached beyond it.

"That is surely the little gentleman that sat in front of us in church to-day," said I to Miss Ducklet, as she bowed to him.

"Yes," said she, "the same; a very remarkable man, Dr. Mouthit."

"Remarkable!" I echoed; "how? in what way?—for his attention to dress?"

"O dear no," replied my companion; "but remarkable generally—I don't know exactly how—but his name is always in the newspapers, and every one has a very high opinion of him."

"He speaks and writes well, perhaps," I suggested.

"I never heard him speak," was the reply, "nor did I ever read anything he wrote, but he's very clever. He is secretary to everything, and agent for everything else."

"Ah, I see," said I; "a sort of universal genius, that can turn his attention to anything."

"And then he does so much to enlighten the natives," said Miss Ducklet, "by publishing Bengali books and such like."

"He is a good Oriental scholar then," said I.

"Well, it's really very extraordinary," was the reply; "but Major Subjanta, the great linguist, says Dr. Mouthit doesn't know a word of Bengali; but I suppose the natives write the books, and he revises and corrects them."

I did not consider this very probable, if he did not understand the language; but, anxious not to press the point too far, I made no objection, and in a minute or two we found some other theme of conversation. All this time, Mr. Ducklet had been riding beside us, too much absorbed in the consciousness of his own dignity, as vehicle after vehicle swept by us, to notice our conversation—indeed, his deafness would have prevented his catching it, had he so wished.

At length we turned our horses' heads homewards towards Chowringhee, the west end of Calcutta, the well-built, clean, regular, and European portion of the city; the filthy, irregular, narrow streets of the rest of the town being occupied almost exclusively by natives. As we walked our horses quietly towards Ducklet's house—a palace in this City of Palaces—a young officer joined us, who was apparently going in the same direction. The darkness of night was fast falling over the city, and, as the new arrival and Miss Ducklet kept up an animated conversation in too low a tone to be heard by us, Ducklet and I were soon left in advance, walking our horses side by side—not intentionally so, on our parts, as I perceived at once. A vehicle with the dark liveries of Gorah, Wallah and Co. dashed by us.

"That's Dr. Mouthit, is it not?" I screamed into Ducklet's ear.

"What's that you — yes, Dr. Mouthit, Dr. Mouthit, it is," replied my companion.

"A remarkable man, Miss Ducklet informs me."

"Eh? what's that? Yes, a remarkable man, a very remarkable man, a man I have a great esteem for," said Ducklet.

Effect and cause I thought—the esteem the cause, the remarkable character the effect.

"He has distinguished himself, I suppose," said I.

"What's that you say?" asked the old gentleman.

"He has distinguished himself, I suppose," I screamed out louder than ever, to the amusement of Layjow, the young officer behind me, whom I could almost hear audibly grinning at my endeavours to maintain a conversation.

"Distinguished himself?" replied Ducklet, "O, yes, of course, very much, in every thing. When anything is to be done, Mouthit's the man to do it."

And here our conversation ended, for I had no disposition to minister further to the amusement of the parties behind us. Before we reached the gate, Layjow had taken leave of the fair Julia, and, cantering gracefully past us as he waved his hand, disappeared in the darkness.

A heavy Calcutta dinner of fifteen courses closed the day's entertainment, at which Mrs. Ducklet was sullen, Miss Ducklet in a reverie, and her papa at the *acme* of enjoyment. The servants stood behind us with folded arms like breathing statues, noiselessly gliding about the room, as they changed the plates or removed the dishes; the punkah vigorously pulled, sent the steam of the viands and the fragrance of the rich sauces and *entrées* into our faces, in order to make the contrast greater when the fruit made its appearance, and the cool breeze, wafting the pleasant favour of mangoes, pine-apples, mangosteens, and peaches about, imparted life and enjoyment to all of us.

The former part of the entertainment had been stupid and dull, notwithstanding the perfection of the arrangements, the appetizing character of the dishes, the glare of the costly chandeliers, and the excellence of the wines; but, with the fruit, the heart seemed to be opened—nature made us natural, and as servants disappeared, and when the made dishes of the kitchen had given place to the products of the orchard, all was light and joy.

Mrs. Ducklet's sullenness evaporated, and she quaffed her iced claret with enjoyment, whilst she delicately sipped a mangosteen. Miss Ducklet's reverie was at an end, and she dilated with eloquence on the relative merits of the fruits, whilst her slightly flushed cheek told of pleasing excitement and roused imagination; it was fortunate for me that I had seen on what intimate terms Layjow was with her, or the grace and eloquence of her figure and movements would have gone far at that happy moment to make an impression on my heart. Ducklet had enjoyed the good things of the table abundantly, and as he played with his fruit, his hearing wonderfully improved, and he had a gracious "he! he!" ready for every attempt at a joke.

To me the former part of the dinner, with its tedious removals, had been dull and monotonous, notwithstanding the excellence of the dishes and the sparkling brilliancy of the champagne, but when others became willing to enjoy, my capacity for enjoyment similarly expanded, and I found myself, ere the ladies left the table, cracking jokes, and making abominable puns, and telling Joe Millers, with a freedom and an hilarity that astonished myself. Mrs. Ducklet, however, and her elegant daughter gone, the scene was completely changed.

All was grossness and sensuality on the departure of the ladies—the fruit, and the wines, and the enjoyed dishes, or worse, the only pleasing themes of conversation with the voluptuous old Anglo-Indian. I was glad, therefore, when he moved an adjournment to the drawing-room, where we found Mrs. Ducklet dozing over a volume of sermons, and the fascinating Julia performing sacred pieces on the piano. It was now half-past ten o'clock, and we had sat down to dinner at half-past seven! such was Ducklet's usual habit, such the ordinary routine of his life—dinner occupied with him exactly one-eighth of his life-time when private and domestic, but a much greater proportion when he entertained friends or went to the entertainments of others.

Such was fashionable life in the City of Palaces! I had seen enough of it. Life more absolutely sterile or trivial, more monotonously dull and pretentious, is not probably to be found elsewhere. Good eating and drinking, much show and little comfort, its prevailing material characteristics; a supreme contempt for those whose darker skin proclaims their relationship with the children of the East, its grand ruling dogma. An existence combining all the vulgarity and prejudice of American life, with the languor and vegetating inertness of the tropics, but without that energy and vigour which renders the rudest Americans remarkable, to whatever class they may belong. I had lived a week in this atmosphere of fashionable vulgarity, and had had enough of it. The following day I removed to quarters of my own.

A fortnight later, I read in the *Bengal Hurkaru* the following mysterious announcement :—" We understand that yesterday, about mid-day, Mr. L., of the Bengal Horse Artillery, eloped with the daughter of a gentleman high in the Civil Service in Calcutta. The youthful pair are said to have crossed the river, to have been united in the bonds of matrimony at Howrah, and to have started express to join Mr. L.'s station up the country. This affair has caused a great excitement amongst the fashionable circles of Calcutta, the young lady's papa and mamma having been known to be decidedly opposed to the marriage."

I had little difficulty in convincing myself that Mr. Layjow and Miss Ducklet were the parties alluded to, and on calling a few days afterwards on the parents of the young lady, Mrs. Ducklet herself, with many wailings, confirmed the truth of my conjecture.

CHAPTER XII.

NEWSPAPER-EDITING IN THE FAR EAST.

A MAN who has once been editor of a newspaper can scarcely cease to write afterwards. A holiday of a week, a month, or even a year, may be acceptable. He throws down the pen, and pushes away his desk, with the air of a man that has had enough of it, and is determined, for the future, to eschew perorating, puffing, and criticizing. For a time, his release from the daily routine of the office is delightful, and he luxuriates in the bliss of being entirely his own master. He no longer finds a heap of effusions, and a pile of newspapers, before him daily, which *must* be looked over, however cursorily; letters from anxious correspondents about manuscripts of which he has no recollection; queries from inquirers who expect him to be a walking encyclopædia—an epitome of all knowledge, bound in broadcloth and linen; lines, verses, sonnets, and poems from unfortunate poetasters, who *will* not be persuaded that he does not wish for such; diatribes against unknown offenders from unknown assailants, all anxious to see their attacks in the columns of his paper; together with cautious puffs of friends and their productions from knowing ones, who do not wish to pay for them as advertisements.

All these the editor in the far East has, with his own eyes, to glance at or wade through. In some instances the most superficial glance is sufficient; in others, he reads through two or three pages of crabbed manuscript, only to find in the end that the production is of no use or value. All these he flies from and avoids, when a holiday season gives him an opportunity of forgetting the cares and fatigues of editing, to indulge in the luxury of doing just *what* he likes *when* he likes.

But the *cacoëthes scribendi*, the itch of writing, has been acquired. In time, he sits down to indite some article more than usually piquant, which has been troubling his brain for a day or two, and *will* be born, *will* struggle into existence, let him determine, never so resolutely, that it shall not. Some happy simile, some telling period, some brilliant allusion, some irrefutable argument, some stinging retort, that he thinks it would be a pity to strangle in its birth, is issued into the world by the quondam editor, and raises a storm of debate, indignation, or abuse. The whilom silent voice is recognized by some, and a reply appears. The holiday-maker smiles as he contemplates the hubbub from the quiet of his retreat; an answer to the reply is necessary, and he buckles himself again into the old business, but "only for an article or two," as he sagely whispers to himself—"only for an article or two, and then I shall have done."

Vain resolution! The answer to the reply calls forth an attack, and a rejoinder to that attack is absolutely necessary. He is fairly in for a storm, and he must weather it as best he can. He composes himself at his desk as of old, seizes the damp papers with the avidity of former days to see what his rejoinder has called forth, and, having read, ruminates over the line of argument to be adopted in his reply. Thus is he almost insensibly led into the vortex of newspaper-discussion, the arena of literary combatants, in which drops of ink, not of blood, are lavishly shed daily all over the civilized world—a perfect hurricane of words, sweeping ever faster and faster over the cities and towns of Christendom, repressed here, only to thunder in louder and more long-protracted gusts there; ever blowing, ever whirling, in constant, dustiest commotion.

Poor man!—he feels the tumult, and is well-nigh blinded by the dust. Who shall tell the anxious inquirer where the diamond truth in all this sea of dust is to be found? Nay, is it not the very province of some writers, just as it is of many most respectably be-wigged lawyers, to throw this same dust vigorously into the mental eyes of all who will regard them, that the said diamond truth may *not* be discovered at all, but hid rather from the sight of every man, if possible?

When I arrived in Calcutta, it was with the intention of eschewing broadsheets and leading articles. I had to lecture on History and Logic to a fine, intelligent body of young men, who crowded the upper classes of the Hindoo College—as acute and as intelligent a body, for the most part, as could be found in any similar institution elsewhere, and, as long as the inquirer searched into their intellectual developments and progress only, satisfactory too. As for morals and morality, that was another matter. I say nothing about that here; when I come to talk about the creeds and want of creeds in Calcutta, it will be time enough to touch upon that subject. The duty then was agreeable; that is, it was as agreeable as any duty to be performed in the midst of an extempore and never-ending bath could be. With the thermometer at 90°, I lectured and perspired, for about a year, incessantly.

But the *cacoëthes scribendi* was on me, and I must be dabbling with the newspapers, and other periodicals. I wrote for the *Calcutta Review*, about Confucius and Lord Wellesley; for the *India Sporting Review*, about the bagging of alligators and elephants; and for one of the daily papers, about politics and the Sikh war. At length, it was announced by a publishing firm of great respectability, in the City of Palaces, that they were importing a steam-press from London—the first steam-press that had ever rounded the Cape—and that they were about to establish a cheap daily paper, that was, of course, to be as far superior to any other ever established in Calcutta as the steam-press was to the paltry hand-presses of the other offices. It was, on the whole, as pretty a piece of puffery as even this age of puffs could produce.

To my surprise, I was asked to undertake the editorship of this mighty organ, that was to drown the paltry pipes of all the other organs in Calcutta—nay, in India. I had a considerable portion of my time unoccupied, it is true. I wrote an article daily for another paper; but I had never edited anything but the *Ceylon Herald*—that small twice a-week folio of four pages—that was, to a Calcutta daily paper, what the barn-house Macbeth of some strolling company is to the Macbeth of Drury Lane or the Princess'. I represented to the proprietor that the editor of a daily paper ought to be able to devote all his time to the work, and that the terms he offered were not sufficiently liberal to enable me to do that.

"Never mind," said he; "we have a military

officer to undertake the war, and all about that. You'll only have the local politics of Calcutta to attend to. We can manage the rest."

The Sikh war was then the principal event in progress, and, as they had a military officer to undertake *that*, the duty was comparatively light. I agreed.

Let me remind the reader, however, that a daily paper in London is a very different thing from the daily paper of Calcutta. In London, all is upon so grand and large a scale, that no comparison can be instituted between the two. A circulation of a thousand copies daily is a large circulation for the Calcutta paper—a circulation of only a thousand daily would be regarded as a very paltry affair in London. Nor do they differ more in circulation than in size. An ordinary copy of the *Times* contains about ten times as much printing as an ordinary copy of a leading Calcutta paper, such as the *Englishman* or the *Hurkaru*.

Such was the arrangement, then, under which I was installed as editor of this wonderful periodical, that was to shine like the moon amidst the lesser lights of the Calcutta literary armament—its steam-press particularly making it at once all that could be desired. I read the announcements over again, and sighed as I recollected that it fell partially to my lot to fulfil all these magniloquent promises about "literary articles of the first class, to be combined with the fullest discussion of all subjects of political interest," and such-like. I sighed, and thought of what the world would expect from the steam-press.

At length, the first issue of the new paper was sown broad-cast over Calcutta.

"They shall have plenty of copies," muttered the proprietor and publisher; "there shall be no lack of copies, seeing that our steam-press is in full working order now."

"I must see this same steam-press that is making such a noise in the world," said I.

"Certainly," he exclaimed, proudly, "certainly. Come along; this way, sir, this way. I'll show it to you myself."

We descended into the lower regions, through narrow staircases and dark passages, such as, from time immemorial, have invariably belonged to all printing-offices everywhere. At length, we emerged into a damp, vaulted apartment, the smell from which was by no means of the pleasantest, where I saw the printing-press —the great steam-press—in active operation.

To my extreme surprise, however, I heard no sounds of an engine working, no clanking, and fizzing, and whirling, to indicate the proximity of a steam-engine—nay, on further and more minute inspection, I discovered a man turning a wheel, and thereby setting the celebrated steam-press in motion! I was astounded. There was nothing to distinguish this mighty engine from the ordinary press that I could discover.

"It is worked by hand?" I enquiringly suggested to the proprietor.

"It is," said he, pointing to the words *Napier's Steam Press*, on a part of the machinery.

"This arrangement is but a temporary one, then, I suppose," said I; "you have not got the engine ready yet. Perhaps it has not arrived?"

"Why, the fact is," said he, taking me a little aside, "the fact is, we don't intend to have an engine to work it—at least, not at present."

He then proceeded to point out its peculiar

excellences and advantages, not forgetting to mention the large sum it had cost; but to all this I was by no means attentive. My mind was taken up with the onslaught, which would soon be made most justly upon the new comer, by all the other papers. It *was* a "steam-press" it was true—the words were plainly visible upon a conspicuous portion of the machinery; but it was not worked by steam, nevertheless, and when this fact became known, I foresaw that a great storm would be raised.

It came at length. From Madras and Bombay flattering notices of the new paper poured in, but particularly of the enterprize of the publishers who had introduced printing by steam into India. Up to this moment the other Calcutta dailies had been silently watching the progress of events, and the course steered by the new paper that was to cut them all out with its cheap price and its magnificent *steam-press*. But now the moment came for the premeditated onslaught, and right vigorously were we belaboured—right vigorously, and most justly, from all sides.

"The Madras *Athenæum*," indignantly wrote the *Hurkaru* (one of the Calcutta daily papers)—"The Madras *Athenæum* congratulates the proprietors of the new cheap daily on the enterprize they have displayed in introducing printing by steam into Asia. It was natural enough that our Madras and Bombay contemporaries should have been misled by the puffing announcements about the steam-press, &c., &c. What will they think when we assure them that the new paper is no more printed by steam than their own, or than the *Hurkaru?* Yet such is actually the case. There is neither steam-engine nor any place for a steam-engine in the new daily's office, any more than in our own!! Here we leave the matter with our contemporaries and the public. Let them judge whether such a paper is worthy of support, whether the false pretences on which it seeks to secure public favour, are not in themselves sufficient to make all honest men eschew it."

This was severe, and yet, perhaps, on the whole, not too much so. It was necessary, however, that my part in the transaction should be explained; so, slipping into the grand editorial *we*, I perorated after this fashion:

"Our contemporaries seem to think that, because this paper is not printed by steam, a promise, implied in our prospectus, has not been kept. It is a matter, we dare say, respecting which the public is profoundly indifferent, but we feel it due to ourselves to afford a little explanation. The prospectus, which had been drawn up and issued before we joined the paper, stated that the new daily should be printed with one of Napier's steam-presses, imported for the purpose! This promise *has* been kept. One of Napier's steam-presses has been imported, and with that the present sheet, like its predecessors, has been printed. It was never intended, however, as our contemporaries seem to have expected, that the press should be worked by steam. The 'steam-press' is a new and improved printing-press, which may be driven either by steam or by hand, at option—at present it is not the intention of the proprietors to have it driven by steam. Whether at some future period it may be so, is another question. To all who are curious on the subject, however, we give this general invitation to come and witness the performance of the press for themselves. A practical man will point out to them its superiority to the ordinary hand-presses, and they will not require spectacles to discover the words *Napier's steam-press* boldly raised upon a prominent portion of the machinery."

Such was the defence—a lame enough one I admit, but what more could be said upon the subject? If people chose to fancy that a steam-press must necessarily be worked by steam, that was not my fault. I should have most probably fallen into the same error myself, had my eyes not been opened to the nice distinction between a steam-press and a press worked by steam, at an early age of the discussion. To this day the question is an open one in my mind, and there are hundreds of lawyers who, if asked their opinion of the merits of the case, would probably reply like the late Lord Plunket in a similar case—"I should be very glad to have £100 for arguing the question upon either side."

Notwithstanding this little difficulty, and numerous others with which the infant paper had to contend, its subscription list increased steadily, and when I finally resigned the editorial pen of the cheap daily, its prospects seemed bright and cheering enough. Even at a later period, when I left Calcutta, it was still flourishing apace in all the vigour of early youth.

CHAPTER XIII.

ANGLO-INDIAN COMFORTS.

DURING that period of the year which is, by a pleasant fiction, called the "cold season" in Calcutta—extending from December to February—the temperature is bearable. The European can then walk out in the mornings and evenings with comfort, walk out and enjoy the exercise, or ride briskly and not feel himself gradually sinking into a state of liquefaction. He must not, even then, however, tempt the sun's rays during the heat of the day; if he do, medical men "will not be answerable for the consequences." It is the "cold season," to be sure, but it is the Calcutta cold season, and, in such a climate, we must expect to exist only, not to enjoy.

The musquitos, too, during this cold season, swarm by thousands into the houses; they are driven in by the *cold*, any old yellow-faced, liver-diseased Anglo-Indian will gravely tell you; nay, not only gravely tell you so, but positively appear aggrieved if you do not appear at least to believe it. Those only who know what the delights of being a favourite with the musquitos are, can fancy the incessant state of activity in which the devoted object of their attentions is kept during a long evening.

The large fan which, for three-fourths of the year, swings heavily backwards and forwards in the room, suspended from the ceiling, is now at rest, and the little plagues have it all their own way. They persist in settling on your hands, or tapping your forehead, with a perseverance which, if you be an entomologist, will considerably enlighten you as to the nature of insects generally. You find that a flourish of your handkerchief is one of the best means of preventing their settling—they cannot endure a breeze, and they dislike being caught in the folds of even a cambric or silk trap—so you flourish your handkerchief, innocently, often.

If you have the misfortune to wear shoes, they will soon discover the fact, and settle accordingly upon the instep and by the side of the foot—they prefer the fleshy portion. By skilfully manœuvring your feet, however, you easily detach them or prevent their settling effectually, that is, by gliding one foot over the other softly and leisurely, as if you meant nothing particular. Acute smarts you must expect, for, to be a favourite with the musquitos, is an honour involving much that is disagreeable, like many other honours—acute smarts, followed by intense itching; but you see old Anglo-Indians making light of musquitos, and you do not like to be considered a grumbler, so you say nothing about your own sufferings, feeling none the less, however.

One cannot be always flourishing his handkerchief about, gracefully or ungracefully; one cannot be always sliding the right foot over the left, and the left over the right, quickly or slowly. There is a limit beyond which the most determined musquito-hater cannot carry these resources, but there is no limit to the ravages of the little blood-sucker. When you take your stockings off at night, you will be able to trace the outline of the shoe upon your foot, by the bites, the little red spots forming the centres of small circles of inflammation; the neat way in which these bites will be found crossing your instep and running round by the side of the foot to the heel, will enable you to decide at once as to whether your shoe is properly and evenly cut.

Nor is it during the "cold season" only that the musquitos thus abound in the houses. During the months of August and September, that is, after the rains, they are to be encountered in swarms. You have then, however, the resource of the large fan swinging over your head, and by sitting beneath it, the upper portion of your figure is safe from their attacks, as long as a sufficient current of air is kept up to drive them off, which will be as long as the fan-puller is awake. As to your nether limbs, if you wear shoes after the first few days of Calcutta life, you must then be one whom experience will *not* teach, and if you do not have a pad at the knee, beneath your tightly-drawn nether garments, to prevent the little monsters from assailing you there, it is your own fault.

Nor will you heedlessly sit on an open-worked cane-bottomed chair any longer than is necessary to convince you that you have made a mistake. However large the company, and however stiff, be not afraid to convey your person at once to a softer horse-hair or leather-covered seat. True, every one is well aware why you have moved—never mind that,—the old Anglo-Indians may smile a little internally or externally, but all those who have not become yellow with "liver" (as the disease of that organ is curtly called in Calcutta), will sympathize with you—ladies as well as gentlemen—for musquitos know no distinction of sex, and would as soon commit their depredations on the shapely ankle of the belle of the season, as on the nose of the moustachoed and bewhiskered officer who solicits her hand for a dance.

The heat in May is intense, but, as Ducklet said, and as all the old Anglo-Indians will tell you when you complain of it, "it is a fine dry heat, without anything disagreeable in it."

"But the thermometer is at ninety-four degrees," you argue, "in the coolest part of the house."

"Is it?" asks the yellow-faced consoler, imperturbably; "is it, indeed: ah, well, at ninety-four degrees it *is* hot, certainly, but it will do nobody any harm—a fine dry heat, I assure you—it is not by any means disagreeable."

"Not by any means disagreeable!" you repeat; "why, I'm melting, even, under the fan."

"O, but you mustn't mind that," urges yellow-face, "you'll soon get accustomed to it: why, if you complain so much now, what will you do in August and September?"

"But they say this is the hottest period of the year," knowingly remarks the new-comer, determined not to be taken in.

"Well, so it is, so it is; but wait till August and September," soothingly observes imperturbable yellow-face, "and then you'll find that this is not so bad, after all, because it's such a nice dry heat; but then the thermometer, perhaps, is a degree or two lower, and yet the heat is infinitely more disagreeable—unbearable, you would call it—but it's not unbearable by any means,—only disagreeable, because every thing is steaming after the rains—the ground is steaming, and the vegetation is steaming, and the houses are steaming, and you're steaming, so that the air is loaded with moisture, and the perspiration is not carried off imperceptibly, as it is now."

"Imperceptibly as it is now!" groans the griffin, wiping his forehead, to contemplate his misery.

He only gets laughed at, however, for the old Anglo-Indian is right. In May, the heat is excessive, but the air is dry; in August and September, the heat is perhaps not quite so great, but it is infinitely more felt, because the air is already saturated with moisture, and cannot relieve the oppressed sufferer of the load of liquefaction which threatens to drown him.

The Englishman likes to contemplate the misery he endures, and so he always has a thermometer in his house, and by no means in the coolest part of it, either, which he always looks at during the hot season. When the temperature is agreeable, when he can exist without inconvenience, he forgets utterly that there is a thermometer in the house at all. I have already shown how he gets on *in* the house, let us now watch him abroad during one of those grilling days in May, when yellow-face has assured him that things are by no means so bad as the griffins are anxious to make out.

Making his way to the door, in unexceptionable white from his black neck-tie to his boots, he takes a peep at the thermometer as he seizes his hat, and sighs as he perceives the mercury above ninety degrees. His hat is the ordinary black European one, of all others the most unsuited to the climate; but, let him boast as he will, John Bull is the very slave of custom, and wears the ugly black hat in all climates with pertinacious discomfort. His buggy stands at the door, the slim Arab or more muscular Australian champing the bit, and anxious to be off.

All without is one fierce glow of heat and glare—a glare to which that of the fiercest dog-day in England bears no comparison whatever. The houses are all white, and, as the sun shines upon them, they reflect his beams with dazzling lustre. The road has been formed of half-burnt bricks, and if not watered, is covered with a whity-brown dust almost blinding in its fiery glare; if watered shortly before, then, from every nook and crevice, gleams shoot forth of reflected rays, whilst the whole shines brightly in the sun. The probability is, however, that the road is *not* watered, or that if it has been, all trace of the watering has disappeared, for two hours of a vertical sun will dry up a road that has been deluged.

The glare, then, is almost blinding, but a breeze is blowing that one fondly hopes will be agreeable as it makes its way into the buggy and drives off the stifling heat; but the breeze is most probably loaded with dust; is so loaded in the hot season, five times out of six; and as the melting charioteer, with half-shut eyes, takes off his hat to enjoy the luxury of the pleasant breath of air, he is covered with a thousand minute particles of brick-dust. His face and head are by no means dry; and, once wafted on him, these particles remain there. He takes out an unspotted handkerchief, and as he wipes his face, he finds it is clammy and whity-brown, whilst his hand assures him that he has but drawn figures on the dust-besprinkled oily exudation that covers him.

It is nonsense endeavouring to maintain the pleasant state of cleanliness in which he left the bath that morning, and soon the attempt is given up in despair. He resigns himself to his fate, and with eyes half closed and clenched teeth, he faces the wind and the dust grimly, but with John Bull pertinacity. Nor is the breeze only to be deplored for the quantity of dust which it bears upon the unfortunate buggy-occupant—if it have swept over the ground before it reaches his face, it arrives like a blast from a furnace, heated, suffocating, stifling—John mutters no blessing on the climate of Calcutta as he drives along—no blessing at all.

He resolves, however, that he shall use a buggy no more in the middle of the day. Next time he encloses himself in a carriage in which he is shut up from the glare and dust.

This is better, certainly. The coachman is left to battle with the external inconveniences, whilst John, within, engages in a vigorous search for coolness, and makes violent efforts to obtain it. Lounging back in the neatly-cushioned brougham will not do: one might as well step for comfort into a heated oven, or repose in the middle of a very hot day between two feather beds, German fashion. No; he sits up, allowing his clothes to touch him as little as possible—he sits up, and taking a small hand-fan, provided for the purpose, proceeds to cool his face with it. In this he partially succeeds—cooling his face, whilst he makes all the rest of his frame hotter and more uncomfortable than it was.

If this be the case in May, when the air is dry, and capable of evaporating moisture as fast as it forms, it may be conceived how uncomfortable the state of things is in August and September, when the ground, and the houses, and the trees, and the people are all soaking; the latter steaming with the oppressive heat, the former after the recent rains. August and September are the most unhealthy months in that most unhealthy of cities—the

City of Palaces. There are not many portions of the earth's surface that can boast more discomfort for humanity than Calcutta; and there is no period of the year, even in Calcutta, that can rival August and September in the amount of unwholesome misery to be then endured.

It was with feelings of gratitude that I found myself, on one occasion, able to escape the misery of these unwholesome months. Business took me to Delhi, and I made arrangements for travelling, at least a part of the distance, by the river. One of the Ganges steamers was to bear me more than half-way.

CHAPTER XIV.

THE GANGES STEAMER AND ITS PASSENGERS.

An Indian river steamer, and particularly a Ganges steamer, is totally unlike all other vessels. It is formed on the American model. Every one has seen drawings of the huge floating towns, with the houses built on deck, which navigate the Ohio and the Mississippi, the Hudson and the Potomac. But the Indian steamers, being fitted for passing shallow sand-banks and half-dry rivers, are built with flat bottoms, and are intended to draw as little water as possible. They do not, therefore, admit of the high superstructures which ornament their American prototypes, nor, of course, of the splendid saloons and commodious cabins of which Jonathan is justly so proud.

Little worlds they are, of a character quite unique—the passengers consisting, for the most part, of Anglo-Indians of all classes and types —the most crotchety of mortals. Every class of Anglo-Indian society differs from every other class; the civil servant from the military man, the military man from the merchant, the merchant from the planter. Each differs much from the other, agreeing only in one thing. They all grumble,—not occasionally, however, as in England, but constantly, in every variety of key and tone.

The civil servants, for instance, who stand at the head of Anglo-Indian society, and are determined that the fact of their so standing shall not be forgotten—the civil servants, I say, have a method of grumbling of their own. Theirs is of the pompous order. They are proud of their order, and well they may be, for it has produced a larger proportion of eminent political men than any similar service in the world. They are proud, too, for the most part, of themselves. The man who, at twenty-two or twenty-three years of age, sees himself at the head of a district double as large as Yorkshire, as its magistrate—who sees European subordinates anxious to stand well with him, and natives of all ranks cringing, with servile adulation, before him—such a man must have a strong head if he is not affected with the homage. If he estimates himself by his deserts only, and not by the factitious importance which a defective political system has given him, he must be a clear-sighted man, not likely to be turned or deceived by any circumstances.

Pomposity, therefore, is to be expected in the civil servant of the Honourable East India Company—it is to be expected, and, truly, those who look for it in India, will not have far to go to find it. On the deck of the river steamer it displays itself in the proud walk, the self-satisfied air, the *odi-profanum-vulgus* look which the great man assumes. If empty-headed—and in such a body there must necessarily be many empty-headed men—the affectation becomes ridiculous and absurd, as it was in the case of one of our passengers, when we steamed up the Ganges in the "Irrawaddy"—a youthful magistrate, of the name of Paugul. The grumbling of the civil servants, then, is of the pompous kind.

The military grumble too, but not so much; theirs may be called the candid, off-hand kind of grumbling—as fine and gentlemanly a set of fellows, these military men, as any army in the world can boast of. As a general rule, they may be said to bear no good-will towards the Civil Service; they do not see why the latter should hold their heads so much higher in the social scale, merely because their monthly income is, for the most part, so much larger than theirs. The military are not more manly and gentlemanly than they are luxurious. No men know the smack of good champagne or superior hock better than your Honourable Company's soldier; nor is there any class in India, not even excepting the planters, who know more thoroughly how to make the nearest approaches to comfort that an Indian climate will admit of. They grumble, as I said, in a plain, off-hand manner, and by no means with that abundance of profane swearing that distinguishes the rougher and more unpolished planters.

The merchants and planters of Bengal are as various in their grumbling characteristics as the same classes in any other part of the world. The latter may generally be known by their diligent eschewing of the black European hat, and the extraordinary substitutes which they use for it. Of these substitutes, some resemble copper boilers in shape, with broad brims, and innumerable air holes; others have a peak in front, and an apron behind, just (as far as shape is concerned) as if a child's pinafore had been tied upon a dragoon's helmet to cover the back of the neck; others rise in the most outrageous manner—cauldron-fashion—as if the unfortunate individual's head had been introduced by mistake into a wooden washing-basin, and had become fixed there; whilst not a few recal to one's mind the helmet of Mambrino, in Don Quixote.

The men who wear these head-dresses are as various as the head-dresses themselves. The majority of them, however, particularly the younger planters, have a rollicking, devil-may-care gait, as if, for their parts, they thought quite as little of the world as the world does of them. They are distinguished moreover by an insatiable propensity to draw the long bow. They will spin more tough yarns in the course of an evening, than a man-of-war's man of thirty years' standing in a week. The most surprising part of the matter is that they seem to think people ought to believe these extraordinary tales, and either naturally look, or try to look, astonished, when people express doubt or incredulity.

The *Irrawaddy* (our steamer) was fortunately not a favourite on the river with passengers, and was, consequently, chiefly employed for the carriage of merchandize, and for the towing of flat-bottomed receptacles for goods, called flats. These are attached, sometimes three of them at once, to the steamer, and are so lugged by the bows up and down the river, just as the tail is attached to a boy's kite, following it in all its movements. Only those passengers, therefore, who were anxious to get up the river as soon as possible availed themselves of the Irrawaddy, the majority waiting for the next boat, the "Sir Howard Jenkins," which was a great favourite, from the fact of the cabins being built upon deck, and the accommodation for passengers being in every respect superior.

The masters or "Captains" of these steamers are a peculiar race, just as the steamers themselves are. They have generally been sailors connected with Eastern vessels, accustomed to Indian crews, and, of course, to giving orders in the Hindostannee language. Excellent seamen, I believe, the majority of them, and it may therefore be easily conceived that they feel, when commanding one of these river-boats, like fish out of water. Their passengers are often of the most punctilious description, and hard set is the honest captain to please them. He generally wishes to follow the latest existing usages of society, and his anxiety to please and make his passengers comfortable ought to cause them to overlook any little breaches of etiquette. But, unfortunately, when people are stewing as if in an oven, their tempers are not of the most equable, and are difficult of control.

Captain Lumba, of the Irrawaddy, was extremely anxious to please everybody, but he was unfortunately endued with such a length by nature that nothing could exceed his awkwardness, and the constant habit of endeavouring to squeeze himself into small spaces had made natural ungainliness still more ungainly. He was thoroughly convinced that the drinking of healths was no longer fashionable, and, consequently, eschewed it as a vice, whilst he could not resist the temptation to apply the corner of the table-cloth to his mouth instead of the napkin, although the latter piece of luxury was duly deposited on his knees.

Our little party consisted of six passengers only, of whom the principal were Mr. Paugul, of the Civil Service, and Colonel Bunder, of the Company's army. Mr. Paugul affected the exquisite, and expressed the most supreme disgust for the Irrawaddy, and for its captain, and, although the esteem was, doubtless, mutual between Lumba and him, poor Lumba could not venture to exhibit it.

Mr. Paugul seemed particularly surprised, not that he should have taken his passage upon such a steamer, but that Government allowed such a steamer to take passengers at all, for the cabins being below, and not built upon deck, were insufferably hot, and unless one had a servant to fan him all night, the heat was really unendurable.

Over and over again did Lumba assure him that the inconveniencies of the steamer were not *his* fault, modestly insinuating at the same time that the next steamer would be much more comfortable, and that any passenger who pleased might be left at the first station we stopped at, to be taken up by it. Colonel Bunder, although he detested Lumba, because he was tall, would here come to his rescue (for he hated the Civil Service with an intense hatred), and say that, for his part, he thought it was not so bad, that one would soon become accustomed to it, and as none of us were going the entire distance of the Irrawaddy's voyage, the passage would not last so long.

Bunder was very little—he had never forgiven nature for making him so; and as he endeavoured to make up for his deficiency in size by the growth of hair upon his face, which gave him a remarkably fierce expression of countenance, he contrived to render himself ridiculous. "His figure-head," as Lumba confidentially informed me, "was for all the world like a hairy baboon's." Furthermore, he was fond of monkeys—anxious, I suppose, to see something resembling humanity smaller than himself, he constantly travelled with a pet; whilst he kept a ménagerie of them at his quarters. It was impossible not to be struck with the resemblance between the two countenances, when he caressed his favourite "Sukchilly." The comparison, however, was unquestionably in his favour, and when Bunder and Sukchilly played together, there could not be a doubt that the man was the better-looking of the two.

Yet Colonel Bunder had a good heart, which Paugul apparently wanted, and had Lumba been a small man, or even a man of any ordinary length, I have no doubt Bunder's sympathies would have been immediately enlisted in his favour, and he would have become his staunch protector.

Mr. Paugul had installed himself as the chaperon of a lady, the wife of a magistrate in the Upper Provinces, a Mrs. Nutkut, who was proceeding to join her husband and family; having been obliged to come down to Calcutta in consequence of the alarming illness of a relative. Mrs. Nutkut was agreeable and unaffected. Nothing could exceed the ease and grace with which she accommodated herself to the numerous inconveniences of the steamer, making as light of them as possible, and turning many of them into sources of amusement, whilst her self-constituted protector made things but more uncomfortable by his incessant growling. It is astonishing with what apparent ease an agreeable, sensible woman becomes accustomed to circumstances which, in any other position, she would find almost unendurable; and it is, surely, only those who are lost to good sense and propriety who cannot take an example from her conduct, and make the best of what cannot be obviated, and must be endured.

Such were the passengers the *Irrawaddy* bore in its grilling cabins and on its well-scrubbed decks, as we steamed northwards, towards the mighty flood of the Ganges—for the Hooghly, which flows past Calcutta, is but one of the numerous streams by which the sacred river discharges its waters into the ocean.

CHAPTER XV.

STEAMING UP THE GANGES.

The number of native servants, the European engineers, and the native sailors, all crowded together in that floating hive, a Ganges steamer, form as strange a medley perhaps as one can witness anywhere, whilst the various languages employed on board—English, Hindostannee, Bengallee, Oordoo, and, perhaps, Persian and Arabic too, tend to make the moving mass a veritable Babel.

"Coaling a steamer" in England is anything but an interesting sight—huge men, and huger cranes deposit sack after sack, or bucket after bucket of the black diamond under hatches in a very methodical and matter-of-fact way. But "coaling" the Irrawaddy was a different matter altogether. The steamer was obliged to anchor at night, the river being too dangerous to admit of proceeding in the darkness. Our captain, therefore, endeavoured to arrive at the coaling station just as night was setting in, in order that the coals might be taken on board whilst the steamer was compelled to remain inactive.

We had arrived at Cutwa, a coaling station half-way between Calcutta and the Ganges. The stars gave as much light as they could reasonably be expected to give. We could just perceive objects on the bank beside us dimly and faintly. Suddenly a dark troop of figures made their appearance, near what we could discover, with a little difficulty, to be a small mountain of coal. The individuals composing the mass of humanity that thus suddenly attracted our observation, appeared to be in constant motion; they were chattering incessantly; each had a small basket in his hand, and it appeared to me that some dreadful quarrel was raging.

"They must be boys," said I to Lumba, who was standing beside me. "They must be boys, judging by their size."

He was intently watching the movements of the chief mate on shore, who came and went, appearing and disappearing with extraordinary celerity, amongst the dark masses, as if in search of some particular individual in the crowd,—which, considering the number, the noise, and the confusion, would apparently be a fruitless search.

I repeated my observation to Lumba.

"Those," said he, smiling, "are all Hindoo girls and women. They carry the coals on board here."

"That accounts then," I replied, "for the incessant talking, the shrill voices, and the size; but what are they quarrelling about?"

"Nothing," said he; "they are not quarrelling, but they are all eager to be employed—there is no keeping their tongues quiet."

"It's all right, sir," shouted the chief mate from the shore.

"Very well, let them begin," replied Lumba, as he walked aft* to give the necessary orders.

* In the river steamers the *fore* part is that occupied by the passengers.

Women and girls! thought I, how strange that they should be employed in such work, and yet how much better that they should be thus occupied, than excluded, as in England, from all out-of-doors employment. Besides, as I speedily perceived, the work was not altogether unsuitable to them. They carried small baskets of coals upon their heads, and came in troops, laughing and chatting incessantly. In fact, from the moment the work began, there seemed to be still more noise than before, made with their tongues. It was altogether a strange scene. Our vessel was a blaze of light.

The chief mate stood at the gangway, to count the baskets that came on board, each containing an Indian measure about equal to half a hundred weight. One by one the erect figures, with the baskets on their heads, emerged from the gloom on shore, and plunged into the illumination of the steamer. Naked for the most part to the waist, they seemed of every shade of colour, from the lightest brown, the hue of coffee with an extra allowance of milk in it, to a deep black—some indeed shining with a jetty lustre that would have eclipsed one of Hoby's patent leather boots.

Talking to each other, some laughing, they came on regularly and without intermission. The coals were discharged into the hold, and still laughing and chatting, and, perhaps, replying to some badinage of the passengers or crew, they made their way in single file on shore again, by another plank. Many of them had fine forms—forms that would have served as models to the sculptor, and the erect posture which they were obliged to maintain in carrying the baskets on their heads exhibited such figures in the best possible way. The quivering of the flesh, caused by the motion and the load, showed off the firmness and elasticity of the frame, as well as its delicately rounded muscular character.

Some, I say—nay, many of them—were thus distinguished, but there were others also, old and withered, whose flattened, elongated breasts hung down to their waists, flapping against their bodies as they advanced, whilst their wrinkled skin proclaimed their age, or the wear and tear to which they had been subjected.

It was altogether a strange, and, to me, unprecedented sight, and yet that which surprised me most was not the contrast between the gloom on shore, and the blaze of the steamer, nor the moving line of figures, nor the fine forms, nor the wrinkled skins—wrinkled although some of them were, from the toes upon their feet to the crown of their heads. All these formed strange items in a very strange scene, yet it was not any one of these that surprised me most. As each threw down her basket to have it filled, she talked to her who filled it, and she who filled it talked to her who threw it down. As each placed the basket on her head, she talked to her who assisted her, and she who assisted her, talked to her whom she assisted. As each walked along, she talked to her before and to her behind, whilst the one before and the one behind talked too. When the basket was empty, and she was returning, she talked more rapidly than ever.

All were talking—all were *always* talking—where the listeners were, I could not by diligent examination discover. It seemed to me that all were speaking, and all were listening at one and the same time. A stranger, a wilder, a more unique scene could not well be conceived.

Leaving Cutwa, we were soon steaming over a portion of the river rich in religious and historic associations. It is here called the Bhagirattee, and is held peculiarly sacred by the Hindoos. On our right we had passed a place formerly famous for the burning of widows, and other human sacrifices. Even as late as 1832, a Hindoo sent for a Mussulman barber to shave him; he asked him afterwards to hold a goat, whilst he cut off its head as an offering to Kali, a bloody goddess of renown. The barber did so, and by an intentional mistake, the too zealous Hindoo cut off the head of the Mussulman instead of that of the goat.

This is not a solitary instance of human sacrifice. A number of Brahmins, not long since, whilst assembled for "religious" purposes in the neighbourhood, began, as Hindoo saints sometimes will do, to drink and carouse. A sacrifice to Kali was proposed and boisterously agreed to by the riotous party.

"Where is the goat?" asked one, a little soberer than the others.

"I will be the goat!" shouted an incipient, though drunken, martyr, from the midst of them.

The offer was accepted with proper devotion and respect—the devotee knelt, one of the party, more zealous or more intrepid than the rest, seized the sacrificial knife, and, in a moment, the head of the drunken saint was severed from his body, and devoutly offered to the bloody Kali. The carousal was continued, and, on the morrow, the survivors found, on awaking from their stupor, that the dead body of their sacrificed companion was still in their midst. The corpse was burned according to custom, and a report circulated that the deceased had died of cholera, but the secret transpired, and English justice seized upon the offenders.*

A little further on, we sailed past the scene of the battle of Plassy, in which Clive, with three thousand two hundred British troops and sepoys, defeated seventy thousand Bengallees,

* These are facts. Vide *Calcutta Review*, No. XII., Vol. 6.

and decided the fate of the most populous and the wealthiest portion of India. The river is constantly changing its course here, and it now rolls over the scene of that extraordinary conflict. Suraj-ud-Dowlah, the reigning nabob, was dethroned in consequence, and the whole of Bengal lay, as the result of that action, at the mercy of the conqueror. On Clive's return to England, he was asked by an East India Director whether Sir Roger Dowlar (Suraj-ud-Dowlah), whom he had treated so cavalierly, was a knight or a baronet!

The scene which bursts upon the view on reaching the river Ganges—which the Bhagirattee, an insignificant branch, leaves almost at a right angle—is one of extraordinary beauty. The mighty stream is spread out before the observer like a vast panorama, clear, placid, and shining, yet flowing ever on to the ocean with wonderful celerity; constantly bearing too, as if in contrast with the natural beauty of the scene, its freight of dead bodies, in every stage of corruption, upon its bosom. Those who are too poor to burn their dead, conceive the shortest road to Paradise to lie through the Ganges, and look upon themselves as having done the greatest service to the deceased, by pushing the body into the stream.

It is a frightful sight to see several of these human carcases, bleached by exposure to the sun and water, and sometimes half burnt, floating past—the eye sockets generally deprived of their contents by ravenous birds, and every ripple of the stream giving the appearance of life and voluntary motion to the corpse. If the face be turned towards one, the impression cannot be removed for a month after—it is as if death and you had stood face to face, and spoken to each other—as if for the first time you had discovered what your lot would be, fearfully and shudderingly. Strange to say, it is in the male corpses only, that the faces are thus turned upwards — the female float with the face down, and the weight of the long hair appears to drag the head far beneath the surface.

The heat had been gradually increasing as we advanced. Every succeeding day, we felt it more intolerable, and before we had reached the Ganges, Colonel Bunder was the only one who maintained his position at night in his cabin. He was already so dried, so shrivelled-up, that an atmosphere at blood-heat around him incommoded him but little, whilst he took care in the mornings, during his dressing, to have a servant constantly fanning him.

We were proceeding quietly up the Ganges, occasionally beating, with great difficulty, round some corner where the current was stronger than usual, but always keeping as much as possible in shallow water, in order to avoid the strongest currents. The passengers had gradually become acquainted with each other, the captain felt himself a little more at his ease, and even ventured to lean comfortably back upon his chair after dinner. In the morning the steam was got up before daylight, and as soon as that dawned—which it did here without any long-continued preparations, but decidedly, all at once, as if there were no hesitation about the matter to overcome—we proceeded. Our breakfast hour was half-past eight, and by half-past seven the passengers were all occupied in going through the laborious operations of washing, shaving, and dressing.

To gentlemen accustomed to a temperature of from fifty to seventy or eighty degrees all the year round, these operations are matters of little difficulty; but where one is steaming in a vapoury atmosphere between ninety and one hundred degrees, these necessary preparations to yawning or smoking through the day, are regarded with horror and detestation. Bunder took it very easily and quietly, like all old Anglo-Indians. He sat patiently, martyr-like, whilst one servant shaved and another fanned him (for although there was very little shaving to do, he was the more particular about having it well done on that very account), unencumbered the while with any other dress than a pair of the shortest of drawers. He continued seated whilst the servant put on his stockings, an operation he informed me he had never once performed for himself during the last twenty years, the fan still diligently going without cessation. He then sat quietly for the space of about a quarter of an hour, to regain his strength, after the labour of being washed, being shaved, and having his stockings put on.

He was sitting thus in the saloon, right in front of one of the port-holes in the bows, to get what breeze could be got from the river during the progress of the steamer; for I need scarcely say, that in the river steamers of India they do not put the cabins aft, in the hinder part of the vessel, to collect all the heat and smell from the engines, but forward in the bows, that the melting passengers may obtain as much fresh air and breeze as a hot Bengallee sun will allow.

And here let me remark, how different the air in England is from that in India. The passenger who adventures a voyage on the Thames from Vauxhall to London Bridge, or from London Bridge to Margate, will find, on a cold, raw day, that the quantity of breeze caused by the advance of the steamer is really surprising. Like so many fine needles does it attack the face and every crevice of the neck which the carefully-folded muffler leaves exposed to its insidious attacks. The colder the air the more indubitably strong and sharp is the current caused by the vessel; but how different on the Ganges! The steamer advances, perhaps, just as rapidly; there is unquestionably as much air for it to cut its way through, and yet the breeze caused by the motion is only perceptible by the most delicate straining of the nerves and of the chin to discover it.

Here is a meteorological fact, which I leave to the learned to account for.

On the morning to which I have referred, the river was calm and placid as a prime minister's face, when something very important is expected from him. The sun had got up furiously, as if roused inconveniently from slumber, hot, red, fiery; we were to have another scalding day. Far and wide spread the water upon every side like a great sea, for the country was inundated by the rains. The banks, where banks still remained, were crumbling and falling into the stream, sometimes gently and imperceptibly, sometimes in mighty masses, with a report like the discharge of a piece of ordnance. The river was coquetting with tne rays of the sun, as if rejoiced to see them again, and ashamed to own it; bright glances were exchanged between the two as the slanting beams shot down variously upon the water—rendering our awning of little use as a protection. My dressing was fortunately over; the deck had been washed by the Lascars, and dried by the sun.

I had nothing particular to do, and for want of something better, I went to the skylight, which rose above the saloon, and looked down. We took our meals on deck, the saloon was so intolerably warm; and it was consequently never used but for dressing in the morning. The cabins below opened into it, and as there was but one lady on board, and she had a cabin on deck, we generally made use of the saloon in the morning, as being a little, and it was only a very little, cooler than the cabins.

Bunder in particular sat here longer than any one else, naked to the waist, sipping a cup of coffee, and dozing at intervals, whilst he was fanned without intermission. I have before mentioned, that on such occasions the only article of dress which he wore, was a pair of the shortest drawers. He was now in his arm-chair, evidently asleep; his wiry, grey moustaches, beard, and whiskers formed a strange contrast with the dried-up yellow skin of the rest of his body, whilst a remarkably hairy chest heightened the contrast.

His *bearer*, or *valet*, had perceived that his master was fast asleep, and being tired of fanning him, had crept into the cabin to smoke a little, returning at intervals to brush off the musquitos, which were fast settling upon the exposed limbs. At length the *bearer*, too, began to feel drowsy, and, remaining longer than usual in the cabin on one occasion, fell asleep there.

Dried up as Bunder was by thirty years' residence in India, the heat was too much even for his frame; the big, round drops coursed each other down his body—he was steaming. The musquitos, too, left in undisturbed possession of the field, began, in an epicurean manner, to inquire whether there were not some portions of his body more dainty than the face and hands, which years ago they had given up as useless to them. Delicate draughts of blood were discovered here and there, and they settled down in such places in multitudes.

Bunder began to sleep uneasily—the excessive heat, the stinging, itching pain caused by the musquitos, and the want of the cool current of air kept up formerly by the fan, all combined to render him uncomfortable. He moved uneasily in his easy chair. He grunted and half growled as he started more and more violently. Paugul was in an adjoining cabin, and looked out to enjoy the fun. He had just finished dressing, was arrayed in spotless white, and had carefully perfumed his handkerchief, previous to making his appearance on deck. He saw me looking down at the colonel, and stopped to observe him. Bunder made a more violent plunge, and growled louder than before. He was wide awake in a moment.

"Hang it!" was his first exclamation.

Paugul jumped stealthily into a neighbouring cabin, to avoid the imputation of having unmercifully enjoyed his torment. Bunder got a glimpse of the white figure vanishing into the cabin, of which the door was still open to his left. A bright copper basin in which he had been washing was at his side, and the water remained in it unchanged. To seize it and launch it after the culprit, dirty water, basin and all, (for Bunder conceived it was his own *bearer* he had caught a glimpse of,) was but the work of a moment.

"Ha! you scoundrel!" shouted he, at the same time in choice Hindostannee. "Are you leaving me to be eaten up by musquitos, and to soak in perspiration?"

The exclamation was hardly out of his mouth, when Paugul made his appearance—

"Even such a man, so faint, so spiritless,
So dull, so dead in look, so woe-begone,
Drew Priam's curtain at the dead of night."

He had received the entire contents of the basin upon his back—the soapy cataract was trickling over his shoulders and down his cheeks, whilst his thin white clothes stuck to his figure with a closeness and a regularity which fully revealed its outlines.

"Paugul!" exclaimed the colonel—whilst his *bearer*, who had crept stealthily out of the cabin, commenced fanning as usual, as if he had never left off. "Paugul, is that you? what, in the name of wonder, made you slip so stealthily into that empty cabin just as I awoke, almost eaten up with musquitos, and melting with heat?"

"O, it's no matter now," said Paugul with melancholy mildness, "but upon my honour, colonel, you ought to be more careful in throwing such articles about; as a magistrate, I really would not advise your allowing your temper to get so far the better of you—the copper basin might have injured me seriously."

"So it might, but it was intended for this

scoundrel," said the colonel, turning fiercely to the *bearer*, who kept fanning harder than ever, but maintained a position carefully out of the reach of Bunder's arm. Indeed, to look at the servant's face, one would fancy that he knew nothing of the occurrence at all, but had been fanning there without intermission from the night before.

"Go and call the gentleman's servant, you fool," said the colonel, endeavouring to repress a laugh as he contemplated Paugul's forlorn condition. Many servants were about, however, and the unfortunate sufferer quickly received assistance in divesting himself of his wet garments, which, by the way, is no such easy matter when they are light and thin.

At breakfast that morning, Mrs. Nutkut was, of course, fully informed of the circumstance—the colonel representing his own conduct in the most favourable light, and impressing upon us the fact that he was not kinder to his dear "Sukchilly" (the monkey) than he was to his servants, and that a considerable portion of his ire arose from indignation that one generally so kind and attentive, should have been so badly treated by them. His table-servant was behind him at the time, heard and understood every word his master was saying, was painfully conscious that scarcely a week passed without some dreadful thrashing being inflicted by the little colonel upon himself or some of his fellow-servants, and yet did not by a look, not so much as by the lifting of an eyebrow, betray his consciousness of either the one fact or the other.

In this respect Hindoo servants certainly surpass all others. Their powers of simulation and of dissimulation are equally extraordinary. Paugul did not make his appearance till breakfast was half over; his dressing occupied an hour exactly by the clock, no very extraordinary length of time, all things considered; and as he had to go through precisely the same routine twice on this particular morning, we were not astonished at his late appearance.

Mrs. Nutkut asked him particularly for his version of the story, and it was amusing to see, that, whilst Bunder's account was intended principally to exculpate himself, Paugul's abounded in abuse of the Colonel's servant, and was elaborate only upon the motives which induced him to enter the cabin. How different the points of view from which different people survey the same scene or the same object! To us at the breakfast-table the motives of Bunder or of Paugul were of little moment, whilst we dilated upon the ridiculous figure made by Paugul on his exit from the empty cabin, and admired amazingly the apparent collectedness and *sang-froid* of the *bearer*, for whom the libation was intended.

Mrs. Nutkut did not fail to rally Paugul upon his taste for the ludicrous and its consequences; and indeed the incident, simple and natural as it was, was a source of much merriment in so monotonous a journey.

CHAPTER XVI.

RIVER HAPS AND MISHAPS.

In the evening the captain and the pilot seemed to differ in opinion with respect to the place where the vessel should stop for the night. In so ever-varying a stream as the Ganges; the steamers, in their voyages up and down, are obliged to take various pilots as they proceed, who, by constantly going over the same ground, or rather the same water, backwards and forwards, are aware of the changes in the river, and where the steamer can most safely and swiftly progress. On this particular evening we had "carried on," as the sailors say, later than usual.

It was already dark before Lumba was thinking of dropping the anchor. The native pilot thought the position we were then in a favourable one, whilst Lumba conceived that we should be safer further inland, where the country was inundated, but where there was quite sufficient water to float a vessel drawing so little as the Irrawaddy. The pilot, however, prevailed, and the anchor was dropped about half a mile from the shore, in rather a deep portion of the stream; a sand-island lay three or four hundred yards behind us, and to our left a deep inundation, like a gulf, stretched into the land.

No sooner was the anchor dropped, than we became aware of the amazing strength of the current of the river. It rushed as through a sluice past the bows of our steamer, curving at each side into graceful arches, as if we were proceeding at the rate of ten or twelve knots an hour. I have said that the steamers on the Ganges tow up barges called flats after them, laden with merchandize, of which the vessel cannot take much, from its peculiar construction. Sometimes, indeed, there are two, or even three, of these monstrous tails appended to the unfortunate steamer, which puffs, and groans, and labours, and strains under the infliction, having to overcome the current, drag up its own weight, and two or three other bodies nearly as heavy as itself, and all this without the slightest assistance from any quarter.

Fortunately, the Irrawaddy had only one of these ungainly appendages on this occasion. Had there been more, they would probably have been lost.

No sooner was the anchor down and the fires partially extinguished, than Lumba commenced running first to the bows and afterwards to the stern, in such a way as caused some alarm amongst the passengers. He had been just promising to rig a tent with sails for Mrs. Nutkut on the forecastle (which here answers the purpose of a quarter-deck), such was the intensity of the heat in the cabins. Her couch-cot was to be conveyed there from her cabin, and she was thus to pass the night in the open air, as we did, encircled only by a wall of canvas.

We were quietly discussing these arrangements over our cigars and brandy-pawnee,* when Lumba's agitation and his abuse of the

* Brandy and water.

pilot caused us to ask what was the matter. The roar of the water as it swept past the steamer soon convinced us that our anchor had been dropped in one of those rapid currents which abound in the neighbourhood of the sand-islands.

"Get up the steam again!" shouted Lumba to the engineer; "lash the flat with the chain-cable!" roared he to the chief officer.

"Ay, ay, sir!" were the ready replies; and corresponding orders were immediately given in Hindostannee to the crew.

"The flat's gone, sir!" screamed the chief officer from the stern, as we heard a crash and a jerk that almost upset us; the noise of the stream and the high wind caused the loud tone in which the orders were given, and proportionately alarmed the passengers, of course.

Lumba ran to the stern; the flat had broken from its moorings, and the stream was, to our astonishment, carrying it away to our right, instead of down the river in our stern.

"I thought so," growled Lumba; "it's a blessed whirlpool we're in;" and he seized hold of the pilot (a native, of course,) to inflict summary chastisement.

"Shall I let go the other anchor, sir?" asked the chief officer.

"The steamer will hold, now the flat's gone, and we must be off as soon as we can, for the flat will be down upon us in five minutes," was Lumba's reply, as the pilot glided away from his grasp. I returned to the forecastle, where Mrs. Nutkut had been left in great alarm, fancying that we were speedily going to the bottom. It was a strange scene. The stars were shining brightly, but fleecy clouds flitted over them with wonderful rapidity. The river was running like a mountain torrent, black and raging, past us, and forming a large circle to our right was the flat (which we could distinguish distinctly by its two lights), borne rapidly along by the current. I heard the engineer telling the captain that it would be fifteen minutes before the vessel could be in motion. The lascars, or native seamen, were running to and fro, apparently more alarmed than we, the landsmen, were, and yet, perhaps, I wrong them; at all events, they talked more, and Lumba, the chief officer, and their serang,* were all obliged to use their canes

* A native officer.

pretty freely, before the incessant jabbering could be put an end to.

The flat had been gradually forming a wide circle far in towards the shore, whilst we were gyrating round our anchor. I saw now what Lumba was preparing for—the flat was evidently approaching us, and there would probably be a collision. Hence it was that swabs and coils of rope were slung so plentifully over the sides, as completely to fence the steamer. As soon as it came within hailing distance, Lumba shouted to the only European on board, asking if they had got their swabs and coils out. They had not done so, but hastened to repair their error.

"Stand by, Mr. Mota," said Lumba to the chief officer, "and jump into the flat when it comes up; that fool Chatters does not seem to know what he's about."

"Ay, ay, sir!" sung out Mota, and he had scarcely said so, when bang! bang! bang! came the flat heavily against the side of the steamer. There was a loud crashing of timbers, as if both vessels were breaking up, and it was gone again.

No material injury had been done to the Irrawaddy, however; the crashing having been entirely confined to the wooden frame on which the awning was stretched above us. We were standing looking intently at the flat during this collision, and watching it as it departed again on its wild whirl, every one of us in breathless expectation of something dreadful, when the rattling of a chain, and the heavy bounding of some soft substance against our legs, caused us to start once more. Mrs. Nutkut screamed and fainted, Colonel Bunder swore, and the other passengers uttered such ejaculations as suited their taste or temper. It was the unfortunate "Sukchilly," Bunder's favourite monkey, who had been quite forgotten in the emergency, and who inhabited the flat. He had jumped on board during the collision, and had just then succeeded in discovering his beloved master. Bunder caressed his favourite, and took him aft to tie him up somewhere; Paugul had dived down into the cabins immediately after the collision had occurred; the other passengers were variously engaged in different parts of the steamer, the majority following Lumba, and I was left to succour Mrs. Nutkut, who had indubitably fainted.

I knew it was a very interesting situation to be placed in, but felt that the pleasure, or rather the interest of it, would have been very much heightened had it occurred at any other time. The lady's *ayah,* or native female servant, was found after some little search, but it took only a moment to convince me that she was useless, being herself in so great a fright; so leaving the fair lady upon the skylight, I dived into the cabin to get the salts and *eau de cologne.* These restored animation after a little, and to my great delight, she sat up and conversed as before.

The steamer, however, was not yet under weigh; our enemy, the flat, which had saluted us so warmly before, was again going its rounds, and I saw that another collision was inevitable. I endeavoured to prepare Mrs. Nutkut for it; and, pale and alarmed as she was, not so much afraid of death as of the horrid alligators, and of the still more horrid Bengallee corpses in the river, she endeavoured to resign herself to her fate, knowing, as she declared, that we should never survive that dreadful night.

I felt rather anxious myself, too, more so

than I allowed her to perceive, for it appeared to me that every thing depended upon the position in which the flat struck us, and that that must depend, to a great extent, on fortuitous circumstances. On it came, its two lights,—which, before we knew there was any danger, looked so interestingly bright, and which we admired as they were wafted gracefully along by the stream,—these same two lights, now glaring upon us like the fire-eyes of a demon, advanced swiftly and yet smoothly and calmly upon us.

And here what a temptation there is to rhapsodize! Every thing, it is evident, depends for its effect upon the aspect in which it is regarded; what is hideous in one point of view, is beautiful in another. "Burn the dead bodies of our parents!" said a tribe of the wildest Scythians to the Roman ambassadors; "we could not think of such profanity. We honour their remains, and we eat them."

Never did two simple lanterns, the one containing a red and the other a white light, appear so utterly hideous to gazing mortals, as the two lights of that flat did to us as it came towards us, swiftly, surely, calmly, as if by its own will and power to destroy us. But the chief officer had got on board of it, and the collision was much less formidable than we had anticipated. There was the same bump, bump, bump, which had so alarmed us before, but unaccompanied by the crash which had formed so alarming a feature of the first collision.

"Are you going to stop here to be bumped in that fashion all night?" roared out the Colonel to Lumba.

"We shall be off in three minutes now, and the flat will not come round any more, even if we were obliged to stay," was Lumba's reply.

The danger was over. The steam was almost immediately up, and we proceeded. As the flat approached the outer edge of the circular current in which it had been whirled round so widely, its anchor was dropped and held it. A boat was sent afterwards to the steamer with a stout rope, and we speedily towed it out of its unpleasant position.

Lumba now adopted the course which, from the first, he thought would have been the wiser one. He steamed away towards the side of the stream into a gulf-like portion of it a-head, where it had overflowed the fields. The tops of the long reeds which grew on the banks, and far inland, were just peeping above the river, and when we had gone a considerable distance in this way, the anchor was again dropped in six feet of water, where the current was, of course, of no very formidable character. Our steamer drew nominally but three feet at the utmost power, and so Lumba, when he had got "all snug," set about rigging the extempore tent for the lady.

This was no very difficult matter for one to accomplish who was skilled in all kinds of capricious contrivances by use, for it seldom happened that he had not more than one lady to please. Sails were placed so as to form three sides of a square, hanging from the poles which supported the awning, and attached, in some cases, to the awning itself. The fourth side was open towards the water on the side of the vessel, whence it was not likely that any molestation could proceed. The lady's couch-cot, with its comfortable-looking musquito curtain, was conveyed into this sanctum, where she and her native ayah hoped to enjoy a sound sleep, untormented by the excessive heat of the cabin.

The captain and I took up our position behind this sacred enclosed space, upon the skylight over the saloon, and the other passengers, with the solitary exception of Bunder, were soon stretched in various positions upon the deck, where each had his own space for his mattress, or mat, or cot, marked out. The fires had been extinguished, and, in a few minutes, every thing was perfectly still.

The steamer and her flat lay like two great logs upon the stream, which rippled past us with a sweet, though rather melancholy, sound. Every thing around was black and dark as a midnight without a moon could make it. The snoring of Mrs. Nutkut's ayah, and the occasional growl of the colonel from below, alone disturbed the silence on board, whilst far away to our right might be heard the hum of insects and the distant roar of the wild beasts from the jungles. Pondering on the late encounter between the flat and its steamer, and thinking how dangerous it might have been, I fell asleep.

How long I had been asleep I know not,

but I was instantaneously awaked by a wild shriek from the lady, who was only separated from us by the intervening sail. Lumba started up too, but the snoring of the ayah continued as regular as ever, without the slightest intermission.

"What's the matter, ma'am?" asked Lumba, "can we assist you in any way?" and he went close up to the tent.

Now be it known unto all whom it may concern, that in the East, where covering is not required on one's bed, the gentlemen sleep decently in wide loose muslin or silk trousers, called "pyjamahs," very similar to those Mrs. Bloomer would have introduced for female use in America, so that there was here no delay to put one leg into a pair of pantaloons, and to tear the said pantaloons with the other, because they would not go on quickly enough, as would have been the case in England. Whether the ladies wear a similar night-dress I am not, of course, able to say, but I presume not, for Lumba prevented our intrusion into the lady's cloth chamber until we heard whether there was an answer.

There *was* an answer almost immediately,

although the lady was evidently very much frightened; the snoring of the ayah continuing as before.

"O, thank you, Captain Lumba, but he's gone now," was the sobbed-forth reply, as she endeavoured to wake her drowsy duenna.

"Who's gone now? who was it, ma'am?" asked Lumba.

"I could not see very distinctly," said Mrs. Nutkut, after a pause, "but I think it was—it was—the Colonel.

"What!" shouted Bunder from the companion-ladder, for he, too, had come from his berth below on hearing the shriek, and had advanced so far when he stopped to listen to the conversation.

"What, Mrs. Nutkut, do you mean to say I intruded into your cabin, or whatever else you call that ridiculous bundle of sails you have got into? I beg to inform you, madam, that my servant has only just ceased fanning me, and gone to sleep, the rascal! and that I put my foot on him in jumping out of bed the moment I heard you cry out."

"Then," said Mrs. Nutkut from within, gradually regaining her confidence, "if it was not you, it must have been that horrid monkey again."

"O, thank you," said Bunder, making his way to his berth as speedily as possible.

It *was* the monkey. The "lovely Sukchilly," as Bunder called him, had again made his escape, and seeing the enclosure on the fore-castle, with the characteristic curiosity of his race, had been anxious to penetrate its mysteries. He had crept stealthily over the ayah's body to the side of the couch-cot, which he had slightly shaken, sufficiently, however, to awake its inmate, and when Mrs. Nutkut turned her head round, she saw, to her horror, an ugly, hairy face staring at her through the curtains. Hence the scream. With some difficulty Sukchilly was again secured and made fast, and in a few minutes every thing had relapsed into quietness on board, the occasional loud snore of some noisy sleeper being the only sound that broke the stillness of the vessel.

Next morning, as usual, the steam was got up before daylight, and about half-past five we were under weigh, Mrs. Nutkut having, of course, previously retreated to her cabin, and every vestige of the tent having been speedily removed to make way for the men weighing the anchor. We had not been going on more than a quarter of an hour, when I saw plainly, from my position on the skylight, that something was again wrong. What it was I could not make out for some time. On looking carefully at the water, however, as the light increased, I perceived that the reeds were now considerably above the surface of the stream, and that we were making very little way, although the engines appeared to be going with full power. Lumba was again abrupt and sharp in his orders, whilst, when things were going on well, as they had been for the week previous to the late unlucky evening, he was the personification of coolness and dryness.

It was evident that the river had been falling during the night, and that on advancing this morning, the vessel had got aground upon some bank, but so gently, that no one on board felt it. This was an alarming prospect; the rains were now apparently over, and the river was not likely to rise again till next year. We were far inland, and if the water still continued to decrease, and we remained where we were, there was every chance of the Irrawaddy and her flat being left till next inundation, high and dry upon the shore, in the midst of a fine open country, a quarter of a mile at the least from the river, when confined to its ordinary channel. Such things *had* happened before, and poor Lumba was to be pitied. In escaping one evil, he had fallen into another.

As for us, some other boat belonging to the same company, the Great Bengal and Bahar General Inland River Steam Navigation Company, (generally written the G. B. B. G. I. R. S. N. Co.), there was no doubt, I say, that some other boat of the same formidable company would take us to our destinations, but there was still a loss of time to be dreaded, which the commercial and military passengers could ill spare. An anchor was sent off in a boat in the direction of deeper water, and it was hoped, by the aid of the steam and the windlass, to draw the steamer off the bank and float her again, by "kedging," as it is technically called. The flat was sent adrift, and was speedily wafted into deeper water by the current, where it awaited the steamer.

All that morning did the Lascars unceasingly ply the windlass, in the vain hope of drawing the steamer from its immovable position. We were all impatient of the delay, and yet, impatient as we were, we could not but feel more for Lumba than for ourselves. To us it was a delay of a few days at most; to him it was probably ruin. The "kedging" was of no use; the river was evidently falling, and the steamer every hour became less likely to be dragged off. It was then attempted to lighten it sufficiently to make it again float, and boat-load after boat-load of merchandize was despatched to the flat, which was now two miles away to the south-east.

All that day the most strenuous efforts were made, in a variety of ways, to prevent the evil which appeared almost inevitable, but without success. Towards evening, fortunately, another steamer made its appearance; we could not tell at once to what company it belonged, but as it ultimately proved to be one of the G. B. B. G. I. R. S. N. Co.'s fleet, we were considerably relieved. Had it belonged to the rival company, the Great Ganges and Brahmahpootra River Steam Navigation Company of India, there was very little chance of any effectual assistance being offered.

The "Sir John Pelham Smith," which now so opportunely made its appearance, was proceeding down the river to Calcutta; this did not prevent it being of essential service to us, however. A rope was speedily passed from the Irrawaddy to the Sir John Pelham Smith, and at that rope Sir John tugged and tugged again with right good will. The Irrawaddy trembled as if it really was thinking of leaving its comfortable nook—it trembled again—Sir John tugged harder than ever, leaping out of the water almost, in his violent straining, and—at length—the rope broke. Two additional ones were speedily procured, the same process was repeated—round went the paddle wheels of both vessels, madly, furiously, impetuously, and yet neither stirred an inch.

"She's yielding!" shouted Lumba, at the top of his voice—"harder, my boys! harder!" cried he wildly to the Lascars, who were straining at the windlass, still kedging as they had been all day.

She *did* yield—there was a tremor, a shivering, a gentle shaking, a long-drawn sigh as it were, and she was off. Sir John steamed merrily away down the river, as if conscious of having performed a meritorious action. The Irrawaddy captured her unfortunate flat once more—things were speedily set to rights in every way, and, on the following day, I was landed. During the remainder of that voyage Lumba did not anchor either in a whirlpool or in six feet of water, nor, I am sorry to add, did Colonel Bunder, as I was subsequently informed, say a word, except of the most formal and complimentary character, to Mrs. Nutkut. The remainder of my journey to Delhi, which was my ultimate destination, was performed by land in a palanquin.

CHAPTER XVII.

THE PRIEST'S HAREM AT DELHI.

The stranger, arriving for the first time in Delhi, is at once impressed, by the aspect of the town, with the conviction that he is in a city once great and mighty, but great and mighty no more. The remains of past magnificence are strewed around on every side, some mouldering under the heavy hand of time, into their primeval dust, others beautiful in their proportions, and in an excellent state of preservation, but still telling only of what *has been*, not of what *is*. The great palace of Shah Jehan, a thousand yards long, and six hundred broad, is still inhabited by the descendant of the great Moguls, the lingering representative of a dynasty that wrote their names largely on the world's history, and then vanished, to give place to foreign rulers.

In solemn mockery of royal splendour, their surviving descendant, an emperor in form and a slave in fact, maintains the empty state of sovereignty. He has his throne and his sceptre, his palace and his servants, his ministers and his grand officers—the English have his kingdom. He receives like a king his foreign visitors, and decorates them with a valueless collar of tawdry tinsel; he wears jewels and royal robes, and has about him all the paraphernalia of majesty; but the substance has fled, the shadow only has been retained.

The palace, built by Shah Jehan, is a magnificent pile—its gateway is what the entrance to a royal domain should be, grand, imposing, and magnificent. Its gardens, a mile in circumference, are still maintained as in the times when the Moguls wielded the sceptre of India, really as well as nominally, from Cape Comorin to the Himalayas.

But whilst the palace itself betrays little of the fall of Delhi, its immediate vicinity is full of monuments that speak unmistakeably of a city whose glory has departed. Long ranges of buildings, once the palaces of the Mogul nobility, with gilded mosques, richly ornamented pavilions and magnificent tombs, are scattered about in wide confusion, forming a vast scene of ruin and desolation. Two of its streets may still be considered elegant and spacious if not grand, and the others, although narrow, contain many good houses, partly of brick and partly of stone; but every where the wanderer may meet the ruins of past magnificence, in immediate contact with the abodes of present mediocrity—a palace and a cottage in juxtaposition may be met, it is true, anywhere in the East, from Constantinople to Canton, but a palace in ruins and a well-kept cottage together, such as may be frequently seen in Delhi, is but symbolical of the decay of the princes, and the rise of the people, which we may probably regard as the inevitable results of the British conquest.

The Muhammadan quarter of Delhi is far finer than that inhabited by the Hindoos—the very houses show which were the masters—and in this Muhammadan quarter the mosque called the *Jumna Musjeed* is certainly the finest building. It was built by the daughter of Aurungzebe, the greatest monarch the Mogul line produced, and is of red stone, inlaid with marble. Four graceful minarets, each two hundred feet high, rise at the corners, pointing ever to the skies, the fittest possible ornaments of religious buildings Three great domes rise from the interior, of which the central one is by far the loftiest, domes that curve beautifully upwards, ending in a slender point like that of the minaret, and suggestive, too, of thoughts raised far above the earth, to the place where "the wicked cease from troubling, and the weary are at rest."

The central doorway, of lofty and imposing dimensions, is flanked by five arches on either side, that stretch off to the minarets, and above these arches is that elaborate and intricate decoration which the orientals love so well, and which astonishes the European in the Alhambra not so much by its intrinsic beauty, as by the immense quantity of labour which must have been expended upon it.

The neighbourhood of the *Jumna Musjeed* is all that the vicinity of such a temple should be. An extensive square court-yard affords an admirable view of it in front, whilst the sides are flanked with lower buildings, that harmonize well with the magnificent proportions of the mosque. No narrow dirty streets run right and left from the very precincts of the great temple, as in more civilized countries is too often the case — all is repose, quiet, solemnity, and harmonious combination.

But it was not to describe Delhi or its temple that I brought the reader to the *Jumna Musjeed.* We have had descriptions enough of walls and houses, of forts, cities, and harbours, of windows, doors, and pillars. Still life is better portrayed by the pencil of the artist than by the pen of the traveller. It was that we might find subjects of strictly human interest amid the ruins and the mosques of Delhi—that we might see how men and women think and act who profess the creed of Muhammad, and live amid the glare and dust of a tropical city—that I brought the reader up the Ganges to the ancient capital of the Mogul empire. Nay, more, that we might obtain a peep into that mystery of mysteries, a priest's harem.

I became acquainted in this strange city with a Persian—a young man of three or four and twenty—who interested me much by his intelligence and freedom from prejudice. An extensive acquaintance with the world had given Cossim Ali an agreeable manner and a winning address, which made him a favourite with every one, but particularly with the fair sex. In his picturesque conical hat, loose dressing-gown-like coat with slashed open sleeves, and oriental sandals, he might have been chosen by an artist, as a specimen and sample of his race and country. He was tall, well-made, and active, and there was that air of mystery about him which is so attractive, particularly to the fair. Some said he was a Persian agent, appointed by the Shah to reside at the court of Delhi as a mark of honour to the nominal "Emperor," others that he filled some profound diplomatic position in connection with Affghanistan and its interests in the Seikh war; whilst not a few declared that he was merely a Persian gentleman of fortune, travelling for his amusement, who had taken up his abode at Delhi for a time, to inspect its lions.

Cossim Ali cared little what they thought or what they said about him. He sauntered about the streets or into the mosques, rode his fine Affghan horse in the suburbs, and attended European parties, with equal indifference and unconcern. His stock of English was of the smallest, but he spoke Hindostannee fluently, and, as all Anglo-Indians must speak that more or less, he contrived to make himself interesting and amusing to all parties. To the old yellow-faced, liver-diseased English grumbler, who had been shrivelling up into a parchment bale for twenty or thirty years, he spoke of the wines of Shiraz and the cookery of Ispahan, until the old gentleman licked his lips again at the savoury description, his mouth watering the while.

To the English lady he spoke of the beauties of Lauristan, with their fair blue eyes and black hair, and how they were put up to sale in Ispahan and Teheran, as well as of the fabulous prices which they commanded. He described the Georgian vessels, making their way over the waters of the Caspian to the north of Persia, to dispose of their cargo of beauties to the deserving faithful. The ladies were deeply interested, and asked much of Persian harems and wedded life amongst the

Sheahs, to all which Cossim answered glibly, knowing or unknowing, describing or inventing as he found most convenient, whilst his black eyes, sparkling with animation, were telling deeply upon his fair listeners.

To the military man, Cossim discoursed of the horses of Kurdistan and the light cavalry of the Persians, the modern representations of the Parthian troops who had so often driven back the Roman invaders.

Cossim, in fact, was a sort of lion in Delhi; and as he did not like to talk about himself, the little air of mystery which hung around him, rather captivated than repelled. He lived in the Muhammadan quarter of the town, not far from the *Jumna Musjeed*, and, whilst he often attended European parties, spent by far the greatest portion of his time in his own neighbourhood. I had met Cossim two or three times before I had an opportunity of conversing with him. At length, however, we talked together over a game of chess for an hour or so—talked uninterruptedly, he telling me wonderful stories of Persia, which I endeavoured to equal by tales of Europe, and particularly by describing the wonders of

London life. "*Barekillah!*" would Cossim exclaim at every fresh recital, "*Barekillah!*" (praise be to God!) "but the fire-drinkers of London must be strange men—*Inshallah!* (please God!) I'll see them before I die."

"Will you come over and spend an hour with me to-morrow?" I asked, seeing that Cossim and I had really become excellent friends, for I longed to penetrate the mystery that hung over him.

"*Bechushm!* (by my eyes!) but I will," rejoined Cossim, "at the eleventh hour, if it suits your excellency, and hear more of these same fire-drinkers."

"Your servant's chamber will be honoured in your presence," said I, not to be behind him in politeness, and so we separated for the evening.

And here, lest I should unwittingly defraud the reader of his valuable time, let me confess at once that I never *did* penetrate the mystery that hung over Cossim Ali; that, although he gave me an insight into a priest's harem, I never discovered whether he was an accredited agent of the Khan sent to the court of Delhi, or a profound diplomatist deeply interested in the Affghan interests of the Seikh war, or only a Persian gentleman travelling for pleasure, or, as was more probable, a Persian merchant watching the market of Delhi to find profitable fields for investment. It is but right that I should at once confess to the reader that I never discovered which of these he was, so let no one read this chapter to the end in the vain hope of discovering the precise character and employment of Cossim Ali.

Having thus satisfied my conscience, and duly warned the reader, to prevent future disappointment, I now proceed with my story. We shall soon come to the priest's harem. Cossim called as he had promised. I had seen him duly and religiously abstaining from wine at parties, but I was aware that it made a vast difference with many Mussulmans whether there was only one witness or several. I had, of course, no wish to tempt him to break any ordinance of his faith, far from it; but, regarding it as no sin myself to take a glass of wine, I was aware that many excellent Moslems, whether Sheahs or Soonnies, thought likewise, and that, although they might not be disposed to display their disobedience before a multitude and before Mussulman servants, yet that in private they indulged in a moderate allowance.

The wine was on the table—there were two glasses — the servants were not visible. I poured out a glass for myself, and pushed the bottle over to Cossim. He looked at the rich red hue of the claret for a moment—muttered something of the grapes of Shiraz—filled and emptied his glass without ceremony, and threw himself back upon his easy chair, exclaiming, "Barekillah! but it's not bad, although not so good as cherry-brandy."

We talked of different things—of politics, of the war, of the Affghans, of the English, of London, and a host of other topics pleasant and engrossing out of Europe, but stale and unprofitable within its precincts. At length, our conversation turned upon Delhi,—the *Jumna Musjeed*, the palace, the Muhammadan quarter generally. I asked information respecting an old mosque, that had evidently once been handsome and of importance, which had attracted my observation, but was now fallen much to decay. I asked, too, about an old Moollah or Muhammadan priest, whom I had seen entering it, and whose venerable white beard and forbidding countenance had equally interested me.

"I know the mosque well," said Cossim, who was gradually becoming more communicative as the wine flowed more freely, "I know it well. The old Moollah occasionally reads a chapter or two of the Koran there on Fridays, and I have visited one of the minarets before now. *Yah Hyder! yah Ali!** but if it weren't for that minaret, I should have been far enough from Delhi now."

"How was that, my friend?" I asked.

"Well, it's a secret as yet," said Cossim; "but you're my friend, and I will tell you all about it. The Moollahs don't generally like any one to go up to the top of the minarets, you know, except the guardians and themselves."

"Do they not?" said I; "I was not aware of that."

"No," said Cossim, "because they overlook the houses and the harems. But I made acquaintance with the guardian a month ago,

* An exclamation, like an address to a patron saint (similar to the "Holy Virgin!" of the Continent), ever in the mouths of the Persians. Scarcely a sentence do they utter, without some such expletive.

and got up. Delhi, however, is not like our Persian cities, and the people do not in the mornings lie upon the roofs of their houses, so that I was disappointed.

"The neighbourhood of the Mosque is crowded with houses of great size, some inhabited and some ruinous and empty, each containing a considerable number of courts. One of these houses was in the immediate vicinity of the temple; and looking down from the minaret, I could see into its courts and verandahs as plainly as into this empty glass now. The entrance to it, which I traced out after a time, was low, intricate, and confined, leading to a *divan-khaneh* (a public hall), of no great size, but from all that I could see, elegant and admirably embellished. Two large windows, with elaborately carved frames, the remains of better days, opened upon the court; and, *Mashallah!** but who do you think I saw sitting in the corner of this hall more than once?"

"Nay," said I, "how can I tell?"

"None other, by my name! than the old Moollah. Here I saw him sitting more than

* An exclamation of surprise or admiration; literally, "by the hand of God."

once, evidently enjoying himself, and beyond this outer or public apartment, I discovered that there was a splendid suite of rooms surrounding a court admirably kept, with a nice fountain and the prettiest flowers, all belonging to the old Moollah! *Mashallah!* thought I, but the venerable priest knows how to take care of himself, and if that wasn't cherry-brandy he was drinking one day, as he lay in the court near the fountain, watching some dancers, I'm sure it wasn't water.

"That these were the female apartments I saw at a glance—it doesn't take long to open the eyes of the fox when the poultry are near—ha! ha!—the handsome hall at one end, with its stained glass windows, that let in only the mellowest light; the small apartments surrounding the pleasant court; the female attire hung up here and there in the verandah—there was no doubt of it. I watched long and earnestly, for there was an evidence of luxury about the whole affair that riveted my attention, particularly when I remembered that the old priest was the possessor of all these treasures.

"The forms of females were not long in

being discovered flitting about in the court or passing through the verandah from one room to another, and it was easy to distinguish the horrid ungraceful air of the slaves, from the more dignified gait of the mistresses of the mansion."

"Slaves!" said I, interrupting him, "you forget we have no slaves in Delhi."

"No, no," said he, "you don't call them slaves, I know; attendants or servants, if you will; but the harem is sacred, and slaves they are, nevertheless. Well, there was something very interesting about the place—I was never tired of watching it. I went so often up the minaret, that its guardian began to grow suspicious, and followed me up more than once, on which occasions I took out a volume of poems, and read him a sonnet or two of Farduzi, telling him this was the place to enjoy poetry. But when he was gone I gazed again. It was quite useless, however, not a face could I make out, so carefully were they all veiled.

"At length, as the lucky stars of Cossim Ali would have it, I discovered an old house adjoining the east of the harem that had nothing in it, and was all falling to ruins. If I can get on the roof of that, thought I, I'll be able to look right into the hall, and on the beauties of the priest's harem without their veils. *Mashallah!* I lost no time in exploring the eastern side of the court. Yah! but it was a filthy grope I had, through old houses, ugly insects, muddy lanes, and filthy puddles. There were tumbling down walls every where about, quite deserted, with passages that twisted and twined every where, and led no where; rugged excavations, that I thought I should never find my way out of again, and dark holes looking into awful cellars, that made one shiver to contemplate.

"There was one narrow passage, however, that I explored, for Cossim was not to be easily daunted, that led between mud-walls of some height under ground, amid rubbish and fallen plaster, and half-decayed, half-burnt bricks. I followed it until it opened into a cellar under the empty, ruinous houses above, and as I made my way further and further up and on, in the dark, I heard the sounds of a guitar in the distance. I was on the east of the court; there was at last but a wall between me and the Moollah's harem. I distinctly heard the hum of voices within; the wall was thin, but still it *was* a wall, and I might as well be on the minaret, thought I, as here, if I can't get any nearer, or gain any insight into the court. I groped my way forwards, passed a well-closed door, and at length saw light issuing nearly from the top of the wall, coming evidently from the very court I so much wished to inspect.

"Yah Hyder! yah Ali! but I worked then like a dozen men. I piled up the bricks and hardened mud firmly and securely. In the saying of a long prayer I was up on the top inspecting the court-yard within. It was a busy scene and a strange one. Some of the slaves—O no, not the slaves, the attendants—were as ugly as those in any harem between Delhi and Mecca, frowsy wretches, all wrinkles and age. One was cleaning a hookah, another teazing cotton, a third preparing pillaw. In the verandah that ran round it, ladies' trousers, handkerchiefs, and shawls hung here and there to air.

"The slaves were all unveiled, their ugliness had no need of any disguise. But as I was gazing, I saw such a vision—yah, Frank! but it was a vision to turn a wiser man's head than Cossim's. She was magnificently dressed in a close-fitting vest of green velvet, for it was cold then,—a vest embroidered with silver and edged with fur,—whilst an orange-coloured shawl was tied round her waist, and hung down over her white satin trousers. A veil was half on and half off her face, but I could see her eyes were large and black, that her cheek was like the pomegranate, and that her mouth and chin were in shape like one of those statues that you Franks sometimes bring from Europe. I thought it was a Houri the old Moollah had enticed from Paradise.

"She was majestic in her gait, and stood a moment watching the inferior women, her guitar in her hand, then giving a direction or two in the most musical of voices, she turned and walked into one of the side apartments. I had hardly drawn a breath when she was in the court, so eagerly did I gaze, but as she retired into the apartment, I pushed my head against the wall at the side of the crevice through which I was looking, to obtain a longer view.

"I pushed the old wall so hard in my eagerness that a little plaster fell on the inside, and all eyes were turned up at once to the spot—the fair lady's amongst the rest, for she had looked round at the exclamation of the others. But I was secure from observation—the crevice was not wide enough for them to discover me through it—and none but the beautiful houri herself looked twice, whilst the slaves cursed the tumble-down old place roundly.

"But, although the slaves never looked more at the crevice, never thought more, probably, about the circumstance; yet, the lady, the favourite wife, evidently remembered the circumstance, and looked often. Frequently, when I was stationed at my post as usual, did I see her large lustrous black eyes fixed upon the spot—fixed, unavailingly, of course, suspicious of something doubtless, and not displeased, perhaps, to think that she had an admirer, who watched her actions from that dark nook.

"Fatima, for I soon discovered her name, is not the only wife of the old Moollah. I have seen four about at least, but she was evidently the favourite, and no wonder, for, *wallah*, (by Allah), Frank! but I never could take my eyes off her, or look at any other when she was by. I have seen her singing to the old priest whilst he lay in the court at her feet, his grey beard resting on a soft cushion on the grass as she sat by him, his eyes fixed upon her countenance, and her voice uttering notes that would shame the bulbul and make the loory jealous. *Bismillah!* but it was enough to rouse a man.

"Yesterday I witnessed an entertainment given by Fatima to her friends, and never shall I forget it. When the shadows had fallen upon the court, she took her place in the seat of honour, just opposite my hiding-place, the Moollah's three other wives occupying couches near her. Laughing voices and the noise of attendants announced the approach of the visitors, who were ushered into the court. They removed their blue checked veils, and exhibited themselves as well-dressed ladies, as soon as they had reached the inclosure. Some of them were passably fair, others more than ugly, but, beautiful or hideous, I regarded them with indifference. I had no eyes for any one but Fatima, and I thought that she gloried in exhibiting her unveiled charms to the suspicious chink, at which she occasionally glanced.

"Pillaws and curries were handed round—the conversation was general and free—the ladies discussed the character of their household, spoke of their jewels, the numbers of children they wished for, and their hopes of having them—all were merry and cheerful. Sherbet and milk-soup succeeded the substantial viands, and lastly, tea and coffee were handed round. Whilst they sipped at these, the dancing girls were introduced, and as they glided about in graceful measures, or sang plaintive ditties, accompanied by melancholy gestures, the ladies reclined upon their couches and watched them, languidly amused.

"The scene fascinated me. I quite forgot that I was a profane gazer at mysteries that the eye of man should never behold. With my incessant climbing, a large brick had gradually become loosened, just opposite to my face, and, perceiving that I could easily remove it, I gently took it from its place; the plaster adhered to it on the inside, and slowly and cautiously I slid it down by my side. The aperture was now wide enough fully to satisfy my curiosity, but I was much more exposed to the observation of those within than before. As I rejoiced in this discovery and enjoyed the extended view, I saw Fatima's eyes turned upwards to my hiding-place. They were fixed for a moment on my countenance, in a full, brilliant stare, and then, as though she had not seen me, she continued to watch the dancers.

"Emboldened by my success, I pushed still further into the court, my head was fully exposed to view—some pieces of plaster fell upon the flowers beneath, and all eyes were turned upon the delinquent. Yah Hyder! yah Ali! but how they screamed—the ugliest ever the loudest.

"'Treachery! treachery; a man! a man!' sounded on all sides, as if it had not been a man but a wild beast.

"'Fatima, I adore thee,' I shouted out, seeing that my delicious vision was put an end to at last.

"Other attendants came rushing into the court, 'What means all this? What news is this? What is the matter?' they kept screaming, whilst those within, drawing on their veils, rushed about, exclaiming:

"'A man! a man!—O! Muhammad, a man!—Yah, Ali! what will become of us?'

"The confusion was little less agreeable to contemplate than the pleasant party had been before. Intoxicated with Fatima's beauty I was even contemplating forcing my way into the court and defying consequences. But the coming in of two or three male attendants, now that the ladies were veiled, rendered such an idea ridiculous; the old Moollah himself was advancing with a scimitar in his hand. It was a joke no longer. I heard them opening the door that communicated with the dark cellar below the chamber in which I was —there was no time to lose.

"Fortunately the door had not been opened for years, and was half blocked up by rubbish. I was far away among the ruins before they forced their way into the darkness, and, when they had done so, they, doubtless, waited to get lights to explore the place. At all events I saw nothing of them, I was soon safe at home preparing to join the party, at which I met you, yesterday evening. I had the satisfaction of hearing the old Moollah mention the circumstance early this morning to an aged friend, whom I accompanied to the mosque betimes. Was it not enough to make one die with laughter?"

"And the beautiful Fatima?" I asked.

"Is still the wife of the Moollah, O Frank! and likely to continue so."

I never heard more of my friend Cossim after leaving Delhi to return to Calcutta, which I did a few days after he had made these revelations to me. He had promised to write, but I never received any letters from him.

THE END OF VOL. I.

TROPICAL SKETCHES

OR

REMINISCENCES OF AN INDIAN JOURNALIST

TROPICAL SKETCHES

OR

REMINISCENCES OF AN INDIAN JOURNALIST

WILLIAM KNIGHTON

IN TWO VOLUME

VOL. II

GYAN

Published by

Gyan Publishing House
5, Ansari Road
Daryaganj, New Delhi-110002
Phone: 011-47034999, 9811692060
E-mail: books@gyanbooks.com

Distribution Network
gyanbooks.com
India, USA, Canada, UK, Australia, France

ISBN : 978-81-212-4174-8 (Set)
ISBN : 978-81-212-4743-6 (HB)
First Published, London, 1855

2nd Impression 2020

Printed at: Gyan Press, Delhi.

Tropical Sketches Vol. II
Author: William Knighton

TROPICAL SKETCHES;

OR

REMINISCENCES OF AN INDIAN JOURNALIST.

BY

WILLIAM KNIGHTON, M.A.

AUTHOR OF "FOREST LIFE IN CEYLON."

IN TWO VOLUMES.

VOL. II.

LONDON:
HURST AND BLACKETT, PUBLISHERS,
SUCCESSORS TO HENRY COLBURN,
13, GREAT MARLBOROUGH STREET.
1855.

CONTENTS OF VOL. II.

TROPICAL SKETCHES;

OR,

REMINISCENCES OF AN INDIAN JOURNALIST.

CHAPTER I.

THE SEIKHS AND THEIR FOUNDERS.

ANY one who wanders much about Calcutta with his eyes open, will soon be struck with the fine manly appearance of the Seikhs as a body. Tall and well formed, they constitute unquestionably a superior division of the native community, physically regarded. They may be seen about the bazars and the native mercantile establishments with cotton garments, not always of the cleanliest, wrapped round their loins, a close-fitting jacket on their shoulders, and a turban of red or yellow hue—a muslin cloth, in fact,—twisted carefully and neatly round the head. They stand, or lounge about, squatting on their heels, in easy attitudes of indolent repose, when unemployed; but, busy, they exhibit far more of the bustling energy which the European naturally associates with the idea of labour than any other class of natives. Their features are, for the most part, good; their complexion a shade lighter, perhaps, than that of the Bengallee; their eyes dark and sparkling.

Look into that long native shop in the "Burra bazaar," and far away in the gloom, you will see three of them squatted on their heels in animated converse. You are observed, and, in a moment, one of them darts upon you as if you were a lamb appointed to the slaughter—he has made you his prey. He warns you not to allow yourself to be cheated by lying shopkeepers, who puff their own bad wares; he warns you that there is much villany in the Burra bazaar; that if you want to dispose of your money to your own advantage, you have an opportunity in his shop such as cannot be met with elsewhere. His two brethren join in chorus, and, between the three, you will not find it easy to avoid seeing, at all events, what is pressed upon you with so much apparent honesty of purpose and sincerity of confidence.

You meet with civility, politeness, and attention, when you have entered—there is certainly no individual living in Asia or Europe, who will treat you to more civility and polite attention than the Seikh when he is cheating you out of your money, or charging you only double what he ought to charge you for an article. You show that you know the prices of the goods, and his enthusiasm cools at once. It becomes, in that case, a mere business transaction, and he has nothing to do but to exhibit the article, and declare its value. Eloquence would then be thrown away. "Greenness" is the quality he adores most in his purchasers, and the more unsophisticated the customer the more attention and kindness may he be certain of receiving for his money.

No supercilious smile curls the lip of the energetic Seikh if you exhibit frightful ignorance; no ill-disguised contempt, such as makes you disposed to knock down the well-combed and finely peruked individual that exhibits it when he corrects your ignorance in a London shop, blandly and serenely. The Seikh knows better. Be as ignorant as you please of the nature of the article, of its quality and price, and he will not let you leave his shop until he has persuaded you that you have displayed an amount of sagacity perfectly extraordinary, until he has so far flattered your self-esteem as to send you away rejoicing in your acuteness.

You make an absurdly high offer for something you know nothing about.

"Saheb sees that his slave is a poor man," says the seller—the seller of other articles besides those of commerce.—"Saheb sees that his slave is a poor man, and knows that that quality cannot be bought or sold at that price."

You protest that you know nothing of the kind.

"Then Saheb must let poor man live," suggests the Seikh.

You never intended they should not, is your reply.

"Then Saheb will take the other quality at that price, or give me twenty per cent. more for this," he concludes.

You examine the other quality, and even *you* can see that it is villanously bad. Your perception of that fact puts you into a good humour—he sees that he has no nincompoop to deal with, you say blandly to yourself—and so you take the goods at a trifle below his suggestion. No line on his face is suggestive of the imposition he has practised—he merely observes, that as you have driven so hard a bargain with him in that instance, you ought really to take something more from him to make up for it.

This is merely the mercantile side of the extraordinary race. With their military ability, the British became feelingly acquainted at Ferozeshah and Chilianwallah—on the banks of the Sutlej and of the Chenab. Different as the Seikh is from either the Hindoo or the Mussulman of India, however, he is merely a descendant of ancestors of either community. Before the latter end of the fifteenth century there were no Seikhs at all. Education and early training alone have made them the people they are—their physical advantages are due solely to the spirit of their forefathers, and to the high estimation in which they held every attribute or qualification of the warrior.

Even the history of India itself, fertile as it is in romantic incidents, and prolific of the sentiment of wonder, has no stranger page than that which records the rise and progress of the Seikhs from the first preachings of a peaceful ascetic, to their military renown under Runjit Singh. They grew almost side by side with the British in India, until want of subordination and military misrule brought the two nations into collision—unprovoked aggression on the one side, and stern resistance on the other, ending in the overthrow of the aggressors, and in the loss of that kingdom, which the military successes of so many kings had helped to consolidate.

Nanuk, the founder of the earlier and peaceful community, was born in the year 1469, about sixty miles from Lahore, in a village called Maree. His birth, like that of all eastern founders of new systems, was said to have been miraculous, having been prophesied by a *fakir* of great sanctity and renown.

Of the early years of the extraordinary child we hear much that is surprising, if not incredible. He seems, naturally enough, to have been attached to the class of which one had foretold his birth, and to have been extremely fond of them; so liberal, indeed, that his father by no means approved of it, for, although he was ready to give all honour to the fakirs for having given him a son, he had no intention whatever of paying them constantly for it, when that son had grown up to be a promising boy. These fakirs wander all over India, leading the erratic lives of religious mendicants, and often imposing, to an extraordinary extent, upon the unsuspicious villagers. Women assist them most, and women are most deceived by them.

Anxious to wean his son from a religious life, the father of Nanuk prepared a shop for him at Sultanpore, and stocked it amply with merchandize. But Nanuk thought he was born for higher things than buying and selling—he felt an impulse within him which he had no desire to control, an impulse urging him ever on to that religious life which his father so much dreaded, and from which he would not be diverted. His mercantile affairs were by no means successful. Looking upon the fakirs as the servants of God, he invited them to visit him as often as they pleased. They did not take a fancy to anything in his shop which he was not quite ready to part with. One walked off with one article, another with another, by Nanuk's own desire, and, when his thrifty father came to visit him and to see how he was getting on, he found a beggarly array of empty shelves, and little or no money to account for it. In fact, one would almost be disposed to sympathize with the poor man, had he said, "The fakirs gave you to me, they may take you again." But he did not. On the contrary, he spoke kindly to his strange son, excused his want of knowledge, declared that his *forte* was evidently not money-making, and did, in fact, all that he could do to set him at his ease.

He might have spared himself the trouble, Nanuk was perfectly at his ease already. Nothing that he had done had given him the slightest uneasiness—he was quite prepared to do the same again, if he had the opportunity.

"Nanuk is evidently not made for shop-keeping," argued his father, "he shall live at home with us for the future, and we will look out for a wife for him—he will surely not give her to the fakirs."

A wife was accordingly proposed to the passive Nanuk. "I will marry her," said he, quietly, "if it is your wish, O my father."

It *was* his father's wish, and, like the most dutiful of children, Nanuk was wed. His wife was informed by his father of the strange predilection of her husband for the fakirs. She took her measures accordingly, that they might no longer seek out their old friend as they had done before. Things were evidently altered at Nanuk's; there was no longer a cordial reception for them and a hearty invitation to partake of the best of everything, carrying off what they could not consume. No, it was all changed, though Nanuk remained as kind to them as ever.

For a time the musing youth was satisfied with his new life. In the blandishments of an affectionate wife—in the enjoyment of domestic happiness, he forgot, for a time, the religious life which he desired so ardently to live, and which he had resolved on living. It was, however, but for a time, and, when a few months had rolled away, and novelty given place to satiety, repose to *ennui*, he suddenly left father, mother, wife and home—left them all, never to return. He had ever been accustomed to much musing, and they thought little of it for a time, but when day after day rolled away, and no Nanuk returned, father, mother, wife, all became alarmed, and sought the truant everywhere.

He was in the jungle with the fakirs. He was soon found, for they had a strong suspicion of his intentions. The commands of a father were ineffectual—he would not return. The caresses of a wife were next tried in vain —she hung affectionately upon him; he was not to be moved. She even wept, and Nanuk was still obdurate. It was too much; female equanimity could stand it no more.

"Hard-hearted monster!" she exclaimed, "I have been too good to you, unfeeling as you are. You do not deserve the treasure of a loving, faithful, but too-indulgent wife"

"I do not," said he, quietly; "be loving and faithful to me no more."

Had he been made of marble, he could not have treated her affection, her grief, her rage, more coolly. She could make nothing of him, and, feeling no desire to take up her abode in the jungle and surrender all the comforts of home, returned at length to his father's house, to console herself, in due time, with another husband.

Nanuk was now formally devoted to what he had always looked forward to, as his future career—that of a religious devotee and ascetic; the life of him who has renounced the world and its occupations to pass his earthly career in study, meditation, and the instruction of others—a fakir. Not a fakir of the miserable, disreputable class that hang about the large cities of India, living in idleness and filth on their reputation for sanctity, and pretending to reveal the future to confiding and duped women, to whom they promise many children, not always without an effort to render their prediction true; but a member of a far more decent community, who disdain the filth and entire nakedness of the impostors alluded to; who really devote their time to study and meditation, who really reflect on life and on the future, on the good and on the true; whose piety is something more than a pretence, whose religion is a real living principle in the mind, not a hypocritical show without.

Nanuk did not content himself, however, with simple study and meditation, as many of his class do. He became a teacher and a preacher. He preached indifferently to both Hindoos and Mussulmans, urging the former to put away their images and idols, their mutilations and human sacrifices, their hideous and obscene rites, whilst he impressed upon the Mussulmans the absolute necessity of discarding that fiery spirit of intolerance, that thirst for infidel blood, which forms one of their chief characteristics, or rather did then form one of them.

His doctrines, as a whole, were those of pure Deism. He recognized all the prophets that had gone before him—he honoured Menu and Muhammad, Budha and Confucius, he merely added himself to the number, as the latest, and by no means the least noble illustration of the class. He was eminently an eclectic philosopher, and had faith in human nature besides. An eclectic philosopher, however, he was, with some of the prejudices of his

Hindoo race still clinging to him; for, whilst he preached peace to all mankind and reprobated all intolerance, he had no mercy for the slaughterer of a cow!

To *us* a strange dogma, a strange dogma truly, this of Nanuk's about the cow! but *we* were not born in the Punjab; *we* have not been taught Hindooism by fiery fakirs ready to spill their blood before our eyes to prove the truth of their convictions—ready to thrust an arrow through their tongue, if you doubt their sincerity! It is not a man's mind alone that shapes his convictions—it is not his reason only that guides that mind,—we are all of the age and country in which we live,—formed, fashioned, moulded by the society around us,—ever sinking our own individuality in the waves of public opinion—conforming to social practices in which we see nothing but absurdity—upholding social doctrines, of which we see neither the utility nor the necessity. Let us cease to wonder then that the benevolent Nanuk, who so ardently and eloquently preached peace amongst all mankind, should have regarded the killing of a cow as the one crime that could not be forgiven.

He would not believe in the depravity of man. He was of those who saw God in man as well as in nature, and he could not persuade himself that where God dwelt all could be evil and disordered. He rejected, therefore, absolutely, the doctrine of a fall and the necessity of an atonement. The religious systems of the East are divided into those two great classes—the sacrificers and the non-sacrificers; those that believe an atonement is necessary of some kind, and has been offered or may be offered daily, and those who reject sacrifices altogether, and trust in man's unaided powers to attain the good and the true. Where they have believed atonements necessary, they have sacrificed oxen, sheep, or men, as in Druidism, Magianism, Hindooism; where they have ignored atonements altogether, they have placed their faith in the hand or in the heart, in the sword or in the doing of good.

Muhammad endeavoured to combine the two; Gotama Budha, Confucius and Nanuk trusted solely in the latter. The first class of faiths saw God nowhere, or thrust him to such a distance that the poor sinner had no access to him but by the stepping-stones of priests and altars, temples and sacrifices; the second saw God in everything, and most of all, in man. Verily, the lying spirit of untruth has led poor man a strange dance after salvation—a far stranger dance than any will-o'-the-wisp has done, ever yet seen or fancied!

We may learn from it all, however, one useful lesson, which is this—that religion is a real want of, and necessity for, the heart of man, not a foreign device thrust upon him from without, by any means. God is too far off, says the Devil, for you to have anything to do with him—that is *his* atheism; God is within you, is everywhere about you, all is good and excellent if you will only will it so—that is *his* pantheism; and, between the two, all mankind oscillate and vibrate, now verging on the one, now pressing towards the other. Even the truth itself has been twisted, so as to accommodate itself to the one fallacy or the other, in all ages.

At Rome, God is too far off; priests, saints, virgins, confessionals, and convents are necessary as stepping-stones, and in the contemplation of the medium, the end is lost sight of. In Germany, neology teaches, with its open-mouthed and honest-looking eclecticism, that God is within us, that all is God, and therefore all must be good; as to mediators, or *a* mediator, it laughs at the idea—sees no necessity whatever for any such!

The unity of God was the doctrine that Nanuk most urgently insisted upon, and was most zealous in preaching. Muhammadism taught that doctrine, and he showed from the Hindoo Vedas that they taught it likewise; here, then, was a common basis, a foundation laid for a system to combine the two.

"I am sent," said he, for he always insisted, like all earnest men, that he had a mission from heaven to fulfil, "I am sent to the Mussulman, to reconcile your jarring faiths, and I implore you to read the Hindoo Scriptures as well as your own; but reading is useless without obedience to the doctrine taught, for God has said no man shall be saved except he has performed good works. The Almighty never thinks of asking to what tribe or sect a man belongs, but only what he has done." *

Peace, peace with one another; peace with

* Malcolm. Asiatic Researches, vol. xi.

all mankind, was the doctrine which he ever opposed to the hot-headed spirit of Mussulman aggression. Place your reliance on God, said he, for every thing, and live in harmony and love with each other, and then you shall be saved. He acted up to this doctrine, too, throughout his whole life; he accumulated no goods, had no private property, every thing was shared with his followers, he had all in common with them.

One can easily understand how the constant reflection on the evils caused by civil strife and religious animosity had led a naturally benevolent mind to such conclusions as these. He saw a thousand evils springing from hatred and broils; remove these causes of disquietude, he argued, and all will be well. The fallacy was one which has captivated other minds besides Nanuk's—a fallacy that can only tell upon the benevolent and the amiable.

"A hundred thousand Muhammads," he exclaimed, on one occasion, "a million of Brahmas, Vishnus, and Ramas stand at the gate of the most high. These all perish—God alone is immortal. Yet man, who joins his fellows in praising God, he is not ashamed of living in contention with them; verily the evil spirit has possessed him. He alone is a true Hindu whose heart is just; he alone is a good Mussulman whose life is pure."

There was a loftiness about Nanuk's teaching, which was very imposing; a sublime enthusiasm breathed in his words, that captivated his hearers. A poet himself, for he spent his leisure hours in writing poetry, he was fond of poetic expression and sublime imagery, proving, by some of his sayings, that there was a great soul breathing within him, yearning after the good and the true, the beautiful and the excellent.

"How darest thou, infidel," asked a zealous Mussulman of him one day, "how darest thou, infidel, turn thy feet towards the house of God?"

"Turn them, O believer! if thou canst, where the house of God is not," was Nanuk's meek but sublime answer.

Like the Hindus, he taught the doctrine of metempsychosis, or transmigration of souls, almost in the very words in which Pythagoras and his disciples had taught it so many centuries before. Dogs and cats were the animals which the souls of the wicked should animate in future births, whilst those of the good should gradually climb the ladder of existence, attaining to Paradise at last.

CHAPTER II.

THE ORIGIN OF THE SEIKHS—NANUK AND GOVIND.

Nothing could be more simple than the manner in which Nanuk wandered about, discoursing as he went. He gradually separated from the class of fakirs to which he at first belonged, and which he had loved so much in his youth—a change that brought upon him, of course, the violent denunciations of the more bigoted Hindus. Of that, however, he recked little. It was sufficient for him that he considered a course of conduct right or profitable, and he cared little then what the world might think about it.

He was, on one occasion, taken by the soldiers of Baber before that stern Muhammadan conqueror. Nanuk discoursed to him as he discoursed to his followers usually. Baber was pleased and astonished; so much pleased, indeed, that he ordered an ample provision to be made for the Seikh prophet's future maintenance.

"O king," replied Nanuk, "know that I want no provision made for my future maintenance. I trust in Him who provides for all men. A man of truth and piety requires no favour at the hands of conquerors, nor will he consent to receive such." He carried a rude tent about with him in all his wanderings, but it was usually under the shade of a tree that he discoursed to his followers, or sitting beside a wall. Unbelievers in his mission desired to see some miracle in attestation of it. "I have nothing of the kind to exhibit," said he, calmly; "the true teacher has nothing but truth as his sign. The world may change, but the Creator is unchangeable."

But the followers of Nanuk were by no means pleased with this simplicity They were dissatisfied that their prophet should call himself a Gooroo only, or teacher, and not a miracle-worker and a God, so they invented miracles for him in abundance. At eleven years of age, say they, when he was one day tending his father's cattle in the fields, he lay down to repose. The sun's rays gradually became more and more powerful, and would have been directly upon the youth's face, probably inducing thereby a sun-stroke. A hooded snake of enormous dimensions crawled from the jungle, and spreading abroad its hood, stood erect by the side of the sleeping boy, thus shading his face. Some neighbours saw the unwonted spectacle, and went to tell his father. But it did not astonish his father, for his father never forgot that he was the gift of the fakirs.*

Let us take another specimen of these traditions from his later life. Nanuk was one day sitting at the outskirts of a village, and seeing a man, Boda by name, feeding his cows hard by, he asked him for a drink of water, as he was faint.

"The water is at a great distance," said Boda; "but mind my cows, and I will get you some."

"There is a tank near," replied Nanuk; "fetch me water from thence."

"There certainly *was* a tank near," was Boda's reply, "but it is dried up."

"Go and see," rejoined Nanuk. Boda went, and to his great surprise, he found the tank, which had been some time dry, suddenly filled with water. He returned, of course, to worship the prophet, and to become a firm disciple, giving up cows, and family, and all, to follow him.* But the legend does not end here.

Umritzir, or the water of immortality, was the name given to that tank in after-ages; a city was reared upon its banks, which is now the second city in the Punjab, retaining the name (Umritzir) which had been given to the tank on account of the miracle, and that city is at the present day the head quarters of the Seikh faith. In an island in the midst of the lake, which must have marvellously grown since then, is the sacred book of the Seikhs kept in a magnificent temple, and daily read to crowds of worshippers. The following is a description of the temple, taken from the "History of the Seikhs:"—

"The *Durbar Sahib*, as it is called, or great Seikh temple, is erected in the centre of a beautiful sheet of water, above the surface of which it is raised by means of a terrace. The building is a handsome one, and its lofty gilded

* Macgregor.

dome and minarets produce a rich and dazzling effect. Surrounding this temple, and skirting the edge of the water, may be seen the stately mansions of the different Seikh chieftains. The entrance to the temple is by a flight of steps, which descend from one of the public streets or avenues; before entering on these, every person is obliged to take off his shoes, even the king himself was not exempt. On reaching the bottom, there is a causeway leading to the temple, the door of which faces the north. This causeway is almost constantly crowded during the day-time with people passing to and from the temple."

One is almost disposed to ask here how they all get their own shoes and slippers again, or whether people ever go with good slippers on; but our historian does not condescend to such points, and we proceed in ignorance :—

"On the ground-floor, opposite the door, sits the presiding Gooroo, or priest, clothed in white robes, and before him is placed the Grunth, or sacred book, which is open; this book is constantly fanned by the priest, by means of a chourey, or yak's tail, which he keeps waving about, backwards and forwards.

The Grunth is placed under a small arch of gold tinsel, inlaid with precious stones, valued at fifty thousand rupees (five thousands pounds); the rest of the apartment is strewed with flowers, or covered with rich carpets. The doors and walls are gilded and ornamented, whilst the light descending from the lofty dome has a pleasing effect. Above this there are other apartments, with verandahs running round the whole circuit of the building."

So much for the great temple of the Seikhs, and for Nanuk's water-producing miracle. Did you hint a doubt to a Seikh on the subject of this miracle, he would doubtless exclaim, "Why, there is the water itself to convince you; go to Umritzir, and you shall see it," to him a convincing argument.

But even the production of a miraculous lake is by no means the most astounding circumstance related respecting Nanuk. He is declared by Seikh authorities to have had an interview with the Deity himself.

One day, say they, he heard a voice from above, exclaiming, "Nanuk, approach."

His reply was, "O God, what power have I to stand in thy presence?"

"Close thine eyes," said the voice.

Nanuk did as he was commanded, and advanced. He was told at length to look up: he did so, and heard a voice exclaiming, "Well done," pronounced five times, concluding with, "well done, Gooroo."

After this, the Almighty said, "Nanuk, I have sent thee into the world in this the depraved age; go and bear my name to it."

"O God!" exclaimed the prophet, "how can I bear so mighty a burden? If my age were extended to tens of millions of years, if I drank of the waters of immortality, and my eyes, like the sun and the moon, were never dim, still I could not presume to charge myself with thy wondrous name."

"I myself will be thy Gooroo," said the Almighty, "and thou shalt be a Gooroo to all mankind; thy sect shall be great in the world, and I will forgive the sins of thy disciples. Thou must teach to thy followers three great lessons; first, to worship my name; secondly, to love one another; thirdly, to practise ablution. They must not abandon the world, they must do ill to no living being, for into every being have I infused life. It is a blessing to the world that thou art sent in this the depraved age."

Thereafter continues the account. "Well done, teacher; well done, Gooroo," was pronounced again by the Most High, and "Nanuk came to give light and freedom to the universe."

From all which it is abundantly evident that Nanuk's disciples had no intention whatever of allowing him to sink down into the character of a mere teacher, which alone he arrogated to himself, but were determined to place him on a level with the founders of other faiths, such as Gotama Budha and Zoroaster, as a miracle-worker and as a converser face to face with the Almighty.

He had fled from his wife and family in early life, to become an ascetic; but in the course of years he relinquished that profession, and strictly prohibited his followers from forsaking the world and their social or domestic duties. He found another wife late in life, and settled upon the banks of the Ravee, where he died at a good old age, leaving behind him two sons, whose descendants remain to this day. He was buried in great state by his disciples, near his own residence; a magnificent tomb was erected over his remains, and pilgrimages to it were frequent, until the Ravee rose higher than usual one year, and swept it away. He did not leave either of his sons as his successor, but a faithful disciple, in whom he had more confidence, named Ungut.

The precepts which the founder of the Seikh religion gave to his disciples as the rules of their lives and the laws of his faith, were collected into a volume called the Grunth, or holy book. Much was added to it subsequently by one of Nanuk's successors, Govind, who completely changed the character of the sect. Persecution had roused the spirit of defiance and opposition. The peaceful character of Nanuk's doctrines was forgotten, and the sect, previously harmless and benevolent, became one of the most warlike and cruel that even the annals of Asiatic warfare describe.

Nanuk himself is revered by his followers as a species of Deity. They have made him almost equal with the Almighty in the honours which they pay to his memory. Prayers are offered up to him as a saviour and a mediator, and thus, the whole fabric that he erected has been grievously mutilated and altered. One "improvement" after another, one addition here and alteration there, have quite done away with the simplicity he advocated, and the comparatively pure doctrine he taught, until it is difficult to recognize the modern faith as that to maintain which the followers of Nanuk suffered so much.

In 1680, the tenth successor of Nanuk, Govind, the last of the Gooroos, became the head of the Seikhs. He seems to have been a man the very opposite in point of character and disposition to Nanuk. Proud, ambitious, cruel, he began his administration by summoning all the tribe to assemble and arm in order to revenge the death of his father, who had been beheaded by the emperor at Delhi. When they had assembled together, he addressed them in a speech which breathed far other sentiments than those which the Seikhs had up to this period been accustomed to hear from their teachers.

"My father ordered me to avenge his blood," he began, "and with this view I have collected a large army, but money is required for its maintenance. Now, my friends, every one of you must prepare to obey my orders, and to contribute money. Secondly, you must be all of one mind, and adopt the same manners, and have the same religious belief. There must be no castes among you, as amongst the Hindus. You must be all equal, and no man greater than his fellow. You must place no reliance upon the *shasters*. You must not visit the sacred places of the Hindus, nor pay any respect whatever to their gods—to Nanuk Gooroo let your respect be paid, but to none else. The four castes of the Hindus are to be dissolved amongst you from henceforth."

Thus did Govind begin a re-construction of the Seikh tribe, changing altogether its character and principles. Nanuk had taught his disciples the transmigration of souls; Govind said, "Not so, we are warriors now, we must not believe in any such doctrine." The shedding of blood was no longer regarded by them as the greatest of crimes, nay, they soon came to regard it as the most trivial, for, throughout the entire subsequent history of the nation, the cutting off of heads is one of the commonest incidents recorded. The production of the head, indeed, seems to have been the ordinary official intimation of the death of any individual.

There was good policy in much of Govind's reform. The destruction of caste, and the resignation of the Brahminical thread, the sign and symbol of one of the superior castes, was a politic step. It ingratiated the Seikhs with the lower castes, and brought a vast accession of numbers to their ranks, whilst they lost thereby but a few. When he exclaimed against the doctrine of transmigration, he was no less wise, for a belief in that doctrine leads naturally to a horror of the taking of life, and he was determined that henceforth the Seikhs should be pre-eminently takers of life — the cow still respected, however. *Its* life was sacred, but that of man was a trivial matter.

His next step was to select ten men from amongst his host, which now numbered twenty thousand—ten warlike men, pledged to stand or fall by him—and having administered an oath to them, he took upon himself the appellation of Singh, from the Sanscrit for *a lion.* Henceforth he was styled Govind Singh. But he did not confine this appellation to himself, he gave it also to his ten disciples, an honour of course duly appreciated by them, whilst his twenty thousand followers were now first called Seikhs, a corruption of the same root, the name which their descendants have ever since retained—a name which, under Runjit, was the terror of northern India. Thus, in a few days, were the peacefully religious descendants and followers of the simple Nanuk transformed into a fierce military and political tribe, ready to assert their rights with the sword, and not afraid to engage in a contest even with the Emperor himself at Delhi. Two of the three primary duties which Nanuk had laid down as imperative on all, Govind wisely retained—the worship of the one God and daily ablutions. The third, love to all, was changed by him into love to our friends, hatred to our enemies.

In one striking respect Govind imitated Nanuk, or rather the bent of their minds led them to act precisely alike. They both despised wealth, and were ready to give it up without a sigh, or to share it with their followers. Govind's desire was to excite martial enthusiasm in the breasts of his followers, and in showing a contempt for wealth he was but acting politically as well as in accordance with his natural bent.

Several strange anecdotes are told of him, illustrative of this contempt of his for money and precious stones. A Seikh from the South-East brought him two valuable bracelets as a present, valued at £5000, and requested permission to buckle them himself on the wrists of the Gooroo. Govind allowed him to do so, but, on washing his hands shortly after in the river, he dropped one of the bracelets into the water, which was deep there. The Seikh heard of it, and hired a diver for 500 rupees (£50) to search the stream, requesting Govind to show whereabouts the bracelet was lost. The Gooroo walked with him towards the river, and, when they came near the place, taking off the other bracelet he threw it into the stream; "It was somewhere thereabouts," said he, quietly, and then turned away to walk back to his house. "The Gooroo does not value the gift," said the donor to himself, amazed, "I shall not search for it further."

That Govind was a bold, resolute, and courageous man the history of his life abundantly proves. For more than thirty years he was at the head of the Seikhs, and nothing could be more various than his fortune during that period. At one time the leader of fifty thousand men, threatening the Great Mogul himself,—at another wandering, deserted, with only five followers, from place to place, obliged to disguise and deceive in order to save his life.

When reduced apparently to the last extremity, we find him addressing his few remaining troops thus—"If we die, my friends, I shall be esteemed as a warrior, whilst your memory will be revered as that of heroes. If we conquer, the country will be ours. To die as cowards is base, to die as warriors is glorious." Obliged at one time to eat beef in order to prove that he was neither a Seikh nor a Hindu; and imposing laws, at another, upon all the neighbouring princes and governors, he passed those thirty years in a series of alternate elevation and depression, such as even the history of Indian sects scarcely parallels.

He died in 1708, at the court of the Mogul Emperor, some say by his own hand, being weary of life. That he completely changed the character of the Seikhs is a fact fully attested by the history of India—he found them a peaceful, charitable, benevolent community, he left them a fierce military people, daring, cruel and revengeful. He was one of those few heroes who write their own character on a nation, stamping it ineffaceably upon the hearts of thousands, just as the die leaves its impression upon wax or upon the hardest metal alike. A century and a half after Govind Singh, we find the Seikh people powerful, formidable, rich, brave, and courageous; disputing the very possession of India with its foreign lords, and that with so formidable an amount of vigour and ability, that it was for a time doubtful whether the vast resources of the Company would not be insufficient to repel them. Govind Singh himself could not have animated them with a nobler courage than they then displayed, although there can be little doubt, had *he* been then their leader, the contest would not have been so speedily and decisively ended.

For nearly a century after Govind's death, the Seikhs were still battling for existence and for power with the Mussulman rulers of the Punjab, and it was not until Runjit Singh became the ruler of Lahore in 1799, that this supremacy was doubtful no longer. The history of the world scarcely contains a stranger chapter than that which relates the rise and fall of the Seikh dominion—its rise from Nanuk to Runjit, its fall from Runjit's death in 1839 to the British conquest of the Punjab. It took three centuries and a half to attain its culminating point—in seven years afterwards it had become nearly extinct! Sic transit gloria mundi.

CHAPTER III.

ROMANCE OF EASTERN STATE-CRAFT.

No history can look more like romance than that of the Seikhs, from the reign of Runjit to the invasion by the Seikh army of the British territory in India, during the winter of 1845. Not even in Eastern despotisms might such a train of quickly occurring conspiracies and revolutions, elevations and depressions, be expected to occur in the course of six short years. They remind one, indeed, of the exploits of a pantomime, in which the chopping off of people's heads is a joke, the cutting of their bodies into pieces a pleasant episode. The point of contrast, however, is plain enough. In the fictitious, the heads soon rejoin the bodies, or are easily done without, whilst the removal of the severed limbs seems to be but a relief to their temporary owners; in the real, however, the heads once off, cannot be replaced; the bodies once dismembered, we hear nothing more of the intriguing spirits that animated them.

During the entire administration of Runjit Singh, which lasted from 1799 to 1839, the Punjab was a prosperous, flourishing kingdom; its revenues ample and constantly increasing, its power formidable to its neighbours, and itself therefore respected. Runjit was one of those uncompromising, white-bearded, turn-up nosed eastern despots, who, whilst they take their fill of all the pleasures that money and power can procure, yet know how to keep a firm grasp of the reins of government, and to wield with energy the unsparing sword of justice or polity. The Seikh nation required such a ruler, and willingly obeyed the man who proved by his firmness and ability that he was fitted to command. Like a fiery courser, that would unseat a timid ruler, but is obedient to a bold one, they bent their necks tamely to his yoke, winced at his unflinching severity, and admired whilst they winced.

He understood the posture of affairs, too, out of the Punjab—with that far-seeing eye of his, voluptuous in its full proportions, but powerful in its overhanging mass of shaggy eye-brow, he had looked deeply into the exact position of India. He had got together a great army, he had established a vast park of artillery, he was surrounded by French and Italian officers, who drilled his infantry, and who introduced European tactics into his army, men ready to take their oaths on the Bible, the Koran, or the Grunth—it was all one to them—that 'the lion of the Punjab' had but to will it, and the British should be driven from India.

He was surrounded by flatterers, who extolled his power and magnified his resources. He let them flatter, listened to what they said, catching the tones with one ear and letting them go with the other, as he smiled with the smile of a despot at their empty praises.

"I might drive the Ungreez Bahādor (the Honourable English) as far as Allyghur, but I should be driven back soon after, first to the

Sutlej, then out of my kingdom," was his reply, when he was thus importuned to give the order for the destruction of the foreigners.

Of the Europeans in his service, Avatibili, Ventura, and others, he made good use, whilst he paid them well. Cannon were cast in Lahore, his capital; artillery-men were trained; infantry and cavalry were disciplined; but he took care that these Europeans should not get the upper hand, or become the leading-strings by which he, puppet-like, was to be directed. He treated them well, but kept rather aloof from them, not admitting any to much intimacy. They had money, women, command, but not political power—*that* was reserved for himself, and for those of the Seikhs whom he thought worthy of it.

To British emissaries who visited him, whether military or civil, he took care to display his military power. His salutes were fired from a hundred pieces of ordnance, whilst twenty thousand muskets rolled forth incessantly and unremittingly during the booming of the larger artillery. "They would fire better and more quickly if in presence of an enemy," he would carelessly observe to his

English visitor; "but, on the whole, that's pretty well." It was a part of his policy never to permit his European servants to hold commands in the artillery—they might be too dangerous there, he thought. The British have reason to know that this artillery of Runjit's was by no means despicable, and thousands of Her Majesty's and the Company's troops, who rot beneath the sands of the Punjab, are dead witnesses of the fact.

It must be remembered, too, that these Seikhs, whom Runjit governed so well, were but the ruling race in the Punjab—that by far the greater proportion of the inhabitants were Hindus and Mussulmans. The Seikh faith endeavoured to combine the Vedas and the Koran into one harmonious system, and its earlier disciples were, of course, equally persecuted by the upholders of both. Thousands of them had fallen martyrs to their new dogmas, before they finally settled in the Punjab, and became its rulers. Considering then that these Seikhs, of whom Runjit was the king, were but the lords of the Punjab, with the vast majority of the population in serfdom, and ready to rise at any moment against their rulers, there is all the more credit due to Runjit for the peaceable government which he established, all the more credit due to him for holding the Seikh in order with one hand, whilst he restrained the conquered native with the other. Such men do not often make their appearance in any country; still seldomer are they born to a throne. The subsequent history of the state proves how turbulent the Seikh chiefs or Sirdars were naturally—how ready they were to take advantage of the weakness of the ruling power to thrust forward their swords against that power.

It must be remembered, too, that Runjit was King when the British first came into collision with Affghanistan—that he was constantly urged then to attack them—to become the arbiter of India and of Asia. But Runjit saw much further into things than his shallow counsellors. He knew that it was but a small portion of the British power which was marching into Affghanistan—he looked behind the curtain, and saw large armies in Madras and Bombay, European regiments dispersed over the world, but which a powerful fleet could soon assemble; he saw all these things, and replied again, "I might drive the Ungreez Bahador as far as Allyghur, but I should be driven back soon after, first to the Sutlej, then out of my kingdom."

He had met two of the Governors-General of India, Lord Auckland and Lord Ellenboro', and he, doubtless, concluded that the latter, at all events, was not the man to succumb to a few difficulties at first, or to yield India without a struggle.

But though Runjit, with his firm arm and unquailing eye, kept repressed the military spirit of his people, or rather turned it into a proper channel in establishing a disciplined standing army, his successors were not able to do likewise. The Seikhs are, by early training and by religion, a military people. They regard the army as their natural destination, war as their normal condition. Their religion forbids them to adopt any other profession or employment than that of the sword, their early training unfits them for any other. Runjit's task was therefore all the more difficult; and whilst our admiration of him is increased by this consideration, we must, at the same time, feel less astonished at the disorder which prevailed after his death.

It is an essential talent in a great ruler to be able to discover the men best fitted for high office, and in this respect the ability of Runjit was conspicuous. Even when prostrated by paralysis, the result of intemperance and excess, his name was sufficient to govern the kingdom quietly; his name, associated with the administrative talent of those whom he had placed in important positions. Dhyan Singh was his Wuzeer, or Prime Minister—a prudent, cautious man, who found Runjit's name a tower of strength, and could wield the most turbulent spirits in the Punjab by pronouncing it, even when Runjit himself lay unable to utter a syllable; but, when the master-spirit was gone, Dhyan's ability was of little use. Rough men, that cared nothing for diplomacy, but much for warlike talent, started up then on every side, and the peace and quiet that had prevailed so shortly before, became changed into turbulence and discord. Nor is it to be supposed that Dhyan wanted resolution or courage; on the contrary, he was a perfect hero, according to the rude ideas of those rude Seikhs.

The eldest son of Runjit succeeded him, a man resembling his father in outward form, but most unlike him in his mental constitution. For a short time he availed himself of Dhyan's ability, but only for a short time; and then, turning round upon his father's counsellor, dismissed him, and gave the premiership to a spiritless creature of his own. Dhyan was not a man to brook this, and, besides, he knew very well that this was no second Runjit that occupied the throne, so he marched boldly into the durbar one day, with his sword drawn in his hand. There was a something in his eye that told the new king he was not to be trifled with. Walking deliberately up to the favourite—the unworthy favourite, as all accounts concur in representing him—who was stupidly gazing at the intruder, and wondering what he could possibly want with his drawn sword in open durbar, Dhyan then and there smote him to the earth with one blow, cutting off his head with the second.

Rough and ready with their weapons were

those Seikhs; far rougher and readier than suits our western ideas. The new king was alarmed, as well he might be, and surrendering the power into Dhyan's hands, shut himself up in his seraglio. He was dead within the year, not by Dhyan's agency, far from it. He was precisely the kind of king Dhyan wanted; excessive debauchery shortened his days, inconveniently enough for Dhyan, who had all his work to begin over again.

The grandson of Runjit was now placed upon the throne, but the fates were adverse. Returning from the obsequies of his father on an elephant, just as he passed through one of the massive gates of Lahore, some stones from above gave way and crushed him to death, together with one of his companions. The circumstance appears to have been quite accidental, and probably was so, although one cannot help feeling somewhat suspicious about such accidents amongst such people.

The way was thus opened for a reputed son of Runjit (Shere Singh, by name) to ascend the throne, and notwithstanding the opposition of Runjit's widow, Shere Singh was placed upon it by Dhyan. This was in 1841. Shere was distinguished by two ruling passions, a fondness for strong drink and a love of hunting. Before coming to the throne, these propensities of his had been conspicuous; when he had actually become king, he gave himself up to them completely. Shere drank himself drunken, and, when he got sober, hunted that he might have the more zest for drinking again. Dhyan let him do as he liked, and governed the kingdom in his name.

For nearly two years did Shere enjoy his terrestrial elysium of hunting and drinking, whilst Dhyan ruled. But for only two years—nay, not quite for two years. Associated with him in all his excesses, there were two boon companions, whom the dissolute Shere loved amazingly. Their names were Lena and Ajeet. With their master the three formed a worthy trio, worthy of each other and of their company. But even the best of fellows will quarrel in their cups, and as Shere became more and more reckless, and more and more accustomed to do exactly as he pleased, on two or three occasions he threatened the lives of his dear friends, from whom, says one account, he was never separated, neither by night nor by day. The drunken threats of a man who has the power of doing what he pleases, are, however, not to be despised, and Lena and Ajeet, at length thoroughly aroused, resolved to get rid of the tyrant before he got rid of them. Mark the finesse with which they wrought to this end.

To put Shere to death without Dhyan's consent would have been death to them, they knew. In order to gain this consent they dealt craftily. So one day, when Shere was in his cups, they got him to sign an order for Dhyan's execution. With this order, and the king's signature on it, in their hands, they came to Dhyan. First talking to him of all that he had done for Shere, of how he had put that unworthy debauchee on the throne and had kept him there, they raised a high idea in his mind of the gratitude which Shere owed him. To all this Dhyan assented, wondering, doubtless, what this strange preface was intended to introduce. They then hinted that the king was not grateful, that he hated Dhyan.

"Impossible!" exclaimed the premier; "why should he hate me?"

How could they tell; but the fact was indisputable.

Dhyan was still incredulous—he would not believe it. It is some shallow trick, doubtless thought he. The fatal order was produced. Dhyan examined it amazed.

Yes, it was the king's signature, there could be no doubt of that; but he evidently does not mean to act on it, said he, or the seal would be affixed as well.

"It is his intention to affix the seal," they urged.

In that case I must be prepared for the worst, thought Dhyan.

An agreement was at once made between Dhyan on one side and the two friends on the other, that if the seal were affixed he should have timely notice, and Lena and Ajeet should be his friends forthwith, all three combining, of course, against the drinking and hunting king

Delighted with the success of their stratagem so far, Lena and Ajeet returned to the king, apparently his dear friends, really resolved on his destruction. A promise was obtained from him that he should inspect

Ajeet's troops on the morrow. The usual feasting was commenced, to be succeeded by the usual drinking. The dancing girls were introduced as usual—all was mirth and gaiety; the king in great vein, his two dear friends the most cordial of boon companions. At length drunkenness supervened as usual, also, but not upon Lena and Ajeet; they had wisely refrained and continued sober, whilst Shere drank his senses into oblivion.

The propitious moment had arrived. "You forgot, most excellent king, to affix the great seal to this warrant," said Lena to the drunken monarch.

"O don't trouble me with business," exclaimed Shere; "let me have more music and dancing. This brandy is—hic—hic—is fit for the houris."

The cups were replenished, the music and dancing resumed, Shere was fast relapsing into insensibility.

"But the seal, my gracious sovereign," suggested Lena, humbly. "Your slave awaits the seal."

"Lena, you're a plague—you'll lose your head some day if you teaze me this way," exclaimed Shere. "What's the name of that loose-bodiced wench with the fine arms? Hoonda—hic—hic—Hoondawarra, to be sure. I'll forget my own name, next." So saying, the drunken king, leering upon the dancer, took his ring from his finger.

The execution warrant was legalized. The death of Dhyan commanded. Signature and seal, we have them both now, thought the conspirators, as the drunken king looked at them vacantly.

"What was—hic, hic—what was that warrant?" asked Shere.

"Only to order the execution of the slave that killed one of the hounds the other day. Don't you remember?" said Ajeet.

"I do—hic—hic—I do. And, hark ye, Ajeet. Let him be—hic, hic—let him be flayed—hic, hic—and I'll see it, I'll see it."

So saying, the king turned once more towards the fascinating Hoondawarra, who was exhibiting her utmost grace and her solid charms to the hazy gaze of the drunken monarch. In a few minutes he was in a lethargic slumber, breathing heavily. He was consigned for the night to the dancers' care—

the music gradually died away—the conspirators rose to seek Dhyan.

"We told you the seal would be affixed. Behold!" said they.

"There is no time to be lost, then," said Dhyan, inspecting the warrant, and retaining it.

"Give us permission—an order in writing—and we will rid Lahore of the tyrant to-morrow," urged Lena and Ajeet.

"I will," said Dhyan, and in a few minutes the two king's friends departed with the document they desired in their possession.

It was late on the following morning ere the king was prepared to fulfil his promise respecting the inspection of Ajeet's troops. With two attendants, besides the conspirators, he passed out on horseback through the Roshnaee gate of Lahore, and, taking the road towards the parade ground, alighted near a garden in which were pitched tents belonging to his son Pertaub. The corps which Ajeet had recently enrolled was in the neighbourhood, ready to support its general should anything untoward occur.

Whilst Shere Singh was enjoying some refreshment in one of the tents, endeavouring, doubtless, to shake off the effects of the previous night's drunkenness, Ajeet produced a handsome case, containing a new English rifle, which he showed to the king, who was a connoisseur in such things. Shere took it, adjusted the barrel to the stock, and tried the sight.

"It is loaded," said Ajeet quietly.

The king handed it to one of his dear friend's attendants, who stood there for the purpose, telling him to fire it off outside the tent.

Ajeet gave the signal—the rifle was discharged, but its contents were lodged in the chest of the unworthy king. He had but time for a single exclamation, "What have you done, villain?" ere he expired, for the ball had been fired with fatal precision. Ajeet himself severed his master's head from his body.

But what was Lena doing all this time? He also had a head to procure. Shere's son, Pertaub, was at his devotions when Lena entered his apartments, for, unlike his father, he believed in other things than hunting and drinking. Lena's guards were in all the avenues of the palace, the attendants of Pertaub were at a distance. Rushing suddenly upon him with his sword drawn, Lena slew and beheaded him. With the two heads, as witnesses of their obedience, Lena and Ajeet came to Dhyan, exclaiming, "My lord's commands have been obeyed—the tyrant and his son are dead—behold their heads."

Dhyan was by no means unaccustomed to such sights. He did not shudder, but he looked coldly upon the executioners. He had no further use for them, and would now shake them off, as he would shake off a couple of worms from his hand.

"I did not order the death of Pertaub," said Dhyan coldly.

"You would not have the young tiger live to revenge the death of his father," exclaimed they, disappointed.

"It was not right to murder Pertaub," he persisted.

"What would you have?" demanded the friends of Shere Singh. "What would you have? Who shall be king? What shall be our rewards?"

"There is no king now but Dhuleep, the infant," said Dhyan, coldly, walking off.

"Dhuleep shall be king," said they, "and you will be his minister and govern the country, and we—what shall we have?"

"You will be remembered as the murderers of Pertaub," said Dhyan, sarcastically, walking away.

But Lena and Ajeet were playing for a high stake, and were not willing to forsake it because danger stood in the way. Ajeet had a loaded pistol in his belt, his rage was inflamed to the utmost by the coolness of Dhyan, and, as the premier walked off, Ajeet took the pistol in his hand and shot the wise minister in the back.

The ruler of the Punjab fell dead upon the spot, he who had governed the kingdom wisely during Runjit's illness, and who had pulled the strings of the puppet Shere—he who had made Sirdars tremble and Affghans submit—he who had imbibed some of the spirit, and had naturally something of the same talent as the Seikh Napoleon, Runjit. Lena and Ajeet stood over the corpse of the prime minister, the rulers of the Punjab for the time being!

Did I not say truly, then, madam, that this Seikh history is more romantic than anything I have previously related? Did you or I see such incidents acted upon the boards of Drury Lane or the Princess's, should we not be disposed to say that they were rather improbable, that they were something of the nature of Adelphi extravaganzas? When we came to see the signature and seal affixed by the drunken monarch, should we not have been prepared to say, 'It does very well for the theatre, but real life is a different thing.' Nay, madam, I do verily believe you would indignantly throw your opera-cloak over those alabaster shoulders on which the lights gleam with such imposing effect, and say it was "too absurd," as you threw yourself back (gracefully) upon your chair.

Yet these are the truths, not the fictions, of history. Runjit and Shere Singh, and Lena and Ajeet, and Dhyan were living men known to many still alive. The tragedies of Shere Singh's death and Pertaub's, of Dhyan's execution warrant and murder, are facts of history that have occurred within these few years back. There are thousands still alive who have known the men, and who remember the circumstances. Verily truth *is* strange—stranger than fiction, unquestionably.

It is a useful thing for society and individuals to see how the work of centuries may be destroyed in a few months of folly; to see how speedily the kingdom that has been consolidated and strengthened by the labours of genius, and the efforts of successive generations, may be overturned by anarchy and misrule.

Let us pursue this history, therefore, for a year or two more—there is much to be learned from it every way.

CHAPTER IV.

A LEAF FROM HISTORY—THE FALL OF THE SEIKHS.

The infant Dhuleep, who had been mentioned by Dhyan, was the son of one of the wives of Runjit, and was born a few months before his reputed father's death. His mother vehemently protested, of course, that he was Runjit's son. The Sirdars who heard her smiled, and declared they were certain of it. Lena and Ajeet knew that even an adopted son of Runjit would be maintained upon the throne by the Seikh army; much more, therefore, were they bound to place upon it the son of Runjit's wife, whom all the world protested to be an infant very like his father.

Dhuleep was now four years of age—a fine thriving boy. His mother was from the hills, and had once been a dancing girl. In that capacity she had so attracted Runjit's attention in his old age, that, greatly to the scandal of the faithful, he had married her, and, as she had the good fortune to give birth to a son just before his death, she was now the Ranee, or Queen Dowager, and her son was the Maharajah Dhuleep Singh. Both are still alive, though British cannon and British bayonets have driven both from the high stations to which Runjit's senile wantonness had raised them.

Lena and Ajeet began by placing Dhuleep upon the throne, and securing the favour of the Ranee. Ajeet aspired to succeed Dhyan as virtual ruler—doubtless the honour and the power were to be shared with his companion in intrigue. But there was a formidable obstacle in their way, which they endeavoured in vain to remove. Dhyan's son, Heera, was a favourite with the army, and with the European officers in that army especially. He was sent for craftily, but not until Rumour, with his hundred tongues, had busily proclaimed in Lahore that Shere Singh was dead, that Dhuleep was king, and that Dhyan was not at the head of affairs, as was his wont. Heera, therefore, refused to come, but, aware of the character of the men he had to deal with, he hastened off for protection to General Avatibili's house.

Generals Avatibili and Ventura were the two principal European officers in Runjit's army. They doubtless knew well which side was likely to be victorious, and when they espoused Heera's cause, it must already have appeared promising. Whilst a portion of the army was marching upon the capital, with the European officers and Heera at its head, Ajeet had the Maharajah Dhuleep Singh proclaimed in Lahore as King of the Punjab, and himself as Wuzeer or Prime Minister.

With drums beating and colours flying, the army marched by the Delhi gate into Lahore, whilst Lena and Ajeet prepared to defend the fort. But troops and ammunition were both wanting. Lena was wounded in the first encounter. Ajeet saw that effectual resistance was hopeless, and endeavoured to escape. A Muhammadan soldier in Ventura's division saw him, recognized him, and pursued. Ajeet was not very swift of foot, but the soldier was nimble, and gained upon him. Perceiving that his legs could not carry him from the danger,

Ajeet tried his gold—taking off some rich ornaments which he had concealed about his person, he threw them to the Mussulman, begging him to spare his life.

The prudent warrior picked up the ornaments, and cut off Ajeet's head afterwards, taking it to Heera as a proof that his rival was out of the way. Rude fellows those Seikhs were—they were sure a man was dead only when they saw his bleeding head produced, not otherwise. But Heera ordered the body also to be brought, and after having it dragged, in Homeric fashion, through the streets, it was quartered — the pieces being hung up upon the different gateways.

A vigorous attack was now made upon the fort, and it was taken. Lena, still alive, was captured and disembowelled—all the male relatives and followers of the two conspirators were murdered—the women having their noses cut off, that they might no more captivate men, that the conquerors might be the last whom they should please! It is but right that these atrocities should be known. Let it be remembered that these things happened amongst one of the most highly civilized people in India, and then let the question be answered, Whether the Christian people who now govern that country, are not responsible before God and the world for the use they make of their power? are not responsible for the education and the conversion of these races?

They are doing both gradually, does some one, ignorant of India, innocently exclaim. They are doing neither, I boldly reply, confident of being right, because I have seen what they are doing. The Indian Government neither educates properly nor converts—it extracts money, though cautiously, extensively, incessantly. It is a vast money-producing machine, and it keeps the country in peace—that is all it does. As to improvement, it is not an Indian term—it has no synonyme east of the Indus.

It was during Shere Singh's reign that the British disasters in Cabul had occurred; but Dhyan was then at the head of affairs in the Punjab, and, true to the policy of his great master, he refused to attack the English in the time of their disasters. Now things were changed. The Prætorian bands of the Punjab had made Heera prime minister, and they demanded money or plunder. The European officers had no sympathy with the British, rather the reverse, and they flattered themselves that the army of the Punjab was powerful enough to make so strong a demonstration that all India would be in a blaze, if war became inevitable. At the worst, their fortunes were made, and much of them was already invested in France or Italy.

Of the adherents of Ajeet and Lena, Soochet, Heera's uncle, was one of the bravest, the most powerful, and the richest. Heera, after paying his dutiful respects to the infant king and his mother, resolved to get rid of Soochet, and to confiscate his wealth. Soochet seems to have been too unsuspicious for a Seikh, and, though warned of danger, refused to fly. He remained, and was murdered. His head was taken to Heera—it was the ordinary and official announcement of his death—and forty-five wives were burned with his body! But though the life of Soochet had been taken, his property was still in the possession of his family—they fled with it to the British territories. It was demanded by Heera from the British authorities, but they refused to interfere, for Golab, the brother of Soochet, was a firm ally of theirs. He had learned prudence under the instruction of Runjit, and saw that things were now progressing towards a rupture. This same Golab, "who sometimes flayed his captives alive," says an historian, carelessly, was subsequently made by the British, King of Cashmere, and still rules in that lovely valley—the garden of Asia.

The British refused to surrender Soochet's wealth, and Heera doubtless let the soldiers know that they did so, for he was already in want of money. He had made large promises, and he required an ample exchequer to fulfil them. Soochet's wealth would have been a timely addition to his resources. It was useless, however, for Heera to remonstrate with the soldiery, or to protest that he lacked the means to supply their demands.

"Pay us what you promised," they hoarsely answered to his energetic remonstrances—"pay us what you promised, now."

"It is but reasonable," whispered the European officers, "that you should satisfy these brave men."

"I cannot," replied Heera, alarmed, "I cannot, at present, but give me time."

"Now, pay us now, or die," shouted the soldiery.

"It is but reasonable," whispered the European officers again; "quite reasonable."

Heera attempted to fly, but was taken by the soldiers, and his head cut off. To whom it was taken history does not inform us, possibly Signor Avatibili or Monsieur Ventura could.

The choice of a Prime Minister now lay with the Ranee, and she, naturally enough, chose her brother, Juwahir, for the post—a likely man enough as times went, not unlike herself, ambitious, unscrupulous, pleasure-loving, and with a certain share of ability. But Juwahir was not a favourite with the army, the real ruler—the Ranee had evidently made a mistake in fancying that she was actually the prince; she was so but nominally. The army did not like Juwahir, and they proved that fact to Dhuleep and his mother, by killing him before their very eyes one day. Dhuleep wept at the sight, his mother swore, but to resent the injury would have been dangerous—they deplored it, and said nothing further. It was but a way those soldiers had of showing they did not like a man.

All eyes were now directed towards Golab Singh, the man whom the British afterwards made King of Cashmere, and who still reigns there—a crafty old fox, who can tell what way the wind may lay as well as a weathercock, and veer round no less suddenly; the prince of "trimmers." He was, of course, deeply aggrieved at the murder of his brother Soochet, to which the Ranee had been a consenting party. He was asked if he would come to Lahore, from his government in Jummoo, and assume the Wuzeership. He was quite willing to do so, on one condition, that "the power of inflicting capital punishment should be confided to him, without any appeal from his decision."

That was a small matter; it was granted, and Golab, with his portion of the army, a considerable force, marched to the capital.

He remained there not long, however; he saw that the commanding officers of the troops were resolved on invading the British territories, and the British were his good friends. It will be strange, doubtless, thought he, if, after they have conquered the Punjab, they cannot find some province for me to rule independently. He made the best use of his time, however, whilst in Lahore. He could not venture to put the Ranee to death, but all the others who had taken part in the murder of Soochet lost their heads—whether on this occasion he flayed any of his captives alive, the Punjabee historians do not relate.

His rule was a short one; having finished the work he had appointed himself, he left a portion of his troops with the Lahore army, and returned with the remainder to Jummoo—he would have nothing to do with the invasion of the British territories, not he, and as to lending any assistance to the Sirdars, for that purpose, he had no intention whatever of doing so.

It is said that even the Ranee herself was opposed to the invasion, but it was by her orders nominally that the army was assembled for the purpose. Tej Singh was regarded by all men in the Punjab as the best General they had, and he was appointed by the army to the command—even he is said to have opposed the invasion. After it had failed, there can be little doubt that they were all opposed to it—native officers as well as Europeans.

But Tej Singh did not hold the command alone—the Ranee had a favourite of her own, to whom she was very partial—his name was Lall Singh. Runjit had raised her from obscurity, and she had similarly raised Lall—the motive in both cases the same. Her object was to keep Lall Singh near her person as prime minister, but the army knew better than that. They would have Lall Singh to go with them—he was a sort of hostage for the fidelity of the Ranee and her son. Tej and Lall were, therefore, the generals—the former the real Commander-in-Chief, the leader to whom the army looked up as its true General; the latter, nominally Commander-in-Chief, and by the favour of his mistress, dignified with the most sounding titles.

Under such circumstances and so commanded, the Seikh forces marched from Lahore, in November, 1845, towards the Sutlej, to invade the British possessions—to drive the foreign lords of India out of the country! Golab, from his distant government at Jummoo, was indignant, and demanded why the Seikh government broke the existing treaty with the British, and whether the latter had given any ground of complaint? The reply was, that he was not now at the head of affairs, and that those who were were not responsible to him—that he must send supplies forthwith to Lahore, and join the army with all his troops. He promised compliance, but delayed to yield it. The army was in too great a hurry to wait for the dilatory old governor, and marched off without him—he shall not share in the spoil, determined they, if he does not make his appearance at once.

He played a dangerous game, and won. When the army had marched off to the Sutlej, he was ordered to Lahore, and he came very submissively, but with force enough to protect himself against the few troops left there.

"You must join the invading army," said the Ranee to him.

"Of course, if your Majesty wishes it, I must," he replied, "but, remember, then the Punjab will be wholly without troops—it may be invaded from the hills by the Affghans or the Beloochees, and what will be the result?"

"There is some sense in that," said the

Ranee, completety outwitted—"there is, certainly, some sense in that; remain then."

Golab obeyed. He returned to his government at Jummoo once more, and sent off messengers at the same time to the British, to inform them, that, for his part, he totally disapproved of the invasion, and had risked his head by opposing it; that the army was enraged at his remonstrances, and the Sirdars furious; that, in fine, no power on earth should compel him to march his troops against the British.

"Golab is an honest man," said the British authorities amongst themselves, "Golab is evidently an honest man; he must be remembered when we come to divide the spoil, for he is our good friend."

Such was the posture of affairs in the Punjab, when a Seikh army of nearly a hundred thousand men, with two hundred pieces of artillery, crossed the Sutlej—to be driven back again at the point of the bayonet in total rout and with frightful slaughter a few months after.

It is an ill-wind that blows nobody good, says the old proverb; and truly, this Seikh invasion was a great blessing to the newspapers of India, for the times were dreadfully dull, and people were beginning to be tired of incessant editorial squabbles. The newspaper-editors and Golab were those most immediately benefited by the rash measures of the fanatical army.

We were expected, of course, by thousands of readers, to know all about the Seikhs and their religion forthwith. One correspondent wrote to ask why so many of them were called Sirdars and Singhs? another, who the Punches were, and whether they had anything to do with the individual whose treatment of his spouse Julia had often excited their indignation at home? A third asked the breadth of the Sutlej, and its depth at the place where the Seikhs had crossed? and whether there was any chance of their making their way to Calcutta? whilst a fourth informed us, in a mysterious manner, that the Seikhs in the Burra Bazar were thinking of rising and murdering all the English, requesting that we should take the first opportunity of acquainting Sir Henry Hardinge with the fact.

To answer all these questions, it was necessary we should read up all about the Seikhs immediately. We read about them all day, studying Malcolm, Murray, Prinsep, Osborne, Lawrence, Thornton and the Calcutta Review, wrote about them all the evening, dreamed about them all night. Surely, the newspaper-editors, as a body, ought to have come forward unanimously for once, by way of curiosity, to thank them for affording new topics for discussion, just as all the old ones were becoming flat, stale, and unprofitable.

Like the rest, I read much about the Seikhs, and talked a great deal to one of them employed in the office—a peaceful-looking man enough—hence my gossip about them now.

CHAPTER V.

THE "EDUCATED" AND THE UNEDUCATED HINDU.

The religions professed by the various inhabitants of the City of Palaces are as numerous and motley as the languages spoken and the garments worn. Of the various religious structures which arrest the eye in wandering through the town, the Christian churches are, certainly, the most imposing, the Mohammedan mosques are the most picturesque, from their innumerable minarets and Oriental domes, whilst the Hindu temples are massive, ugly, and extraordinary.

Hinduism, or Brahmanism, as it is variously styled, is, of course, the prevailing religious system in Calcutta, as in most other Indian towns. With all its absurd multitude of deities, decent and obscene; with all its contradictory dogmas and ceremonies; with all its fine sentiment and fiendish practice, Brahmanism retains its hold, nominally at least, over some hundred millions of our race. A hundred millions of our race! a hundred millions of human beings! we talk glibly of such numbers when we come to speak of the swarming hives of Asiatic life, of the densely populated plains of China or of India, but it is no easy matter to conceive such multitudes, to form anything like an adequate conception of what a hundred millions of mankind really are. An aggregated mass of a hundred thousand is perhaps as great a multitude of mankind as we can form a distinct and definite idea of at once—an aggregated mass of a hundred thousand, such as thronged the aisles and galleries of the great Crystal Palace, in 1851, when every part of the building was full to overflowing—a thousand such masses, a thousand such congregations of a hundred thousand each, may serve to extend our ideas to the limits of a hundred millions; faintly, however, and dimly at best.

Let us take a specimen from this living mass of a hundred millions, and see in what he believes for this world and the next. Stand forth, educated Hindu! This man is of the highest caste — compared with other mortals he is of the finest porcelain, they of the densest brown earthenware. His white muslin robes set off his small figure well—his head-dress, a neat roll of the same material, is becoming and picturesque. Outwardly, there is nothing to complain of; the tint of the skin is pleasing, not too dark, merely a tinge of brown, a slight tinge, that harmonizes well with the glare around, affording an agreeable relief for the vision. Were it paler, like that of the Chinaman or the European, it would appear sickly to the eye accustomed to the darker livery. His small hands and feet might be envied by many a beauty in England; they are delicate, neatly-formed, eminently feminine in their proportions. The English beauty would not envy the colour, the light-brown tint, but all the Kalydors and washes of London or Paris will never make her hand of that shape, nor will they give it that delicacy of touch, and smoothness of external surface, which are natural to his.

The countenance, too, is rather a pleasing one. Examine each feature in detail, and you will find that they are all well put together; that eyes, nose, mouth, and chin, are admirably chiselled, yes, that's the phrase—all the features of a man's face are chiselled now-a-days, not well formed, or in proportion, but "admirably chiselled." Externally, I say, all is pleasing and agreeable; but internally, alas! the contrast is striking. This man has been "educated" by the paternal government of the East India Company. He has been an alumnus of the Hindu or Hooghly "college," and what is the result? Why, nominally, he is still a Hindu—nominally, he still believes in the Vedas and the Shasters, in caste and Brahmanism, with its three hundred millions of gods, and in a salvation to be worked out by the most trivial or the most debasing practices. Yes, nominally, but in truth he believes nothing of the kind. This man has been "educated," I say, and has studied Shakespere and Bacon at "College," and what is the result? Why, he returns to the world to uphold the prejudices of his father's faith, because he finds it convenient for him so to do, and to believe in nothing but *rupees*.

Rupees are his deities now, and he would willingly have them as numerous as his Hindu gods. He laughs at Brahmanism with Europeans, he laughs at Christianity with Hindus —he hates Muhammadism—he has no faith, no religion, he believes in nothing that is elevated. And that solemn humbug, the Council of Education of Bengal,* pronounces this man

* "In 1842 the Committee of Public Instruction was superseded by the present Council of Education, consisting of civil servants of Calcutta of high grade, two natives of little influence, a judge of the supreme court, all unpaid, and a salaried secretary, who is, *de facto*, the council itself. This secretary is a striking illustration of the manner and the extent to which offices are heaped upon favourites by an Indian government. Besides being a member and the secretary of the Council of Education, and having, in consequence, to conduct the correspondence of all the colleges and schools under the government of Bengal, he is a Professor in the Medical College, the Secretary of that College, Government Book-agent, Inspector of Schools, and First Physician to the new Fever Hospital." (Capper's *Three Presidencies*, p. 432.) In a recent review, the *Friend of India*, after quoting the above passage, admits that the statement

"educated," and recommends him to go forth as a deputy collector, or a deputy magistrate to govern his fellow-countrymen, although he is without principle to guide his conduct, without a religious conscience to direct him!

The Hindu or the Hooghly "college" has removed from him the slight restraints his own religion imposed, and has given him no other to supply its place—nay, zealously excluded any other, taken excellent care that no other *shall* be given in its place! Why, it is monstrous, do you exclaim, good reader—well, it is, at all events, quite true; without a single principle to guide him aright, without any higher motive than his own interest to influence his actions, the youth steps forth from his "college" to be a débauché, and a magistrate; a profligate character in domestic life, and an honest collector of revenue for the East India Company.

contained in it is true, whilst he endeavours to defend that prince of pluralists—the secretary. Well might the *Examiner* exclaim, in reference to the same officer, that in India only could such abuses exist.

Such is my excuse for calling the *Council* of Education of Bengal a "solemn humbug"—is it not sufficient, gentle reader?

There is no use in taking such a man as a specimen of one of the classes. He is a specimen only of the "educated" Hindu; those who will not be allowed by that respectable old lady, the Council of Education, to believe in their own faith, and will not be taught any other—those who pretend to be Hindus in their own families, and will eat beef and drink brandy and water with their European friends—carefully trained infidels for the most part, who believe in no deity at all. We must have a specimen of a real Hindu—one who actually does believe in something more than rupees, in order to see what kind of a faith his is, and to what kind of actions it leads him.

We shall find thousands of such men in Calcutta. Here we have one—he is a Hindu merchant of the old school. *He* has not unlearned his religion in learning literature, and geography, and history. This man is a Hindu in more than name, and, horrible as may be his faith to our eyes, disgusting and revolting its practices, he stands on a higher footing than the unreasoning infidel, who believes in no God, and laughs at all systems. Faith is too high and holy a feeling for the mind to do without altogether, and not lose completely its balance. The man who wholly wants faith is fit for all that is bad, for little that is good. He may be intellectually acute, intellectually cultivated; but let him lose his faith in everything above himself, let him have no belief in the exalted, the noble, the true, the unlimited, and the mind retreats into itself; feeds ever on its own resources, and comes to regard all other things but its own ease and comfort, as matters too trivial for a thought. Self is the god of its idolatry, becomes enthroned on the altar of its judgment, and to that self, sacrifices are offered up a thousand times more horrible and debasing than even Brahmanism can inculcate.

Therefore it is that I look upon this old-school Hindu, with his prejudices and his want of enlightenment, as a superior being, morally considered, to the model semi-Hindu whom the Council of Education, in its solemn annual farces of examination and prize-giving, turns loose upon society, crammed with odd scraps of poetry, and a good deal of mathematics; a man who can calculate an eclipse, perhaps, and yet is unable to perceive a God in nature, because the Council of Education has not dared to teach him there is such! In such a heart the sweet sympathies of domestic life cannot exist—the state in which such a man finds himself is wholly an abnormal one, and, like all unnatural things, must be a source of ever-increasing evil to all around.

But the poor unenlightened Hindu has been awaiting inspection some time. Let us come to him. With that keen eye of his, you may be sure the man is one who conceals considerable intellectual power under that simple and rude exterior. He appears to be wholly engrossed in his business, but he is watching us attentively, nevertheless, and wondering, too, what we can possibly want with him. This man, then, with his bare shoulders and uncovered legs, his spectacles on nose, and his old-fashioned *pugree** on his head, is a specimen of those who believe in Brahmanism, with its three hundred millions of gods. His sacred books are the *Vedas*, which he never reads; they are left solely to the pundits, whose whole life is spent in the study of their

* The Indian turban.

vast and complicated religious system. Of these vedas he has heard a great deal, but he knows little definitely. They are very voluminous; they are written in ancient Sanscrit; each of them—there are either three or four of them, for even on that point there is a diversity of opinion—each of them is divided into two parts, the one hymns and prayers, the other rules for the regulation of a religious life.

The pundits might have told him too, but they have not, that these vedas contain an infinitely purer system than they teach—contain explicit instruction as to the unity of the Deity, and far better teaching on a thousand other points than our old-fashioned Hindu merchant knows any thing about. The *Shasters* are the only religious books he has ever studied, and they are full of absurd stories about hosts of imaginary deities—deities whom the most unbridled Eastern imagination alone could suppose to exist. As to Brahm—the first principle whence all things proceeded—our old-fashioned Hindu knows little, and cares nothing about Brahm at all. He has heard that it was from Brahm that Brahma, and Siva, and Vishnu proceeded; how, or when, or wherefore, are questions it is not for him to ask, or discuss.

This he knows, however, that ablution and prayer are the two things he has most to practise in order to secure a good position when, in some other form, he returns to earth. Moral duties he also knows he has to perform, and remembers that many sublime exhortations on that point are constantly to be met with in the *Shasters*, but he cannot help wondering why the gods were not more moral. However, that is a question that does not immediately concern himself, and he turns away from it to his own duties.

He is a strict observer of the requisite ablutions and prayers, although he knows that the people around him content themselves with crying out the name of their patron deity incessantly whilst they take their morning bath. But for him that is not enough, and oblations, ablutions, processions, festivals, study, he engages in all, and has faith in them all. He has a faint hope also of a Paradise to which he may possibly attain on quitting the world, and before he has again to return to it—transmigration-wise.

He cannot look for the blessed state to which the *fakir* or devotee may aspire, but still he has a lingering hope that there is an account kept somewhere in which he has a heap of merit to his credit, far more than sufficient to counterbalance the moral derelictions into which he has fallen, and that when the balance is struck, there will be a considerable amount on the proper side. Besides, he purposes leaving a large sum to provide for the necessities of indigent Brahmins, and that, he trusts, will make an important item in his favour.

These *fakirs*, or devotees, he regards with especial reverence. Those of them whom he sees are men who have abandoned the world and devoted themselves to the practice of asceticism, and to wandering about the country in a horrible state of filth, their long hair matted into snake-like locks with mud, their naked bodies bearing the marks of their horrible penances, and their whole appearance suggestive to the European rather of insanity than of piety. In abandoning the world these men have often little to forsake, so that, save in the penances which they endure—self-inflicted penances—they have little hardship to undergo, for all classes of the native community are anxious to assist them. The women, especially, ever the most benevolent and pious, crowd round the disgusting devotee, and minister to his wants with untiring devotion.

Some of these men will hold an arm aloft until it can no more be placed by their sides; until it has become a stiff, wasted limb, ever standing up hideously and unnaturally, in rigid immobility. Others will clench their hands till the nails grow through the skin, and the fingers have lost the power of being straightened again. A knife, an arrow, or a thin sword will he thrust through the tongue; or the insane devotee will stand on one leg, with his hands clasped above his head, his eyes fixed upon the blazing sun, in open, blinding gaze. These things require an amount of moral resolution of which our artificial life in Europe knows nothing. Such men must truly have strong convictions, however mistaken. We may be certain that they have faith in other things than rupees, to endure such living martyrdoms voluntarily.

Our old-fashioned Hindu has a devout reverence for such men. He regards them as sure of Paradise hereafter, and wishes that he, too, had resolution sufficient to enable him to make some such sacrifices for his religion. These, however, are by no means the most horrible features of this horrible faith. Our old-fashioned Hindu knows that there is a huge Juggernauth's shrine in Orissa, sixty feet high, annually drawn forth on a massive car by thousands of men, women, and children, who regard it as a high and holy privilege to touch the ropes. He knows that numbers of devout people of both sexes will throw themselves—and do annually throw themselves—under the wheels of this monstrous idol, getting thus crushed to death, and staining the road with their blood. He knows that all this occurs, but he has never himself seen it. He has been a frequent attendant, however, on the *churruk-poojah*, or swinging festival, and would go to the great car of Juggernauth, were it within visiting distance, or were Indian roads more practicable.

This swinging festival is truly one of the oddest contrivances man has ever invented for getting rid of the burden of his sins. Not a whit more monstrous, it is true, than many other rites of Brahmanism—not a whit more cruel, and by no means so destructive to life as the great car of Juggernauth. But it is stranger and more absurdly ridiculous than anything else that even Brahmanism teaches its votaries to practise. Some rich native, our old-fashioned Hindu, for instance, determines on an act of merit. There is a particular season for this as for all other acts. It is the time then when swinging festivals are all the fashion, just as in England the children fly kites at one season and whip tops at another. Let us suppose the proper time has arrived.

Our rich native provides a place for the ceremony. A wide open space of ground is best, which can accommodate the thousands who crowd to the unholy rite. In the centre of this space a stout post, like a scaffold pole, is fixed firmly in the earth—it may possibly be twenty or thirty feet high, not under twenty, often above thirty, but most usually between the two. A strong bamboo pole is fixed on the top horizontally—its centre resting on the top of the perpendicular post, and so constructed that it can revolve freely. A rope depends from either end of the bamboo, the one ten or twelve feet long, the other reaching to the ground. At the end of the shorter one hangs an iron hook, intended to be fixed into the back of the devotee. So far the preparations are complete. The wide open space is ready for the people. The perpendicular pole supports the horizontal bamboo with its two ropes dangling, one at each end. By catching a hold of the longer rope which depends to the ground, you can easily move the bamboo round. It revolves on the top of the post as on a pivot.

The devotee only is wanting now, and then everything will be complete, and the swinging can proceed at once. There are never wanting men ready to offer themselves for the purpose—let our old-fashioned Hindu prepare the T-like apparatus and a devotee will soon offer himself—although, in these degenerate days, he will expect to be well paid for his performance; at which evidence of irreligious avarice, our old-fashioned Hindu groans inwardly. The bargain has been struck, however--for twenty rupees or less, this unfortunate wretch will consent to have the iron hook affixed into the muscles of his back and to be swung aloft, and spun round and round by means of it until the whirling motion has rendered him well-nigh insensible.

He prepares himself for the performance, however, by partaking plentifully of stimulating drugs or liquors, which the master of the ceremonies, our old-fashioned Hindu, must provide.

Thus prepared—half stupified by the drugs or liquors of which he has partaken—the devotee enters the space prepared for the ceremony. He shouts when he sees the apparatus, shouts with exultation. The people have collected in great numbers, and they, too, shout vociferously. All is excitement; eager, anxious, "religious" excitement. A ladder is procured, and by means of it, the iron hook is passed through the fleshy part of the back —a band being also tied round the body and attached to the hook, lest the muscles should give way and the man be killed, when the English courts of justice might give the aiders and abettors in the matter some trouble. In native states, however, and under native rule, I have been told that this band is dispensed with. The hook, I say, is affixed and by means of it the man is suspended horizontally; his head turned from the pole, his feet towards it. They do not touch it, however, being far removed—he hanging freely in mid-air. He endeavours to retain this position throughout, by keeping his body rigid. Round his waist is attached a small bag of berries, into which he dives his hand, in order to take out a handful.

Great is the rejoicing of the multitude; vehement and exciting the shouts. The longer rope is seized by three or four active fellows, and they run round with it with all their might. The bamboo spins round on the top of the perpendicular post, and the devotee attached by the iron hook flies through the air, revolving rapidly round and round, centrifugal force sending him far aloft over the heads of the shouting multitude. As he swings he scatters the berries, and great is the crushing of eager men, women, and children below. These berries are sacred to them, and of great virtue. Those who obtain them are preserved thereby throughout the entire year—their sins are forgiven, their merit is increased. It will not be difficult to fancy then with how eager an anxiety these berries are sought, how tumultuous the crushing to obtain them, how great the joy when they are obtained. The first hand that touches them is that the owner of which is blessed; given by another they lose their virtue.

The devotee, as he whirls round and round with frightful rapidity, shouts madly with excitement. The young men who run round, dragging the other rope, and thus making the bamboo revolve, shout and yell horribly as they run. The people who see the devotee spinning above them shout vehemently as he appears above their heads occasionally; and as a few berries fall around, all are excited, and the excitement is precisely of the same kind as that which fills the fields with groans and shouts when thousands congregate in America for religious exercises, during the enthusiastic and maddening "revivals of religion" as they are called.

The people see in that half-frantic devotee,

who whirls above their heads, a heaven-sent messenger—a blessed agent of good. They by no means see in him what we see—a half-drunken, half-mad, ignorant performer, who is paid so much for his horrible performance. Our old-fashioned Hindu smokes his hookah, and looks on with admiration at the entire spectacle. He is acquiring merit fast by the display, and who knows, may he not whisper to himself, but this act of merit on my part may be the means of securing me a good berth in another world?

To him, with his quiet rumination and self-satisfied reflections, that eager pushing of the crowd, that crushing and swaying hither and thither, as the sacred berries fall around, is by no means a disgusting spectacle. It is true the weakest have little chance, the strongest are almost sure to secure the largest amount of blessings for the year, but that is not his fault; it is of the nature of things, and they must be content. It is true that that poor woman, who so anxiously strives, despite her weakness and the precious burden she carries in her bosom, to obtain one berry, has little chance of success. The rough excited crowd press upon her unfeelingly — she is driven hither and thither by its swaying, helplessly and hopelessly. She begs for mercy and for air in vain, for the excited shouts drown her cries, and every one is too anxious for himself to heed the anxiety or distress of one.

These are things our old-fashioned Hindu knows must be, but she is a Sudra, he would tell you, if you mentioned the poor woman's case to him, and Sudras have no right to attend religious festivals at all—they were intended solely to be the servants and slaves of the higher castes. At length the legs of the devotee fall; his arms drop, he can no longer maintain his rigidity of body or his horizontal position. He has become an unsightly object—head, arms, legs, depending flaccidly, the back held highest aloft by the iron hook. He has fainted. The revolution of the bamboo ceases. The young men who hold the rope stand still and breathe hard. The devotee is taken down, and means are employed to restore him to consciousness and to strength. A few more stimulating drugs—an additional glass or two of arrack, and he is eager for the performance again, nor will he desist until his strength has utterly failed, until he finds it utterly impossible to maintain, even for a moment, his horizontal position as he swings in mid-air.

Such is the *churruk poojah* or swinging festival! By such means does poor fallen man hope to propitiate the Almighty and to obtain pardon for his sins. A more monstrously absurd method was probably never invented by his irregular imagination—a more ridiculously nonsensical plan not even a wild-eastern imagination could probably invent. We can understand that sacrifices of other animals may be supposed grateful to the higher powers. We can understand that even the sacrifice of man may be regarded as acceptable, supposing the Deity to be a revengeful being like man himself; but what feeling could have prompted so ridiculous an imposition as that of the *churruk poojah*, it is not easy to discover.

And yet it is impossible, utterly impossible, to make a Hindu sensible of this absurdity. He sees in it nothing incongruous, nothing ridiculous. You argue with him about it, and he coolly replies, "Ah, Saheb, your ways and our ways differ—your custom one custom, our custom another. All men not think same thing." Anything more explicit or more to the point you will probably not draw from him by any amount of talking.

I was on one occasion spending the day at a friend's house in Calcutta. He was a missionary—a zealous, devoted missionary of the gospel. A *churruk poojah* was about being celebrated exactly opposite his house, in some waste ground that lay there. Everything was prepared—the promoters of the exhibition saw us watching them from the verandah. They doubtless thought we were admiring their dexterity, and were quite willing to help them to have the affair pass off satisfactorily. A ladder was wanting—a short step ladder, such as is used in houses for reaching to lamps and upper windows. We saw a respectable native approaching the house. He asked to be allowed to speak to the missionary. His request was, that the reverend gentleman would lend him a step ladder, in order that the devotee might be attached to the iron hook which was waiting for him!

Our friend's indignation at the request may

be more readily imagined than described. Yet to the natives his refusal was evidently incomprehensible. They regarded him as an arrant churl — perfectly acquainted though they were with his sacred character.

CHAPTER VI.

MINERVA IN CALCUTTA.

Towards the end of September or the beginning of October, a festival is celebrated by the wealthy natives in honour of the Goddess Doorgah, the Hindu Minerva. There is no occasion on which the Hindu Rajahs and Baboos spend their wealth more freely than during this Doorgah-poojah. Our old-fashioned Hindu friend would as soon think of allowing a day to pass without making his customary ablution, as of allowing the Doorgah festival to pass without its annual display. Feasting and merry-making form essential features of this ten days' carnival, but this feasting and merry-making are accompanied with a lavish expenditure for shows and dances, that proves how much the Hindus are still under the influence of their old faith.

The house and its approaches are brilliantly illuminated with oil lamps, hung in various devices. In the central court, which is covered in for the occasion, the Rajah or Baboo receives his guests, and has amusements prepared for them. All his European friends are invited to the ceremony, for he is anxious to display to them his taste and wealth together. A monstrous image of the many-armed Doorgah stands on a raised platform at one side of the court, surrounded by a gilt halo or glory. Steps lead up to the sacred image, at the head of which a Brahmin stands sentinel, that no unhallowed feet may tread the sacred precincts of the goddess. Gaudy as paint and gilding can make her, Doorgah stands against the wall in unredeemed monstrosity, with her hundred blood-stained arms, to be sunk in the sacred waters of the Hooghly as soon as the festival is over.

It is nine o'clock in the evening; the Europeans have had their dinner for the most part —half-past seven being the usual hour for that meal—and they now begin to appear in the covered court-yard; admittance being obtained by tickets previously sent by the owner of the house. Crowds of natives block up the way outside, eager to see something of the shows—great is the crushing, overpowering the excitement. The master of the house goes from one to another talking, and laughing, amusing and being amused—he certainly seems the impersonation of happiness. An attendant goes round to sprinkle the guests with rose-water, or some other perfume—an agreeable and refreshing operation to all, where the heat is at times almost unendurable, and the odours by no means of the most savoury.

The nautch or native dance begins. A native female, accompanied by three or four musicians, occupies the centre of the court—a carpet having been previously spread for her reception. On a sort of drum, beaten by the fingers, and on a kind of flute or clarionet, the musicians play, accompanying the notes with their voices, whilst the nautch-girl attitudinizes. Her performance cannot be styled dancing, in our sense of the term.

She places one hand on her hip, and elevates the other gracefully above her head, advancing and retreating as she does so a step or two, and looking smilingly on all around. She draws her gold-embroidered muslin skirt aside, which hangs fully in front, to exhibit her ancles, easily seen through the thin fabric, whilst she disposes of them awkwardly or gracefully according to the taste of the beholder — awkwardly according to European ideas, for the most part; gracefully according to those of the Hindus. In this attitude she turns rapidly round, or glides more slowly into her former position, allowing her skirt to take its natural position, and again bringing her hands into attitudes by no means devoid of grace—the musicians all the time yelling forth monotonous notes, and playing with frightful energy on their instruments.

The women of the household are, of course, not to be seen by the visitor's eyes, but they, too, are enjoying the merry-making, inspecting the Europeans, and watching the dancers from a balcony above, which appears to be wrapped up in cloth. Invisible to all below, they can yet see distinctly from their elevation all that goes on there. The nautch-girls are selected, chiefly for their personal charms, particularly for their fine figures—the symmetry of which is fully apparent through the thin coverings in which they are enveloped. Many of them are almost as fair as Europeans, quite as fair, indeed, as an Andalusian brunette, and of the same rich tint of skin. Their hands and feet are beautifully formed—indeed, Hindu women generally, even of the lowest classes, have hands and feet which an English belle might envy for their delicate proportions.

Some of these nautch-girls are said to be women of good character. They get large sums for their performances, if eminent in their profession. I heard one of them—called the bulbul or nightingale, on account of her fine voice, rather powerful than melodious, so far as I could judge—who, I was informed, obtained five hundred rupees a-night, £50, for her performances.

During the dancing and singing, refreshments are handed round to the guests—the master of the house and his sons often officiating as servants on the occasion, to do them the more honour—refreshments consisting of sweetmeats, European and native, champagne, cherry-brandy, beer, and soda-water. Of cherry-brandy the Hindus are immoderately fond, and even the Mussulmans are not proof against its intoxicating sweetness.

The amusements at the doorgah-poojah are by no means confined, however, to the exhibition of fine forms and the melodious utterances of harmonious voices—tumbling, exhibitions of *diablerie*, and feats of strength are not always excluded, although by no means so common as the nautch girls. . I have even seen at the festival a troop of European equestrians performing their usual feats, of riding—in every possible way except that which is most easy and natural—jumping through hoops, dancing grotesquely on horseback, riding two horses at once, with such other performances as constitute the delight of little boys and girls at Astley's. And all this is in honour of the goddess! Verily her godship is easily honoured!

To turn, however, from this, the practice of Brahmanism, to its theory, is a grateful task. In the system laid down by the Vedas, we shall find no such horrible rites as those of Juggernauth and the churruk-poojah; no systematic corruption and degradation of women enforced; no practices permitted similar to those by which a Brahmin of high caste may support himself by marrying a great number of women of inferior castes but of rich families,—women who live with their fathers, whilst the husband visits them occasionally, receiving a handsome fee for the condescension—for such is the ordinary life of a poor Kulin Brahmin! In the Vedas, I say, no such system is taught—these are the modern corruptions of a corrupt priesthood, who inculcate practices and principles that tend to the destruction, body and soul, of the devotees who obey them.

There can be no doubt, however, that the division of the people into four castes, of which one was to be servile, is an institution of primitive Brahmanism—an institution conjectured by some to have arisen from the conquest of the country by the three superior castes, and the degradation of the fourth into slaves. But the monstrous polytheism which forms so striking a feature of modern Hinduism, has certainly no foundation in the comparatively pure system of the Vedas. The attributes of the Deity, as taught by those works, were thus summed up by a learned Brahmin—"Perfect truth; perfect happiness; without equal; immortal; of absolute unity; whom neither speech can describe nor mind comprehend; all-pervading; all-transcending; not limited by space or time; understanding all; the first of all causes; the Creator, preserver, transformer of all things, such is the Great One."*

In judging of the system of the present day, however, it is, unfortunately, that which is practically influential on the minds of the people that we have to consider, not that which was taught long ago by men whose teaching has become since a dead letter. It is not saying too much, perhaps, to assert—and it is in solemn sadness that I assert it—that there is no system of religion, of which we have any certain account, professed by any large body of mankind, so deleterious in its influence, so soul-destroying in its rites and ceremonies, so corrupt in its teaching as Brahmanism. The books which it would put into the hands of its youthful students are such as

* Sir W. Jones.

no decent family in Europe could have read in the vernacular—such as were they literally translated would be liable to seizure by the police in England, and their vendors to punishment, as being injurious to public morals!

And yet this system, so gross in its teaching, so horrible in its rites, is patronized by the Government of India, whilst the missionaries who would uproot it and plant a purer faith in its stead, are coldly looked upon or openly opposed! This system, bad as it is, is even maintained in a Government Educational establishment in Calcutta—the Sanscrit College! and this Sanscrit College is under the direct control of the Council of Education in Bengal.

Surely, it is right that the people of England knew these things; surely it is right that those who permit and sanction such teaching should be called to account for their conduct. The following account of this college is from Capper's Three Presidencies of India:—

"Connected with the Sanscrit College, there is no European officer who holds any appointment involving supervision and arrangement. On field-days, when some notability is expected—a *burra sahib* or influential personage —an imposing appearance is presented by this strange institution.

"The 'Professors' of 'Vyakarana,' of 'Sahitya,' of 'Alankar,' of 'Jyotish,' and of sundry other things equally euphonious and intelligible, muster in great nubmers; and, what with robes, turbans and ornaments, make a great display, looking solid, learned and profound as Sanscrit 'professors' ought to look. The students repeat amazing quantities of unintelligible lines and sentences, and answer unintelligible questions with equally unintelligible replies. The *burra-sahib*, profoundly ignorant of the language used, is quite satisfied with their proficiency, bows to the 'professors,' who bow in return, and then departs, delighted to be able to speak and hear his familiar English once more.

"On any ordinary day the visitor will see, on a table in the midst of a small room, one of the 'professors' sitting in Oriental fashion, after the manner of tailors with us; his head is bare, his shoulders are bare; the day is hot, and the roll of muslin which envelopes his body out of doors has been removed; the ample rotundity of his stomach heaves regularly above the muslin folds which encircle the loins and thighs. The shaven crown of the worthy 'professor,' and his broad quivering back glow with the heat; whilst a disciple, standing behind him, plies the fan vigorously to and fro, and produces a current of wind that keeps the huge mass partially cool.

"Around the table are squatted numbers of dirty-looking youths, carefully enveloped in their muslin dresses, as prescribed by the rules, and droning, one by one, over a manuscript page, which is passed from one to another in succession. The majority are dozing, and well they may, for it is sleepy work—the same verses nasally intoned by one after another with unvarying monotony, and, doubtless, with similar errors. The 'professor' seldom speaks, for he, too, is dozing heavily on the table, anxiously awaiting the bell that is to release him to liberty and dinner. The same scene is being repeated in other rooms, where similar 'professors' are likewise dozing and teaching, and where other youths are similarly shut up."

Such is a picture of the Sanscrit "College!" in which, "whilst the Bible is diligently excluded, the religious books of the Brahmins are allowed to be studied—a College in which there are no European officers, but which is as much under the power of the Council of Education as any other educational institution in the country."*

It is for the people of England to say whether such things should be—the people of England of all classes and sects, whether of the Church, whether Roman Catholics, Methodists, Baptists or Independents—it is a question in which, morally speaking, all are equally interested.

Let us turn, however, from this subject—one which none but the unfeeling can write about without being moved—let us turn to other faiths and other creeds. Next to Hinduism, Muhammadism is, perhaps, the most prevalent in Calcutta, numbering a very large proportion of the inhabitants within its folds. Muhammadism, however, is a creed of which the Eastern development becomes more and more impure the further it spreads from

* Government Education in India, p. 23.

Mecca. The Malays of Java and Malacca are nominally Muhammadans, true Muhammadans in some respects—in their uncompromising hostility to other faiths, for instance,—in their lofty estimate of their own privileges, in their zealous anxiety to destroy idols and make their own prophet the supreme religious teacher. In these respects the Malays are true Muhammadans—but they have mixed up with their faith much superstition which he, whom they pretend to obey, would have rooted out fiercely with the sword.

The Mussulmans of India are chiefly remarkable for the rigour with which they keep the fast of the Ramezan—a terrible annual penance upon those obliged to labour under a burning sun for hours daily, or for a whole day together. During that fast, which lasts twenty-eight days, they must not eat or drink between sunrise and sunset. It does not always occur in the hottest seasons of the year, but, when it does, the sufferings of the labouring classes are intense.

Soldiers engaged in war, travellers on a journey, the sick, nurses and pregnant women are alone exempted from the rigour of this terrible penance. Bathing is permitted if the head be not immersed, and that must doubtless be a considerable relief to those who are parched with thirst, but men involved in the trammels of daily labour cannot always get away to bathe, nor are they always where bathing is possible. Smoking and the smelling of perfumes are as strictly prohibited as eating and drinking during these fast days.

The sufferings endured during this fast by the labouring classes are much more terrible than those accustomed only to the moisture of a temperate climate can conceive. The sweltering sun is shining hot upon the poor labourer—the perspiration has been oozing plentifully from his exposed body—his lips and tongue are parched—he feels faint, feverish and thirsty to an extraordinary degree, but no drop of water must touch his lips till the sun, which has produced his distress, is gone. And yet these sufferings are submitted to by thousands, nay, by millions, of poor ignorant natives without a murmur!

The men who are capable of such self-sacrifice cannot be altogether vile, must, in fact, have something nobler within them than mere animal desires and barbarous passions. A spark of the divine light which first lit up man's soul is found within them, even when that light appears outwardly to be wholly extinguished. This fast of the Ramezan is, like the penances of the Hindus, terrible and dreadful in its nature; but this must be said of it, that it is not demoralizing in its tendency like the practices of Brahmanism—it is rather a lesson in self-control, in the restraint of self, difficult to learn doubtless, but not wholly without use when learned.

It is followed, of course, by feasting and merry-making. Booths are erected by the sides of the roads most frequented by the Mussulmans, in which sweetmeats are sold, preparations of curry and curry stuff of every kind, spiced meat and piquant delicacies, with coffee as a drink, for the most part. In the houses of the wealthy Moslems, too, shows and exhibitions are presented to the multitudes, who crowd them partly for the sights to be witnessed, partly for the good cheer to be obtained. The conclusion of the Ramezan in India is, in fact, the Doorgah-poojah of the Muhammadan.

Like all other religions, however, Muhammadism is split up into two rival sects which detest each other—the Sheahs and the Soonnies. Both equally hold with Muhammad, and profess to obey implicitly all that Muhammad ordained—they differ, however, in their opinions respecting the orthodox successor of the prophet. The Sheahs acknowledge Ali and his immediate descendants as the lawful successors of the founder of their faith—giving the name of Emauns to these successors. The Soonnies regard the Caliphs, as Omir, Aboubekir and others, as the true leaders of the faithful, subsequent to Muhammad himself. There is little difference between the points of faith of the two sects, very little—it is a mere difference of opinion on an historical fact, yet because the more insignificant in its origin, it is all the more keenly contested now-a-days.

Sheahs and Soonnies cannot meet at religious festivals without quarrelling. From words they come to blows — sticks, whips, ropes, missiles are snatched and brought into play, and the looker-on might fancy himself witnessing a faction-fight in Tipperary, or some other such favoured abode of civilization and

Christianity, were it not for the dark skins and the half-naked forms. Instead of "Hurra!" "at thim agin, boys!" "the dirty spalpeens!" "we'll lick them, so we will!" he hears such cries as, "Marro, marro!" "Salawallas!" "Soonnie, koob marro!" "Sheah marro juldee!" and such like. Ali and his followers are, of course, the patterns imitated by the Sheahs, whilst the Soonnies follow the example set by the Caliphs. In their respective methods of ablutions, and in their manner of bowing and prostrating in their devotional exercises, there are also some minor points of difference.

The difference between the two is, however, important in a political point of view, because each sect would rather league with the Christians against its Moslem rival, than with the latter against the Christians. It was but the other day, that a news-writer from a native court, that of Lucknow, wrote thus to the *Calcutta Englishman*:—"The war between Russia and Turkey engrosses the conversation of most natives, even here. The King and his court, who are Sheahs, all hope for the complete ruin of the Turks, who are Soonnies, and therefore held in even greater detestation than the Russian infidels." So much for Moslem charity to Moslem !

The Persians too are Sheahs, and have therefore little sympathy with the Turks. In India the two sects are about equal in point of numbers, although the native courts are, for the most, Sheah. As a general rule, we might indeed assert, that western Moslemism, from the Atlantic to the Persian Gulf, is Soonnie; whilst the eastern, from the Persian Gulf to Java, is Sheah.

CHAPTER VII.

THE LOST SCHOONER.

There were few Anglo-Indians in those days who did not, at some period of their career in the East, seek health at the Cape or in Australia. England denied to them, which they could not visit without sacrificing their situations in the Company's service, they preferred going to the Cape or Australia for a year or two, on sick leave.

When I first visited Cape Town, its Dutch aspect struck me at once most forcibly, as its peculiar characteristic. Founded by the Dutch, and in their possession for nearly a hundred and fifty years, it is no wonder that their air of solid stability and utilitarian massiveness should pervade its streets and public buildings. Your true Dutchman is a broad-backed, stable, portly individual, not to be easily moved by common events, solemn and phlegmatic even when most enjoying himself—the Turk of Christendom—whilst your true Dutch *frau* is of large and massive dimensions, ample girth, particularly at the shoulders and hips, and steady, plodding, and formal gait.

Every thing Dutch partakes more or less of the same character. A Dutch lugger is a thick-set, squat, short-masted, broad-sailed vessel, that can be mistaken at a distance for nothing else, except, perhaps, an improved Chinese junk. A Dutch church is a massive structure, with walls six or eight feet thick, and not more than fifteen feet high; its windows sunk deeply into the ponderous brick-work or stone, its benches made with such an evident regard to strength, that one would be disposed to regard them as intended only for hippopotamus-like individuals of equal width and length; its whole air and aspect that of solidity without elegance, of disproportionate breadth without sufficient height. A Dutch town is exactly like the church and lugger, on a larger scale—wide streets (scrupulously clean, however), regularly laid out, intersecting each other at right angles, shaded, if possible, with dumpy oaks and elms; broad massive houses, of red brick or stone, and never more than two stories high, rise on either side, with here and there a public edifice, that looks like an ornamental gaol, with its broad turret, or angular spire, of so solidly square a base, as to defy earthquakes.

Such are the usual characteristics of Dutch colonial towns; and those who have visited Cape Town, will not fail to recognize some of them as the most obvious features of that pleasant seaport. I trust I shall not be mistaken, but if one only smiles at anything ludicrous now-a-days, he is set down forthwith as wishing to bring down contempt upon every thing connected with it: let me therefore explain. In the first place, I have a profound admiration for much that is Dutch. This very stability, this massive broad-based perpetuity, is it not a thousand times more praise-worthy than the flimsy pasteboard, lath-and-plaster work of modern English towns? And if the Dutchman *be* traditionally broad and massive himself,—and so he is, and so he has been for ages, or Dutch painters, Van Ostade, Gerard Douw, and Brauwer are not to be believed,—why should he not leave his impress behind him in Africa and Asia, a perpetual reminder to succeeding ages that he, Herr Holländer, has been there in times past?

It avails nothing, good sir, that you assure me Amsterdam is an elegant town, and the Hague a beautiful watering place. Unfortunately I have never been at either one or the other town, nor do I pretend to predicate any thing respecting them. I speak of Dutch colonial cities only, and those who have visited Cape Town, Colombo, and Chinsurah, will, I am sure, agree with me. Even when the Dutchman puts up a verandah before his house in a tropical country, he does it with a solidity unknown to other men, undreamt of by men in tropical climes generally. No flimsy pillar, however graceful, will satisfy *his* fancy; he must have an upright, downright, massive thick block of wood or masonry, that looks firm and immovable as himself; and as Herr Holländer throws himself back in his easy chair, with his never-failing pipe in his mouth; blowing cloud after cloud of the densest smoke from his well-filled cheeks, he eyes the pillar with gratulation and self-satisfaction. It is an honest, steady pillar that, mutters he to himself, when he feels equal to the exertion of muttering any thing, and then he smokes again, contemplating it for an hour together silently.

From Fort Knokke—a Dutch fort, of course, as its name implies—from Fort Knokke the spectator can enjoy an excellent view of Table Bay. The fort is to the east of the castle, and connected with it by a rampart called the *Sea-lines*. Looking out from Fort Knokke, then, the idle Anglo-Indian may watch the troubled waters of Table Bay. Several vessels ride at anchor in the Bay, vessels from all climes, some of the larger visiting this half-way house between the Eastern and the Western world only to take in water and provisions, others coming close up to the jetty to discharge their cargoes and receive fresh ones.

At most periods of the year, but particularly in summer, that is to say, in December and January, the Bay presents a busy, cheerful, animated scene. Boats from the various vessels constantly pulling in to the town, manned by their own crews, or boats from the shore broader and more Dutch-like, for the most part manned with tawny, half Hottentotish seamen, pulling out with supplies to the distant Indiamen.

The sun shines brightly, almost fiercely, upon the scene, but neither the European sailor nor the acclimatized Hottentot minds that. The spray glistens as the oars cast it off into the air to be reunited after a little with the abyss, the wind catches it before it falls, the sun illumines it, and sparkling, twinkling, shining prettily in the warm rays, it is whisked off over the sea far and wide. The oars descend again, the crew pull as one man, each bends forward, and draws back in unison with the others; the little ripples, with their white-capped tops, are cut through by the advancing bows, and a line half black, half white, behind, indicates the track that has been left—altogether as pretty a sight as the old liver-diseased Anglo-Indian has seen for many a day

As he views it, and feels the fresh sea-air fanning his yellow cheeks, he thinks of the time when he, too, could enjoy such exercise and glory in it, when fresh muscular force demanded play and activity; but that time has long gone by, never to return, and as he mournfully smokes his hookah and watches the dancing miniature waves playing with each other, like wanton children, he sighs to think of what he is and what he has been; he sighs, as he asks himself whether lakhs of rupees can atone for a wasted frame and a diseased liver, whether poverty and health are not better than wealth and illness? he sighs, and gets no satisfactory answer from asking never so often.

But when the westerly winds prevail in the middle of winter, that is to say in July and August—when the westerly winds prevail, and the long rolling surf comes bowling into the bay in huge masses, that follow each other eagerly and rapidly, then the scene is very different. There is now no warm sunshine, there are no pleasant rays tinting the white foam with their own many-coloured reflection; no little wavelets dashing into each other's faces, and loud splashing as they dash; no pleasure-boats making merry on the sunny water. Nature has thrown off her festive garb, and put on the robe of solemn sternness and gloomy mourning for destruction past and future. A heavy swell comes with incessant iteration from the South Atlantic, and bounding into the bay with unceasing regularity, threatens ships and sailors with destruction. Chain cables are then required, and the large Indiaman, with eighty or ninety fathoms of the cable run out, strains uneasily at her anchors, as if anxious to be off into the open sea, away from rocks and treacherous coasts.

Best bower anchors and kedges will hardly hold the unlucky craft that has but rope cables, and her crew must stand by to lower another bower, should she drag at all. The wind howls dismally through the rigging and along the sides of Table Mountain, whilst the sea, black from the reflection of the threatening clouds, is evidently much disturbed by its raging.

It was January, however, when I was gazing upon the bay from Fort Knokke, and no such gales, no such dangers, were yet anticipated. A prettily-rigged schooner was standing gallantly into the harbour, and had reached the usual station of the large East Indiamen, when the sea suddenly rose. A black cloud came rolling from Table Mountain over the blue expanse of the sky; and what had been all joy and happiness a few moments before, was suddenly changed into gloom and threatenings. The sea seemed to feel the change as much as the seamen, and heaved tumultuously even before the strong western blast had arisen. Large waves came tumbling from the ocean into the bay in irregular succession—large waves, foam-capped, that broke but to give place to others, which followed with frightful rapidity. It was evident that one of those sudden storms so violent in their character, and so destructive in their effects, which sometimes visit the South Atlantic, was bursting upon the stormy cape.

The schooner, then entering—a little before so gracefully tacking to beat into the harbour—naturally attracted our observation. She was a sharp, long-hulled, rakish craft, that floated duck-like on the undulating water. Her master had evidently seen the approaching danger, and hastened to avert its effects. The canvas fluttered for an instant, preparatory to its being brailed up, whilst the schooner rolled uneasily in the chopping heavy sea. Down came the wind as if from a port-hole of the skies, raging furiously upon the agitated bay; down with especial fury upon the schooner, driving her, even without her sails, rapidly towards the shore. Her pilot had evidently intended taking her farther in to a securer berth, but the storm was too violent to admit of delay.

Her anchor was cast out at once, and she swung round to it merrily, like a bird that sweeps against its foe. Another anchor was let go after a little, whilst all the other vessels that could get an offing, were standing out to sea to weather the gale, rather than trust the treacherous shelter of the bay. But the schooner had no means of doing so—she had neared the shore too much to admit of her wearing round and beating out. There was no help for her but in her anchors.

For a few minutes we supposed it was all right with her, as we gazed intently upon the surprised vessel, sympathizing little with the others, all of which were either secure in the neighbourhood of the jetty, or already standing out fearlessly to sea, where they might laugh at the storm. But the ill-fated schooner was by no means secure. All her anchors were evidently out, and she was still dragging, still drawing nearer to the dangerous lee-shore that wooed her to destruction. The heavy swell of the sea rolling in, mountain upon mountain of water, drove her ever nearer to the land, and nearer to us as we watched her from Fort Knokke, whilst the wind howled dismally around, as if sounding her death-knell. It was an anxious time for the brave fellows on board the little craft—an anxious time truly, for it might be but the turning point between the life past and the eternity to come; the waves that surged and gurgled around them might be their graves, the howling storm their only burial service.

It was evident that the dangerous situation of the little schooner was perceived on shore, and that the harbour-master was doing his utmost to afford her assistance. A barge or lugger was launched with an additional anchor for her, and a life-boat, in case the former was unable to make the passage. Guns of distress were fired in rapid succession by the schooner, whilst on one side of her we saw the crew launching their long-boat.

It was evident they anticipated the worst. She still kept driving towards the shore, which here shoaled rapidly, every huge wave advancing her nearer to destruction. In the mean time succour was rapidly approaching; the barge or lugger with the anchor, however, was obliged to put back, she narrowly escaped being swamped as it was, but the life-boat held gallantly on. The only question was, would she reach the schooner in time?—the only question for a few minutes that must have appeared ages to the anxious crew. It was soon all over, however. Drifting with every wave, with every blast, nearer the shore, the schooner at length drew near a portion of the bay, where the water shoaled almost immediately, from three or four fathoms to one, from one fathom to a foot.

To the crew on board it was no doubt an age of anxiety, to us watching keenly from the fort, it was over in a moment. The schooner's bottom evidently touched the sand or a rock beneath lightly—a heavy sea lifted her over in an instant upon her side. She turned—filled—and the next wave bore her, bottom up, dismasted and dismantled upon the beach, bore her there to play with her as the cat plays with the mouse, to cast her up for one moment and seize her the next, to let her go for one instant only that she might be caught hold of the following!

There was nothing at all extraordinary about the circumstance. Such things constantly occur. At the very moment when I am writing, or you, good reader, are perusing these lines, some gallant ship may be going down to the grave of vessels, sinking to rise no more, whilst the breathless carcasses of her whilom crew float away here and there to be the prey of hungry sharks. This was only a small schooner, with half-a-dozen hands in her, no more! A mere trifle in the sum of human life which war, commerce, avarice, or enterprise daily offers up as its sacrifices.

"They are all drowned!" whispered an anxious voice, that sounded in my ear like the death-knell of the poor sailors.

"They are all drowned!"—under such circumstances, the simplest expression conveys the gravest meaning, suggests the saddest thoughts! And so it appeared, indeed, for the time being, gazing as we were from Fort Knokke most earnestly at the scene.

"They are all drowned!" I muttered to myself, as I looked at the wrecked schooner, faintly discernible as a black spot on the billow that was breaking over the beach.

"They are all drowned!" we whispered, as we glanced over the tops of the heaving waves, that rolled in rapidly in irregular succession.

We were too quick in our conclusion, however. In the valley between two of these large waves, the small boat of the schooner had been hid from our observation. The life-boat was up with her almost before she crested the huge mass of water that was advancing, and, before we had had time to lament the loss of the brave fellows, as they ought to have been lamented, we saw that they were safe. It was a strange instantaneous revulsion of feeling that—almost enough to make one laugh heartily, unsuitable as laughter was to such scenes and such emotions.

To see the gallant fellows whose loss we had commenced to mourn, safely borne over the waves by the life-boat, after we had felt sad at their fate, was enough to produce a strange commotion within us, and, as we drew a long breath—I and my companion—and watched the steady progress of the life-boat, we smiled, and said, "they are *not* drowned." To *us* it was only a difference of word and a passing emotion—to each of the brave fellows themselves, it was the difference between a life lost and a life saved!

My companion was an old Anglo-Indian, who had lived for twenty-five years in Calcutta—a specimen of a *genus* which the increasing facilities of travelling, and the alterations now progressing in Indian life, will soon render extinct. He had become so thoroughly wedded to the unnatural life which he led in Calcutta, that none other was tolerable to him. His servants and his iced claret, his rich curries and pillaws, his noon-day couch and luxurious naps, were to him necessaries of existence. But however much the mind may accustom itself to such a state of things, the body soon proclaims feelingly that it is non-natural—that, in fact, it is all very fine, but won't do in the long run.

Illness was gradually making Mr. Kabob but the shadow of what he had been—he could not enjoy, as in times past, his iced claret and his prawn curries, and he sighed sadly as he found that things were altering with him—sighed mournfully at the want of appetite that showed his digestive apparatus was out of order, and would not be set right without some great change. Where dinners are the great events of the day—the sole blessings worth living for—it may be fancied how sad the diner when he finds himself incapable of enjoying them; how grievous the conviction, when it will force itself upon the mind, that the great event of the day is a blessing no longer.

"Nothing but a complete change of air will do for you, Mr. Kabob," said the doctors; "you must leave Calcutta and go to the Sandheads."

Kabob sighed as he heard the sentence, nay, groaned rather. But he was a man of resolution, and so he said resolutely, "I *will* go, doctor."

The "Sandheads" is the name given to the estuary of the Ganges, where it disgorges itself by many mouths into the sea. Pilot brigs are stationed there, some with lights to warn ships from the dangerous banks, some cruizing about to supply vessels making their way to Calcutta with pilots. 'To go to the Sandheads,' meant, then, to remain in one of these pilot brigs, in the hope that the sea-breeze might blow him into health again. It was to forsake his luxury, to give up all that he held most dear, and live in an offensive brig, where people would think nothing of disturbing him at night,—where men looked upon eating and drinking as altogether a secondary consideration!

"I *will* go, doctor," said Kabob, nevertheless, heroically; and he *did* go. He was to have remained at the Sandheads three weeks at least, so said the doctors. In ten days after his departure, Kabob, like a tall ghost, made his way into my office, with a face of the yellowest ghastly hue, and an attenuated frame.

"Kabob!" I exclaimed, in surprise; "back already! why, I thought the doctors warned you not to return before three weeks were over, at least?"

"So they did, my friend," said Kabob, choosing out the easiest chair he could find, and seating himself leisurely, whilst he put his feet on another chair that contained letters and papers in admired confusion—letters and papers from anxious correspondents, who were, no doubt, each hoping that the Editor was attentively perusing his or her communications at all events, whatever else might be neglected. Down upon sonnets, and the first five chapters of a new novel, written in an exquisitely neat hand; down upon facetious diatribes, and laughable expostulations intended to be grave and serious; down upon them all went Kabob's feet, for he knew their value.

"So they did, my friend," said he, as he seated himself; referring to the doctors and their commands; "so they did, but I could not stand it any longer; fowls and ducks one day for dinner, ducks and fowls the next; nothing but ducks, nothing but fowls, every day. 'I will die comfortably in Calcutta,' said I to myself, 'rather than live here in this miserable way.'"

It was true enough, absurd as it may appear, good reader. Good fare was with him the one thing needful, bad fare the one thing abominable, to be eschewed above all others. He preferred dying comfortably in Calcutta, to living "abstemiously" at the Sandheads—the abstemious living, be it remembered, consisting of good wines, fat ducks and plump hens in abundance. "But where are the side dishes?" asked Kabob sorrowfully, and so he returned!

However, death to be looked in the face is no joke; and although Kabob had, in his sadness of soul, resolved to endure death in Calcutta rather than live moderately out of it; yet, when he found that he actually *was* sinking, and that the cemetery in the Circular Road would certainly receive him if some sea-going vessel did not; he magnanimously made up his mind to break up his establishment and depart to the Cape. Advertisements appeared in the Calcutta papers, stating, that in consequence of Mr. Kabob's approaching departure from Calcutta, Messrs. Screwthem Tight and Co. had been instructed to dispose of his valuable household furniture, plate, horses, carriages, &c., &c., &c., by public auction.

It so happened that I had arrived at the Cape before Kabob's departure from it. He was intimately acquainted with the commanding officer at Fort Knokke, and thus we had happened to be spectators of the loss of the little schooner, and of the gallant rescue of the crew by the life-boat.

An advertisement in the Cape papers the

following day informed the public that subscriptions would be thankfully received by Messrs. Roggeweld and Stallenbosch for the crew of the life-boat which had so gallantly made its way to the distressed seamen, and for the seamen and master of the schooner, who had lost all that they possessed. I showed the advertisement to Kabob, who was rich enough to have reimbursed them all, without feeling the expense himself.

"Very proper objects of charity indeed," said the Anglo-Indian, "very proper. I particularly admired the courage of those fellows in the life-boat. It's marvellous that men should risk their lives in that way for a few rupees."

"They did it to save the lives of the wrecked seamen," I urged, "not to get money."

"And they *did* save them, and they'll get money besides—which is all very right and proper," urged Kabob. "I really do not think this claret is equal to what we had yesterday—it's genuine Lafitte, no doubt, but still it's not that first-rate quality that the other was. It smacks of the cask too."

"I'm going to send a small subscription for these brave fellows to Messrs. Roggeweld and Stallenbosch," said I, "shall I put down your name for anything?"

"Of course you will," said Kabob; "I'll give the life-boat fellows ten rupees for their gallantry."

"And the poor seamen of the schooner, that have lost their all?" I urged.

"Why, yes, as you say, they must be badly off—let me see, five rupees for them and five for the life-boat fellows, that'll do;" and Kabob quaffed another glass of claret, as he formed the generous resolution.

I called on Messrs. Roggeweld and Stallenbosch, in order to gain some information respecting the unfortunate schooner and her crew.

"A very sad thing, sir," said the clerk; "the poor fellows have lost all, and the islanders too; their whole year's produce was in that schooner."

"What islanders?" I asked.

"Why, you see, Sir, the schooner came from the Tristan D'Acunha Islands, and the men in her belonged to them. They come over every year with their produce, and after disposing of it here, take back the few things they require."

"Indeed!" said I, as I walked away, after paying my subscription and Kabob's—"indeed!"

* * * *

There are few things that men are more disposed to conceal than ignorance. It requires a good deal of resolution to say—"I don't know anything about it," when your companion makes an observation that puzzles you.

"Strange that they should put a contralto and a soprano together," said a gentleman who was sitting beside a friend of mine at one of the concerts in Exeter Hall the other night—a friend utterly ignorant of the very elements of musical lore.

"Very strange indeed," was his reply, whilst he had no very definite idea as to what either a contralto or a soprano was, and, therefore, could not see, of course, why they should not be put together.

"Very strange indeed," was my friend's reply, as he looked into the face of the gentleman who had made the observation to see that he was quite serious; he had not the moral fortitude to say that he really did not know what a contralto or a soprano was.

Do you think, under similar circumstances —supposing such an amount of ignorance possible in your case, good sir or madam—do you think, under similar circumstances, you would have answered more honestly—would you not mutter "Yes" or "Hem," or some other unmeaning expletive of assent, rather than confess that you did not see anything strange in it? If you would say so—as, perhaps, nine out of ten would, from various motives—some not to give offence, some to avoid the appearance of ignorance, some to be polite —if you would, then do not be astonished that I walked out of Messrs. Roggeweld and Stallenbosch's office without asking where the Tristan D'Acunha Islands were, or without informing the clerk that, up to that moment, I was profoundly ignorant of their existence.

Verily, human nature is a strange thing, and we, living representatives of that human nature—you and I, good sir, you and I, good madam,—are strange people. Let me conclude with Shakespeare, however, "an odd man, lady, every man is odd."

But although I felt my ignorance, and was ashamed of it, I had no idea of sitting down quietly under it and suffering it; no, I made up my mind to rout it forthwith, not to endure it on any account.

CHAPTER VIII.

THE EMPEROR NAPOLEON AND KING GLASS.

"THE Tristan D'Acunha Islands," I muttered to myself, as I made my way that day through the streets of Cape Town to my lodgings in the suburbs—"the Tristan D'Acunha Islands, where *can* they be?"

I met Mrs. Dordrecht, my good landlady, on the stairs, as I made my way to my sitting room.

"Where are the Tristan D'Acunha Islands, Mrs. Dordrecht?" I asked.

Mrs. Dordrecht did not know—had never heard of them before—was not quite sure that such islands were in existence at all—smiled faintly as she replied, to show that she discovered some profound witticism in the question, a witticism hidden from the eyes and understanding of an ordinary mortal like myself.

"You really don't know?" I asked again.

"I don't know," said she, with the prettiest foreign accent, and as simply as possible.

"The Tristan D'Acunha Islands!" I exclaimed, as I threw myself on a couch, when I had reached my room, "where *can* they be?" The few books I had brought with me to the Cape did not include a Gazetteer, nor had the deceased Dordrecht, worthy man, left a Gazetteer amongst his books to his excellent spouse, now a widow, my landlady.

"I *must* discover where those islands are," said I, putting on my hat, and sallying out again; "how stupid I was, not to ask the clerk something about them."

I bent my steps directly to the library in which I was accustomed to see the papers, and to chat with such idlers as presented themselves.

"Do you know anything about the Tristan D'Acunha Islands?" I asked of the librarian, who daily retailed the gossip of the Cape to all quidnunc loungers.

No; he did not know; had some faint idea

that he had heard of such islands before, but where they were situated was to him unknown. We walked over to a map of the world that was suspended against the wall, but an inspection of it tended little to enlighten us on the subject. We found there, as usual, all sorts of names in large type, that every one knew before, but nowhere the mysterious islands which we sought.

"I have it!" said the librarian, clapping his hands.

"Where?" I asked, looking intently at Siberia, as I thought I saw him directing his eyes to that quarter.

"The Edinburgh Gazetteer," said he, again, "will tell us all about them."

"To be sure it will," was my reply; and away we marched to search for the unknown shores in the pages of the Gazetteer.

Mr. Vangeyzel found it after a little.

"Tri, Trip, Tris; here it is, Sir, here it is—TRISTAN D'ACUNHA—there you have all about it," said the benevolent librarian, delighted at the discovery, as he pushed the Gazetteer to me.

I read as follows:—

"Tristan D'Acunha, the largest of three

islands in the South Atlantic Ocean, about 1500 miles from any land either to the west or north, very lofty, and about 15 miles in circumference. Long. 15. 40. W. Lat. 37. S."

"That's all about them," said I, as I threw down the volume.

The map of the world was again referred to, and there, at the latitude and longitude indicated by the truthful Gazetteer, we found the Tristan D'Acunha Islands—south-west of the Cape, and nearer to the Cape than to any other land. I went to the Gazetteer again; not a word more was to be discovered respecting them, than those which I had already read—

"Tristan D'Acunha, the largest of three islands in the South Atlantic Ocean, about 1500 miles from any land either to the west or north, very lofty, and about 15 miles in circumference. Long. 15. 40. W. Lat. 37. S."

Mr. Vangeyzel and I pored over the notice with apparently equal interest.

"It doesn't say a word about any inhabitants on them," I observed.

"Not a syllable," said Vangeyzel, as he turned over to the title-page. The study of the title-page evidently gave him a new idea.

"The Edinburgh Gazetteer," he read out, "or Compendious Geographical Dictionary, containing a description of the various countries, kingdoms, states, cities, towns, mountains, seas, rivers, harbours, &c., of the world."

"It says nothing about islands," he continued, quite seriously, and looking me full in the face.

It was evident he regarded his discovery as an important one, for, receiving no answer, he reiterated—

"It says nothing about islands."

"No," said I, seeing that he was really *not* joking; "no, but the &c. would include islands."

"Ah, to be sure, I never thought of that," replied the librarian, puzzled again.

Next morning I went betimes to Messrs. Roggeweld and Stallenbosch's office, to make further inquiry about the schooner and her crew, as well as about the Tristan D'Acunha Islands.

"I don't know much about them," said the clerk; "but I'm quite sure they're inhabited, for they send their vessel over twicc every year with wool, seal skins, blubber, and otner articles too numerous to mention—that schooner as was lost as per advertisement."

"Can you tell me where the master of that schooner is to be found?" I asked.

"Certainly, Sir, if you wish to satisfy yourself respecting the truth of the statement, and the entire loss of the vessel and cargo, you will find him at —— "

The address was given, and in half an hour I was sitting in a private room in a public house frequented by sailors, with the master of the ill-fated *Enterprize*, for that was the schooner's name, opposite to me. He was a dark, weather-beaten young man, who had evidently seen much service.

"Inhabited!" he exclaimed; "faix an' yer honor may say that, an' the divil a lie in it, anyway. Shure there's near a hundred of us on that same Tristan D'Acunha—there was eighty-six when I left it, and I suspect there's eighty-seven or eighty-eight by this time."

"You're an Irishman, Mr. Brody," I observed.

"An Irishman—O begor it's thrue for you, but how did you come to know that at all at all?"

"By your language—there's a touch of the brogue in it still."

"Why thin, now, I dare say there is," suggested Mr. Brody; "but it's fifteen years since I was in the ould country, and isn't it mortial strange that I should hould to the ould talk still?"

"And how long have you been in Tristan D'Acunha?" I asked.

"Ever since I was a spalpeen, the height of a capstan. My father was out on the island in Bony's time and Mr. Glass', and so you see that's the way that I kem to be livin' there—I was brought up to the say, so I was; and they made me masther of the Enterprize, so they did, two years ago, an' if it hadn't been for that infernal pilot (savin' yer presence), I'd a been masther of her now, so I would."

"In Bony's time and Mr. Glass'?" I repeated. "Do you mean Napoleon Buonaparte?"

"To be shure I do—wasn't he livin' in St. Helena for six or seven years?"

"And Mr. Glass?" I asked.

"Oh, maybe you never heard of Mr. Glass at all at all?"

"Not a word that I remember," was my reply.

"Well, now, see to that—isn't it wonderful? Why, Mr. Glass was livin' in Tristan D'Acunha when Bony was livin' in St. Helena."

"And who or what was Mr. Glass?"

"He was a corporal, so he was."

"Perhaps Tristan D'Acunha was occupied as a military station then, by the British?" I suggested.

"To be shure it was, all the time that Bony was at St. Helena, and when he died they wanted to give up Tristan D'Acunha altogether, but Glass had taken a fancy to it, do ye see, an' he sold out, so he did; an' he got all his kith and kin to go with him, an' my father among the rest, an' there they are in the island now; an' bad luck to me! but it's me they'll be shaking their heads at when they hear the beautiful schooner's gone to the bottom, an' all our fine wool and seals' skins, and all the rest of it—O murther! but it'll break the ould man's heart, so it will."

I was astonished at Mr. Brody's account, and deeply interested in the information he had given me—the unaffected sorrow he displayed, not so much at his own losses as at those of the island, where every one had some venture in the little ship—all opened up a scene so new and striking, so different from what one sees every day, that I formed the resolution of seeing Tristan d'Acunha and its strange inhabitants with my own eyes, if I could.

Mr. Brody's account was strictly correct, as subsequent inquiries convinced me. There, far away in the South Atlantic, so far, that a vessel was seldom seen except an odd whaling ship, lay the strange islands. A company of artillery, with their wives, had occupied it when Napoleon was at St. Helena. Glass had been one of those soldiers—a corporal; and the desert island had taken his fancy so much, that he resolved, Crusoe-like, to live there all the rest of his days. Government aided him in his enterprise, and with his wife and family, as well as all of his friends that he could get to join him, he was taken back to his own island, fifteen hundred miles away from the nearest inhabited land.

It had never been inhabited before the soldiers had taken possession of it, but their occupation had somewhat prepared it for the little colony. He landed in 1823 with six companions; they were all married, and there were amongst them eight children. In 1829, as I perceived from an official account I discovered at the Cape, there were altogether twenty-seven persons in the little state, seven men, six women, for one of them had died, and fourteen children.

In 1849, according to Mr. Brody's account, there were eighty-six inhabitants. Glass was still alive, the monarch of the little empire. Land was tilled; they had six hundred acres in cultivation; their cattle and farming stock had increased more rapidly than the inhabitants, for their original five oxen (four cows and a bull) had multiplied to a hundred; their dozen sheep had become three hundred; the swine and goats introduced by the soldiers were to be found wild all over the island Every thing was prosperous, and, from Brody's account, it was quite evident that Glass ruled them well. He had all the elements of the sovereign in him—nay, possibly has still, for he may be still alive—he was their prophet, priest, and king. They regarded him as the wisest of sages, whilst they loved him as a father; he had kept them in order, and they feared him with a wholesome fear.

A disorderly whaler was what they most dreaded, for the seamen of the whaling vessels had no respect for the property of others; and for many years, when a whaling boat was observed making for the island, Glass and his companions were obliged to make off to the mountain which occupies half the island—a mountain eight thousand feet high—hide their cattle, their sheep, and their wives in its recesses, and then meet the unruly marauders to make the best terms they could for what was wanted. Delicious water abounds in the island, and a stray vessel would sometimes beat about in the vicinity, whilst a boat was sent on shore for such vegetables and water as could be obtained. At *this* period, however, the inhabitants were strong enough to protect themselves from any moderate boat's crew, but it was not so in times past; and what they now delighted to see—a vessel approaching—they formerly dreaded.

I was so interested in Brody's account, that I introduced him to Kabob. The contrast between the two was amazingly striking. The rough child of nature, fresh from the perils of the sea and from his rude island, where all was healthy work, hard work, too, and wholesome activity, and the luxurious Anglo-Indian, accustomed for more than twenty years to all that could gratify the senses, or could enervate the body. They regarded each other much in the same light as a modern city *belle* and an Indian squaw would regard each other, if an honest, hard-working, independent Indian squaw could any where be found now Yet there were some lingering remnants in Kabob's mind of respect for hardihood and bravery, for enterprise and independence—he even went so far as to declare that Glass must have been a superior man *for his station in life;* as if, being a corporal, a superior man in that grade meant a quite different thing from a superior man in fine clothes, and with finer cloth on his back, and a different title.

So much was I taken up with Brody's account and with all I learned of those remarkable islanders, that I determined to visit them, if possible, and endeavoured even to induce Kabob to contemplate some such expedition. He regarded my intentions as slight indications of lunacy, gravely asking if the Cape was not bad enough? whether I thought Tristan d'Acunha could be much worse? if I really wanted something worse, why I did not make my way to Kamschatka? with sundry other equally facetious inquiries.

I felt convinced that the facts had but to be brought prominently before the public of the Cape, however, to secure a sufficient sum to enable Brody to charter a brig, and to stock it as he had been ordered before quitting the island. I called on the editor of more than one paper —myself an editor, I needed no other introduction. The power of the fourth estate was brought to bear upon the public benevolence. Moving appeals were addressed to the benevolent sympathy of a generous public, even from the editorial columns. The disappointment of the poor islanders—fifteen hundred miles away from any inhabited land—was feelingly dwelt upon; their heavy loss, and the years of toil which it would require before another vessel could be purchased by them; the misfortune of the brave master and crew, who had lost their all—these topics, and others equally suitable, were duly urged.

In the midst of political disquisitions on the policy of receiving convicts, and violent diatribes against the Home Government for wishing to force convicts upon the colony—in the midst of editorial squabbles and party perorations, these appeals to the public formed an agreeable resting-place, the neutral tint that harmonizes the strong lights, the pause in the action of the heroic poem that allows the anxious reader time to breathe freely.

The public was not deaf to the voice of their monitors. Engaged in a contest of no ordinary moment, though they were resolutely determined that their beef and their bread should not supply English convict ships and their guards, heroically disdaining present gains for future purity and freedom from contamination, they yet listened to the details of the poor islanders. Sympathy was excited. Money began to flow in. Great names headed the lists; the names of doughty knights and colonial honourables, each of which was a host in itself. In a fortnight, Mr. Brody was negotiating for a brig, the *Osprey*, then waiting for a commission. In a month his purchases were made; Messrs. Roggeweld and Stallenbosch, the agents of the islanders, supplied him with all that he demanded, and there was still a balance to the credit of the charitable fund—a small balance, it is true, but still it must be remembered that money enough had been subscribed to charter the vessel for a run to Tristan d'Acunha and back, to purchase all that the islanders wanted, and to replace the clothes and personal property of the master and crew.

True, the schooner and its freight were gone —heavy losses for the poor islanders—but a large portion of that freight was represented by the goods taken out by the *Osprey*. A heavy loss instead of partial ruin. All honour, then, to the benevolent Capeofgoodhopians!* They were in this case honest followers of the Good Samaritan.

* What name is to be given to the dwellers at the Cape? They would disdain that of Africans; Capites is unpleasant, Capeofgoodhopians too long. The same may be said of Vandiemanslandonians, but they get out of the difficulty by calling themselves Tasmanians.

CHAPTER IX.

THE LIVING CRUSOES.

I TOOK my passage in the Osprey, bound for Glass Bay, in Tristan d'Acunha, Mr. Brody commander. Before I land, it will perhaps be well to give the reader some further information respecting the group of three islands called generally after the Portuguese admiral who discovered them in 1506, and of which the largest (not fifteen miles in circumference, as the Edinburgh Gazetteer affirmed, but nineteen or twenty miles) bears his name particularly. If the reader will but open a map of the world, and draw his finger westerly from the Cape, a little southerly too, but very little, he will come upon the group of three islands, which Tristan d'Acunha, the celebrated Portuguese admiral, discovered when he was sailing to the East to assume "the Viceroyalty of the Indies."

It is not often that vessels doubling the Cape go so far south as these islands; they do not therefore lie in the ordinary track of Indiamen, or else Corporal Glass and his little colony would be as well known to readers of Indian travels as Mrs. Glass of cooking celebrity to all readers. Besides the largest island called after the discoverer, there are two others, Nightingale and Inaccessible Island, both much smaller, with high bleak shores and forbidding rocky beaches. These islands can only be approached by boats or small vessels in a perfect calm—the landing is dangerous even then. Had they both been called Inaccessible, the name would not have been much of a misnomer. A few swine and goats have been put by the colonists upon both of them, and now live luxuriously there, nothing to do but eat, drink, multiply, and replenish the earth, their great enemy, man, seldom seen, perhaps never, by many of them.

Tristan d'Acunha, the largest of the three, is of somewhat peculiar construction. A mountain, upwards of eight thousand feet high, occupies its southern portion, whilst a wide plain slopes beautifully down to the sea upon the north—a wide plain, with three streams of no great size, but perennial, called the Napoleon, the Wellington, and the Glass Rivers. Such is fame! The mountain to the south is a rugged, precipitous mass of granite, with strange caves here and there, some of which Mr. Brody assured me, had never been thoroughly explored. Its base, and a portion of its side, are covered with lofty trees, some of which are said to form valuable timber. When the artillery lived in the island, several of these were felled, and lately the strength of the colony has been equal to transporting a few of them from the mountain's base to Glass Bay in the north, a distance of nine miles, principally by means of the Wellington, which, after heavy rain, is a perfect torrent.

A voyage in a vessel like the Osprey differs as much from a voyage in one of the large East Indiamen, or Oriental steamers, as a journey through England in a carrier's waggon, from the same journey accomplished in a first-class railway carriage. The small number of hands; the little attention paid to luxury, or what a landsman would be disposed to consider comfort or convenience rather; the tumbling about of the little vessel, like a nut-shell in an agitated cistern, even when the said landsman could discern no cause for such tumbling at all, are by no means the least pleasant features of a voyage of fifteen hundred miles in a small brig. It was altogether dispiriting to the searcher after adventure, to find himself disgusted with what he knew to be inevitable, long before the weary fortnight's journey was at an end.

Yet there was much on the other hand that was interesting and novel in the expedition. The frank sailorly friendship of Brody displayed itself in unceasing attempts to render the passage pleasant and agreeable to his solitary passenger, whilst his Irish humour, softened into reflective feeling by his strange life, was a study not easily to be exhausted. His crew, too, all Islanders, were equally subjects for observation. They were so unlike the sailors of the great world, and of ordinary seaports, that I could scarcely fancy myself sometimes in a ship at all. Not that they were peculiarly excellent, or remarkably intelligent, or fine specimens of mankind physically. Far from it. They required to be kept in order just like other sailors — they obeyed Brody from a fear of the consequences should they rebel—they spoke, sometimes with pleasure, sometimes with disgust, of their ocean home, just as the humour of the day suggested.

They were rude, hardy, weather-beaten young men, who had been reared there, whose families, fathers, mothers, wives, sons, and daughters, were almost all alive, and who, therefore, looked upon Tristan D'Acunha as their natural home, upon Brody as their natural "captain," upon Glass as their legitimate sovereign, and upon their island and Cape Town as all the world that they wished to explore. They could not help seeing that they were far better off than the majority of sailors whom they met, either coming in whaling-vessels or at the Cape, and, whilst they grumbled at their position, they clung to it.

"We've got widin sight o' the islands at last, anyways," said Brody, coming into my cabin, early one morning, when the "lively" brig was dancing about a little less outrageously than usual.

I lost no time in getting on deck. There, on the horizon, right a-head, rose the lofty summit of the mountain, forming an irregular line, that resembled the edge of a thick black cloud, shining in the sun. On the right and left of it rose, just above the water, hardly visible, the more even surfaces of Nightingale and Inaccessible Island. Only two of the crew were watching these specks on the horizon, although four of those from the island were on deck. The other two lay listlessly about, waiting for "eight bells" to sound, which terminated their watch and relieved them.

As we sailed that evening into Glass Bay, the inhabitants, who were, doubtless, looking for their island schooner, were surprised at our approach. A boat, resembling the long-boat of a whaler, put off from the shore, with some casks of water, potatoes, cabbages, and the other vegetables which they usually supplied to the ships, in exchange for left-off clothing, and utensils of various kinds.

Brody's greeting, as they drew near, informed them of their mistake, and, as they recognised the voice, they saluted it with a wild "hurra!" a genuine English "hurra!" that sounded pleasantly from fellows that looked so foreign in their unshaven faces and various head-dresses.

As they clambered on board, I should have mistaken them for pirates, had not the recognition assured me that they were the true Islanders, some of the very men whom I had come to see. They were armed with pistols and cutlasses in their belts. Their hirsute faces, trimmed with the scissors only, made them look to my fancy, depraved by civilization, like savages. Their dress was of the most various and irregular description possible. One big fellow, that seized Brody's hand with the grasp of a vice, and whose grizzled beard and erect bearing told him to be what he was, an old soldier, looked particularly threatening in a rough fur cap, woollen sailor's shirt, and wide trousers, well patched, evidently made out of an old sail. Another had a small military undress cap upon his head; a third, a glazed sailor's wide-awake; whilst a fourth rejoiced in an unshapely piece of sheepskin, which had been rudely converted into a head-covering.

Nor was the rest of their dress less various than were their caps and hats. One sported a pair of black cloth pantaloons, that had evidently belonged to the full-dress wardrobe of some careful landsman; another had a pair of leather inexpressibles of the most nondescript character, and of most original design. It was evident that convenience and necessity, not fashion, had moulded their clothing. There was but one point similar in the attire of each—that was, in the extent of patching; there could be no doubt that the Tristandacunian females were adepts with the needle. This extent and variety of patching, however, might partly have been accounted for by the state in which these clothes, are usually obtained by the islanders. Ships' crews exchange these articles of clothing for water, potatoes, turnips, cabbages, and pigs—exchanging, of course, only that portion of their varied wardrobes which has already been condemned as useless, or nearly so.

My curiosity to see the island and its inhabitants was, in no small degree, increased, by the aspect of this boat's crew. If the men are clothed in so original a manner, thought I, how will the women be covered? Ships' crews have not usually much female attire to exchange for anything, however useful or necessary.

I was, of course, an object of interest to the islanders as much as they to me. When Brody had given them an account of how the schooner had been lost, and how I had interested myself in procuring for them the brig, exaggerating my little services a hundred-fold, one after another shook me warmly by the hand, and hoped that I would determine upon taking up my abode with them altogether. I was as cordial as they were, squeezing the rough horny hands that grasped mine as well as I could in a vain endeavour to emulate their warmth of feeling, but at the hint of stopping there altogether I shook my head.

"You want married men amongst you," said I, "not unprofitable bachelors, such as I am; and, besides, I dare say you have no newspaper for me to edit, and that's almost the only thing I can do."

Brody had my portmanteau put into the boat, and, leaving the brig to be brought to her anchorage by his father, the tall fellow in the rough fur cap, who was also an excellent seaman, he accompanied me on shore to introduce me to the great man of the place — the venerable Glass. As we pulled into the bay, I saw the huts of the islanders scattered about the mouth of a pleasant stream. An elevated semicircular mound behind, was occupied by a pleasant-looking house, built more after the European fashion than I had expected to find any in this out-of-the-way place.

"That is Mr. Glass's house, I suppose," said I to Brody, pointing to the European-looking residence I had noticed.

"No," said he, "Misther Glass lives in a house here beyant; you can't see it yet, jist round the bluff on our right—that one was for the officers of the artillery, when the soldiers was here; there was two of them, so there was; and it's our church now."

"Your church?" I exclaimed "and who officiates there?"

"Mr. Glass, of coorse, who else?" rejoined Brody, surprised at the question.

"What an extraordinary man," I half muttered to myself.

"It's thrue for ye, sir, an' it's an extraordinar' man he is, all out; but shure that's no throuble at all at all to him, for he has the larnin', an' he taught every mother's son of us how to read, so he did, when we were spalpeens, only he niver could get the ould talk off my tongue, an' my father an' my mother talkin' the same way kipt me in it."

"Mr. Glass taught the children, too, then?" I observed.

"He did, sir, shure enough, it's thrue for ye, an' a man that knew more it wouldn't be aisy to find in these parts."

As we drew near the landing-place, doubling the bluff which concealed the best part of the little colony, I observed two or three women and several children coming down to the beach, towards which we were approaching. One of them Brody recognized as his wife, who had evidently determined to discover at once if there was any information about the schooner or her husband forthcoming from the brig. She and her companions were dressed as women of the lower orders in England would be dressed; there was nothing whatever remarkable about their appearance, save that the handkerchiefs tied round the head instead of a bonnet gave them a slightly foreign aspect. Each of them wore, too, under her outer cloak or shawl, an apron, like a child's pinafore, of sail-cloth, not unlike that worn by the factory-girls in Manchester and other manufacturing towns—but this I did not observe till afterwards.

The cottages were better, and their vicinity kept in neater order in this sheltered nook behind the bluff, than those which dotted the mound topped by the European-looking house. Their walls, as I afterwards found, were formed of shingle and loose stones, cemented by mud, and they were thatched with a long grass abundant in the interior of the island. Their glass windows were put in scientifically —the frames smoothly formed and accurately fitted. It was evident, at a glance, that some one in Tristan D'Acunha was acquainted with carpentering. Around the cottages, which were seven or eight in number, were pleasant trees and bushes, principally apple trees and gooseberry bushes, which had been planted by the colonists, the seeds having been originally brought, like almost all that they had, from the Cape.

Affectionate greetings were interchanged between Brody and his wife on our landing—he was informed that a day or two after his departure his household was increased by the advent of a thriving boy, whilst he, on his side, had much to communicate respecting the loss of the schooner and the substitution of the brig. All this delayed us for some time upon the beach. Whatever idlers there were in the colony—principally children—were soon collected around us, many of them with no other covering than a loose coarse shirt, but all with the ruddy glow of health and the bronzed tint acquired by constant exposure. One urchin climbed up Brody's knees as he told his tale, another hung on by his jacket behind, whilst a third got between his legs. Many occupied themselves in leisurely surveying me, evidently regarding me as a curiosity imported for them to stare at

The news of the loss of the schooner spread

from cottage to cottage, and as we advanced slowly towards the central house of the little village, anxious faces peered forth from the open doors, or interrogated the passers-by in broad Scotch, in Cape jargon, a kind of Dutch-English, in the Yorkshire dialect, or the rich brogue of Ireland, just as if they had only recently left their native shores. Even of those born in the island the majority appeared to retain the distinctive provincialisms of their parents, varied only a little by a few slang or Dutch terms imported from the Cape or from the whaling crews that occasionally touched at Tristan D'Acunha.

At length we reached the residence of the great man, the founder and president of this little commonwealth. We ushered ourselves in without ceremony—the cottage was empty, but the daughter of the illustrious chief, now the wife of one of his companions and the mother of a thriving brood, was in the garden behind it, looking after some poultry; she speedily made her appearance.

"My father's jist gone to dig a few potatoes doon in the field beyond—rin, Sandy, rin," said she to a little red-haired urchin beside her; "rin an' ca' yer grandfayther here, my bairn."

Sandy disappeared at once.

It was quite true. Cincinnatus-like, the king, chief-justice, priest, and schoolmaster of Tristan D'Acunha was digging potatoes in a field at some distance from the cottage! Mrs. Macrae, his daughter, introduced us into her humble abode, and gave us such chairs and seats as were available—rough and of substantial form, for the most part, but deficient decidedly in elegance.

"It's an airly season, ye see, sir," said she, addressing me, "an' the potatoes must be got ready for the *Enterprize* betimes."

The name of the schooner brought forth from Brody an account of its loss, the third I had heard that day. Some good oaten bread and cold bacon were soon produced, together with a flask of Hollands gin, and, as we were partaking of these luxuries, the patriarch of Tristan D'Acunha himself—the venerable Corporal Glass—made his appearance. We all rose to welcome him. Even the little urchins who loitered about the door and watched our performances on the oaten bread and the bacon, grinned forth a welcome to him.

Glass was not at all what I had pictured to myself he would be. His appearance was venerable from his white hair and beard, neither of which was long, but, with this exception and that of his keen grey eyes, there was nothing to distinguish him in appearance from any ordinary English farmer of the lower ranks. He wore high boots that reached almost to his knees—a pair of leather breeches and a snuff-coloured coat, short, wide, and well-patched. His white shirt alone distinguished him from those around me, his white shirt and his blue cloth cap, which, monarch like, he retained on his head till he joined us at the table.

The loss of the schooner was again detailed, this time with tedious minuteness. It was bad enough to have been a witness of the catastrophe, but to have it rehearsed four times in one day until one's ears and mind were both tired and sick of it, was a trial of patience, that I felt irksome enough.

"A bad business eneugh," said Glass, "Aweel, aweel, it canna' be helpit. We maun jist mak the best o' it. We'll ha'e anither cargo ready for you in a week, my lad, an' you maun just bring a few men wi' you fro' the Cape to tak' the brig back again, whin you come. We'll have anaither schooner ready by next year—there's plenty o' timber in Tristan D'Acunha."

It was evident how Glass had got on in the world—not by brooding over misfortune or sitting down to repine, but by gallantly facing the evils that could not be averted, and as gallantly overcoming them.

"An' noo, Brody," said the chief, "ye'll be wantin' to gang till yer family, my lad. Leave the brig to yer fayther, and the rest to me. As for the gentleman, Lizzy," he continued, addressing his daughter, "we must get the Lieutenant's room ready up at the church, an' much beholdin' to him we are for a' that he's done."

I was comfortably enough located in what was still called the Lieutenant's room—a small chamber adjoining the European-looking house on the mound, which had formerly been the bed-room of the commanding officer of the little garrison when Tristan D'Acunha was held by a military force. Everything then used had, of course, been removed—it was stocked with furniture from the Corporal's store-room, or from the superfluities of the best houses in Tristan D'Acunha. A good mattress, not too soft; two substantial chairs; a small round table; a stool with a metal basin on it for washing, and a diminutive looking-glass, constituted the luxurious furniture of this aristocratic chamber; for *luxurious* furniture, and an *aristocratic* chamber, both were certainly considered to be by the worthy islanders.

CHAPTER X.

THE ISLAND OF THE LIVING CRUSOES.

AFTER the tossing about of the little brig upon the waves of the Atlantic, I slept deliciously in this strange apartment, lulled to sleep by the hoarse roar of the sea as it rolled upon and retreated from the pebbly beach.

In the morning, after completing my toilette, in the natural and simple manner rendered necessary by the unsophisticated habits of the Tristandacunians, I sallied forth to take a walk before breakfast. Pathways led between the different enclosures down into the interior of the island as far as the cultivation extended. It was altogether a beautiful scene that met my gaze as I left the house and stood upon the mound to take a survey of the island. In the bay, sheltered by a projecting cliff, which rose almost perpendicularly from the deep water, lay the brig quietly at anchor, her own boat and one of those owned by the islanders both at her side, being laden with cargo to be conveyed on shore.

All around on land was perfectly still and composed, hardly a sound but the twitter of the birds singing in the early sunshine. South rose the dark mountain, capped with clouds, that occupied nearly half the island, ending the view in that quarter; the fields in the neighbourhood were rich with crops that were only awaiting the sickle—in some of them, indeed, the islanders were busily engaged in reaping wheat and oats, their staple produce, which seemed to ripen here, in sheltered situations, as early as potatoes. Extensive pasture lands lay beyond the corn-fields, in which the oxen and sheep browsed undisturbed. Here and there women made their way amongst the former, milking, occasionally tying up some unruly cow to a tree, or getting a sturdy urchin to assist them whilst the operation progressed.

The only men visible were those working at the brig, at this distance only faintly discernible, and the few, half-a-dozen, perhaps, who were reaping. One lounger, apparently an idle ne'er-do-weel, I noticed afterwards, lolling on a bank, half-dozing, half awake, when he ought to have been engaged in some description of work. The idle children who were about, speedily made acquaintance with me ; the bashful timidity of children brought up in civilized society was altogether wanting amongst them, and when they had once broken the ice of restraint, which they were not long in doing, their attentions were far from agreeable. One insisted on examining my watch, whilst a second pulled out my handkerchief, and displayed it to the rest, laughingly.

I was in danger of being utterly despoiled, when Mrs. Macrae's kind interposition saved me from further annoyance.

"Gude mornin' to you, freend," said she, "I ken ye'll be havin' an appetite for your breakfast the mornin'."

"Indeed you are quite right," said I ; "I feel hungry enough. I wanted, however, to have a little walk before I took it, to see something of your fine island."

"Aweel, aweel, you'll dae jist as you like 't

Wull ye tak yer breakfast wi' us or in yer own room? Mayster Glass 'll be always glad to see you, you ken, when you like."

"Thank you," I replied; "I'll take my breakfast in my own room this morning, if you please."

"Vera weel, and gude mornin'. My dochter will see till 't presently, but I've muckle to dae, I ken, an' I must not be standin' gossippin' here. Awa' wi' you, Jock; awa' wi' you, Barney, an' let the gentleman gang his gait in quietness."

Jock and Barney slunk away at the command, unhesitatingly. It was evident that Mr. Glass's family inherited his natural capability for governing, for Mrs. Macrae was a formidable woman in the colony. The idle loon who had been lounging on the sunny bank before, on hearing her voice, was labouring strenuously in a little garden adjoining, before her departure.

My appearance still excited considerable interest in the huts and cottages I passed—many of which, though differing much in external appearance, according to the industrious or idle habits of their inmates, were comfortable within. The women and children gazed on me as I passed through the fields or over the narrow pathways that led from the cottages towards the mountain, gazed upon me with interest, as Londoners would gaze upon a North American Indian in his national costume parading the streets of their metropolis.

But though rude in manners and unpolished, there was a healthy, hopeful air about everything in Tristan D'Acunha, that spoke eloquently in favour of the system of government which prevailed there. Prosperity made them contented for the most part. On the return of the schooner, Brody had informed me, drunkenness was the besetting sin of the colonists; for every family had its own supply of gin, which was imported of excellent quality from the Cape. It was Glass's policy, however, to prevent the distribution of the cargo until the vessel was laden again, a service which occupied the majority of the able men; and although there was much grumbling at this arrangement, there had never been any open revolt.

All the cargo, duly labelled, was stowed, as it arrived, in an empty cottage adjoining

Glass's residence, and one of the crew was obliged to mount guard in the neighbourhood, till the distribution took place, in order to give timely notice of any attempt at robbery. Such was the good sense of the majority, however, that attempts of this kind were rare; irregularities were severely punished in the most summary way, and, as the delinquents were shunned by the great mass of their friends when in fault, there was little temptation to outrage. The pressure of a full population, much less of any surplus, had not yet been felt, could not be felt for years—when it does, and Glass has been summoned to his fathers, who can tell what anxiety and outrage, violence and crime, may not prevail in the island? But that is a distant contingency, to which none of the colonists as yet look forward.

My breakfast was of the same homely, yet comfortable character, that pervaded all the arrangements of my abode. I waited, of course, upon myself, for such a thing as a servant was unknown in Tristan D'Acunha; and although Mrs. Macrae's daughter, a girl of thirteen or fourteen years of age, with the blue eyes and flaxen hair of the Highlands, and the tanned skin of the colony, would not disdain to bring me all that was requisite for breakfast—for it was woman's province in Tristan D'Acunha, as elsewhere, to look after the domestic arrangements of the table—yet she would have been highly offended at being required to do more than convey the necessary viands and utensils to their destination, and remove them when the meal was concluded.

I felt doubtful, indeed, as to whether I should not be expected to wash up the cup and saucer, the knives and plates I had used; and, lest I should give offence, when my young butler returned to remove them, I exclaimed,

"Wait a little, I havn't washed up the things yet."

"No, no, man," was her reply, for her Scotch was by no means so broad as that of her worthy parents; "no, no, man; I'se no want you to do that. Leave that to the lasses."

Having so said, and having wrapped her head up again in a handkerchief, she placed the breakfast things on a board, that answered the purpose of a tray, and tripped off lightly with them to her grandfather's, which was at some distance; her bare arms—already covered with a fine coating of hair—displayed the muscles that she had inherited from her robust parents to advantage.

I was engaged in smoking a contemplative cheroot after breakfast, wondering whether King Glass would do me the honour of visiting me or not, when I saw him advancing towards the house; it was not, however, with the intention of calling upon me that he came there, but to open the school-house—the large room of the building, which answered the purpose of the school-house, church, town-hall, and concert-room, for Brody had informed me that a few of the islanders had musical instruments, and gave concerts in the autumnal evenings.

Several young urchins, with the shaggiest possible heads, were playing about on the mound, not far from the door of my room, which always stood open, according to the habits of the colony. I thought these youthful gazers had been attracted there solely by my presence, and that they came to amuse themselves with a long leisurely stare, which they enjoyed, whilst I enjoyed my cheroot; but when the door of the large apartment had been opened, they rushed in tumultuously, a bell sounded, and other children, boys and girls, came bounding up the mound from all directions.

I left my cheroot forthwith on my portmanteau, and went into the school-room. Nothing could be more impressive than the aspect of the room as I approached it. The venerable chief stood, cap in hand, reverentially repeating the Lord's Prayer, whilst the little crowd of children, twenty to thirty in number, knelt here and there upon the floor, repeating it after him. A young man, whom I recognised as the lounger of the morning, was also present. Glass had installed him as his successor, not in the government of the island, but in that of the school; and, although his learning was by no means extensive, yet the young man was well qualified for the post, inasmuch as he spoke English better than most of the others in the island, and was fond of reading. It was apparent, however, that his increase of knowledge had by no means taught him content.

The Bible was the only book Glass read himself. He was not at all literary in his tastes, but his grandson had a history of the

French revolution, procured at the Cape, and Glass would occasionally listen to the account of the battle of Waterloo, in which his father, an artilleryman like himself, had lost his life. Napoleon, Wellington, and Glass, were the three heroes known to Tristan D'Acunha—they had heard of none others, and they were content with those three. Napoleon's captivity had caused the occupation of Tristan D'Acunha. Wellington and Waterloo had caused Napoleon's captivity, and Glass was the result! Such was their political creed, and they asked about nothing else.

Illiterate as he was, however, Glass made up for his want of cultivation, by the strong current of good sense and piety combined, which formed the most prominent characteristics of his disposition. He trusted in God and in his own strength, not without feeling a little proud of the position he held and the respect he commanded in his colony. He knew that he had been the suggester and the artificer of the scheme, and, as he looked around upon the smiling fields and comfortable cottages which occupied the northern plains of the island, he, doubtless, felt that he had much to be proud of, and that it was not every day that the world witnessed so complete a triumph; in a good and beneficial cause.

He was by no means a communicative man, rather, indeed, the reverse—reserved and of few words. His deeds spoke for him. Every cottage in Tristan D'Acunha, every field, every planted bush, every fence and hedge, spoke eloquently of what he had done—why should he, too, speak? He left it to these to proclaim what he was; he contented himself with managing wisely, and talking little. The rough, unrefined, illiterate good sense which he himself possessed, he had impressed upon the colony. All strove to imitate the hero of the island—after jealousies and quarrels had ended, and he had been unmistakeably acknowledged as the hero—all wished to be like him, naturally enough, and he was plain and unaffected, a man of one book, of much doing, and of little talking.

In subsequently conversing with Brody and his father, I found that the respectable inhabitants were quite contented with their lot, looking upon it as being far from a miserable one. There were others, however, who grumbled, as Englishmen always will; who regretted that they had ever set foot or been born in Tristan D'Acunha, and declared themselves and all around them wretched; but they were the idle or vicious, for the most part—those who did not labour with hearty good will, and, therefore, found their time hang heavily on their hands. Between the elder Brody and Glass there seemed to subsist a warm friendship. Each had the most entire confidence in the other—they were the only two remaining of the first male colonists. Of the women who had originally settled in the island, three survived.

Sunday was observed as a day of rest at Tristan D'Acunha — of rest, of meditation, and of innocent recreation. At noon the little congregation assembled, of thirty or forty persons. Glass read a chapter to them from the Old Testament. They then sang a hymn—one of the collection of Scotch psalms attached to the Scotch bibles. Another chapter was read from the New Testament, and a short commentary upon it by the young schoolmaster. A prayer was then offered up by the patriarch of the colony—a simple, earnest prayer, in which all the little wants and difficulties of Tristan D'Acunha were detailed, and the blessing of the Almighty invoked upon their labours. Lastly, a hymn was sung, a blessing was pronounced, and the congregation departed. Such religion does the heart good to contemplate. It is altogether different from religion in purple and fine linen—in fashionable assemblies of finely-dressed people, gazing and worshipping—altogether different from too much that one sees everywhere under the name of religion.

The rest of the day was spent by these, the more respectable part of the population, in walking about the fields—every one scrupulously neat and clean, even the children, rough sons and daughters of nature, had some little piece of finery on, to remind them that it was Sunday. Of the others, however, not a few were drunk.

I was not a witness of any burial in the colony, but the little mounds, with a board at the head of each, on which was painted the name and history of the deceased, showed that in their burials, as in every thing else, a decent simplicity reigned, pleasant to contemplate.

In such a place, however, an idler has no business; and, although I fully employed myself in excursions to the mountain, and in geological researches, yet I was not sorry when the Osprey was under way again. I bade farewell heartily to my honest, simple friends, leaving some little memorial with each; and, on the eighth day after I had landed, was sailing out of Glass Bay again, on my way to the Cape. On arriving there, I found Kabob had already made preparations for returning to Calcutta, and I speedily followed his example.

CHAPTER XI.

A GHOST STORY.

A GUN is fired upon the ramparts of Fort William, in Calcutta, every morning, to announce to the drowsy Anglo-Indians of the neighbourhood the first faint dawn of day. Those who are anxious to preserve their health in so uncongenial a climate, take warning by the gun, and, leaping from their couches, prepare for the usual morning walk or ride, before the increasing heat renders all exercise in the open air unpleasant or dangerous. The European quarter of the town—its "West End," in fact—called Chouringhee, is in the immediate neighbourhood of the Fort, so that the report of the early gun may be heard by most of the Anglo-Indians, if they wish.

Round the Fort stretches, as I have before mentioned, an extensive plain as level as a bowling-green, called the *maidaun*, a plain covered with brilliant green vegetation after the rains, but parched, brown, and sear, during the heats of April, May, and June. The *maidaun* is the usual scene of the pedestrian or equestrian exploits of the good people of Calcutta, first in the early morning, and again at the close of the day, when a delicious hour of coolness after the sun has set is snatched from the night. On three sides only, however, does this plain surround the Fort; on the fourth, the Hooghly, with its turbid, muddy waters, foul with human corpses, rushes along, a long narrow road alone separating the two.

Of all sacred rivers, the Hooghly is the muddiest and foulest. Hoarse-grumbling along on its earthen bed, it rushes on, ever bearing down to the ocean its horrid freight of dead men, women, and children chasing each other along in a race of death—their bleached bodies gleaming in the sunlight, ghost-like, out of the yellow murky fluid which surrounds them, and here and there, too, still more horrid to contemplate, dotted with crows tearing out their entrails, or quietly pluming themselves after their disgusting repast. Ever past the green glacis and picturesque ramparts of Fort William, glides the river sullenly along, the mouths of cannon looking down upon it like the eyes of monsters emerged from its own horrid depths.

Many such iron mouths does the Hooghly see on its course to the Indian ocean, as it hurries past the oriental spires of Moorshedabad, the Muhammadan minarets of Cossimbazar, the Hindu temples of Kutwa, or the Christian churches of Calcutta, for in close proximity to each of these are the death-dealing weapons of modern warfare, frowning grimly upon it, and telling of far other passions than the aspirations and fervour of religious devotion should give birth to.

Past the *dinghy*, or ferry-boat of the Hindu river-man, and the gig of the English merchant ship, and the junk of China, and the coir-bound uncouth bark of the Malays, the Hooghly glides by them all on its course, reflecting each as perfectly as its muddy nature will admit, and dashing its burden of human corpses indifferently against one or the other, as it hurries on with speed to the ocean. An impetuous, persevering monster this Hooghly, that tells the lazy Asiatic, with his luxurious do-nothingness, how work should be accomplished, how success can alone be achieved in these days—a lesson the lazy Asiatic, with his luxurious do-nothingness, will *not* learn, leaves rather for his European fellow-man to learn, and refuses utterly to study for himself—Fort William and the East India Company, English Governors-General and red-tape Members of Council the notable result.

The morning gun has fired, and we must be up and away, to breathe the fresh air whilst yet we may—whilst yet the sun remains hidden behind the salt lake and its vegetation, that lies to the east of the town. I want a companion for my morning's walk, and I insist on carrying off the reader with me—to a church-yard. Believe me, kind reader, we shall see much that is note-worthy at this early hour, as we cross the *maidaun* and make our way towards the road that skirts the river and separates it from the Fort. True, all is at present gloom, and the heavy mantle of night has not yet been fully lifted from the plain itself, or from the surrounding objects, but it will grow clearer, and the forms of objects will be more distinct, as we advance.

Before we reach Government House, the soft grey twilight of early dawn will reveal its noble proportions to us as we pass it on our right. Here, along this well-kept path, on which the drowsy native policeman is yawning himself awake, lies our road; he sees us, this gloomy-looking guardian of the peace, his dark face almost indistinguishable from his blue cotton suit, and the black helmet that reminds one of a japanned box. He recognizes the white dress of the *sahebs*, and is alert, vigorously asking the poor palanquin bearer that comes from his matutinal bath who *he* is!

Government House, the Governor-General's palace, is on our right—a right royal structure—not massive or sublime in its proportions, but large, well-designed, and rich-looking—suited to the climate, too, an important consideration. The Town Hall is also on our right as we make our way to the river, a building devoted to the spouting of enthusiastic orators, European and Asiatic, and to the balls of the fashionable world during the few months in which dancing is endurable in Calcutta.

The noise made by the political assemblies, and that caused by the exercise of "the light fantastic toe," and its accompaniments, are equally lasting and efficacious.

The Supreme Court and its offices of justice —where the blind goddess has long reigned supreme—are on our right too, as we draw near the shore. The history of this Supreme Court remains to be written, or rather of the Supreme Court, Union Bank and Co.—they were intimately united; for was not the Master in Equity of the one a Director of the other, when the shareholders lost their capital, and the constituents of the Bank their deposits, by its failure? Did not Sir Timothy Turtle and Mr. Grasp rule equally in the one establishment and in the other? Justice, however, is proverbially blind, and how could the Chief Justice, Sir Bland Trimmer, be expected to see through stone walls? How, indeed?*

* "What must be the state of society in India, when we find the majority of the officers of the highest judicial tribunal in the country lending themselves to the most glaring improprieties, and in not a few cases, to the most scandalous and heartless transactions? First in the lis of these official defaulters is the late Registrar and official administrator of the court, who, after having been

But we have better things to engage our attention than tales of corruption and abuses, such as those that the Union Bank suggests. Let us forget such, and press on to the Hooghly. Seen imperfectly through this hazy dawn, the tall masts of English merchantmen, that a few months ago towered above the East India Docks on the Thames, may be distinguished, and vessels, too, from a still farther land than England—vessels as noble, as grand, as stately in their swan-like grace,

involved in a variety of joint-stock gambling, wound up by resigning his office, leaving his accounts many months in arrears, and his cash-balance deficient to the extent of seventy thousand pounds. Next comes the Official Assignee and Receiver of the Court, who closely followed in the financial steps of his brother officer; he, too, resigned, leaving a deficiency of fifty thousand pounds, and a corresponding arrears of accounts; *this man is still retained in active employment by the Court.* The Taxing Officer of this tribunal took the benefit of the Insolvent Court in 1847; whilst the Master in Equity, and the Prothonotary of the Court, were both constantly occupied in bank matters and speculations to a great extent, and with ruinous results, in bank shares." *Capper's Three Presidencies of India*, p. 473. I am sorry to be obliged to bear my humble testimony to the truthfulness of Mr. Capper's picture of what Anglo-Indian society *was.*

riding triumphantly on the turbid river, their stars and stripes telling of the far west with its aspirations and its onward progress—a country living, not like Europe and Asia, on the fame of the past, but in the glory of the future—yes, *in* the future, for go where you will in the States, are you not told of what *will be*, not of what *is?*

And, besides these,—the symbols of two of the great branches of the Anglo Saxon race (to which a third and younger brother will soon be added from the far East and South),—may be seen battling with the Hooghly, to hold its place on the waters also, the unwieldy junk of the Celestials, with its two painted eyes staring fixedly, but unintelligibly, from its bows into the gloom ahead, and vacantly asking whither the present is driving *its* country, and getting no response from any quarter, no intelligence from gazing never so fixedly ahead. There is no light to be gained from such staring now-a-days; no light for an old nation, time-hallowed and venerable, shaking off almost effete ways and institutions to try novelties and new ways; no telling what such may result in, any more than if the huge leviathan of the ocean, that has long been safely moored to the shore, should be suddenly cast adrift again, and sent forth to do battle with the winds and waves and rocks, long ago fought with and vanquished—no telling decisively, truly, under such circumstances, but a suspicion of much evil unquestionably.

The Malay prahu may be seen here too, side by side with the American and the European, the Arab and the Chinese. Active Malay sailors are just beginning at this early hour to rouse themselves to the day's toils and struggles. The Malay is, in fact, the most active of Asiatics. He has all the excellences and all the defects of the Italian. A keen sense of the beautiful, and a worship of it — a quick sense of right and wrong,—a ready hand to revenge the latter with his well-kept *kreese* (his stiletto),—a no less quick and impulsive gratitude urging him to cast himself at the feet of a benefactor and adore him—with the depravities of the Italian too, the more debasing depravities, leading to utter destruction of body and soul. He is a worshipper of beauty, and ever-bountiful nature has surrounded him with beautiful forms—nowhere is vegetation more rich and luxuriant, nowhere is woman more delicately moulded, more finely formed, than in Malacca and the Eastern Archipelago.

An Arab vessel is not far off from the Malay, but there are no dusky figures gliding about upon it yet, for your true Arab is a veritable epicurean—stately withal in his devotion to enjoyment, giving a dignity to sensuality, by the thoughtful, preoccupied way in which he indulges in it—religion, woman, and his pipe, the three objects of his devotion, he begins the day with the first, and spends it with the last—they are all three too compatible in his mind, no harsh grating of the conscience disturbing his enjoyment; Muhammad his example, and Muhammad loved like him.

As we draw near the river, groups of talking Hindus and Muhammadans are emerging from it, having finished their ablutions—the women wringing out their long hair, and talking rapidly as they proceed—the men wringing out their wet clothes, and talking rapidly also—all talking, men, women and children—all always talking, as they walk along—no listeners, so far as I can discover.

The road which separates the river and the fort is a picturesque one, at this early hour. A few native soldiers are lounging about the banks or drying their clothes—an occasional European, in ghost-like white, paces stoutly along it, proud of his country and of himself, or gallops past on a fine Arab perhaps, proud of his country, of himself, and of his steed.

The determined seekers after what little health an Indian climate will allow to the exiled Englishman, may be seen regularly pacing, in monotonous lines, up and down the strand at this early hour. Some hold their European hat, the distinguishing symbol of their race, in their hands, that the faint morning breeze may play about their temples; others stalk past them shocked at such impropriety, who would suffer a thousand deaths rather than do anything strange or singular,—in complete costume—every portion of their attire unsuited to the climate. The air and the temperature of the city, the circumstances and condition of the citizens, demand loose robes for covering, but tyrant custom declares that the tight fitting vestures of more northern climes, and the unsuitable head-covering used under a very different sky, must be maintained—and so they *are* maintained.

The natives emerging from their bath in the muddy waters of their sacred river, the perambulating Europeans, the equestrians few and far between, and the occasional lounger in a carriage, yawning past, all combine to form a strangely varied scene, with lights and shadows, frames and fittings, background and foreground peculiar to itself. Out of Calcutta, there is probably no such picture to be seen in living reality as that presented by the banks of the Hooghly at this early dawn.

Let us extend our walk, however. Advancing towards the native part of the city, in a northerly direction, the vessels become thicker, the forests of masts more impenetrable, on our left, whilst on our right we see the bank of Bengal and some imposing-looking warehouses, that tell the stranger the busy commerce of the West has found its way to these distant shores and become a denizen of the soil. Turning up a street to our right, in which only a few servants are yet to be seen at their masters' gates, throwing earthen pots of water over their bodies,—an occasional door open here, and the venetianed blinds of a window opening there, we arrive at length at a burial-ground. There is a large old mouldering wooden tomb in its very centre. There is, as you say, little to admire in the tomb—its worm-eaten aspect and antiquated form tell of other days. Age comes swiftly on, amid the tropical life and growth of Calcutta, its heat and its humidity, and a tomb of fifty years ago looks as aged and venerable as one of centuries old in England.

There is a strange tradition connected with that old worm-eaten tomb. A large building in an adjoining square was erected by government as a residence for their young civilians on arriving in Calcutta. These young civilians are still called *writers*, and the long line of European-like houses was hence called Writers' Buildings, a name which it still retains. It has long ceased, however, to be a residence for the young rulers and judges and revenue collectors of Bengal, and consists now of storehouses and merchants' offices for the most part—the College of Fort William, as it is called, or the place where the neophytes are examined every six months in the vernacular languages, still occupying the centre.

When these Writers' Buildings were inhabited by a number of young men hardly out of their teens, who were being manufactured into magistrates, revenue-collectors, judges and secretaries, in the most economical way and on the shortest notice, there was a party of them collected together one dark night, carousing and amusing themselves with ghost stories. The neighbouring church-yard, that before which we stand, was mentioned as being haunted. A youthful despiser of the marvellous—nervous and headstrong—laughed at the superstitious tale.

"I'll bet you a hundred rupees," said one of his companions, in an overbearing way, "that you won't go and drive a large nail into the old wooden tomb in the middle of that church-yard this dark night."

"Done!" said the nervous aspirant—although not without a shudder at the idea.

It was a dark, dismal night. The wind howled in long melancholy gusts, like the wailings of departed spirits, through the long passages and among the intricate door-ways of Writers' Buildings. The rain, a fine, sand-like rain, was driven in masses by the wind, fitfully—rushing across the square, and into every casement, and against every door-way in the wildest way, as if seeking a refuge from the irregular blasts that lashed it along.

The young civilian wrapped himself up in a voluminous boat-cloak before facing the storm, and, nail and hammer in hand, issued into the square. The door closed behind him. The oil lamps—for the City of Palaces does not even yet boast gas—the oil lamps had been all extinguished. The night was dark, and not a living thing was to be met with in the streets.

Getting more and more nervous, more and more excited, as he advanced, the young man made his way along. He groped through the church-yard; the tombs dancing before him—as the wind swept over them, and the rain flickered in sheets—dancing before him, in a wild, warning maze. It was no joke to walk through the dark church-yard that gusty night, or to reach the wooden tomb in the midst, with the rain gushing like a cataract against his face, and the wind blowing the large boat-cloak about in a voluminous entangling way.

At length, his faculties wound up to a great effort, excitement wild within him, the young civilian gained the wooden tomb. He felt about for a convenient place to drive in the nail. It was a large nail, and the wood was soft. The hammer was raised, and the iron was easily driven into the half-rotten timber. His task was accomplished—but the tombs had been dancing before his eyes in an unearthly reel all the time, and he doubtless fancied a thousand spirits were shrieking at his unhallowed task, as the wind groaned amongst the tombstones, and whistled round the church-porch, and grated through the wire-protected windows. Twelve o'clock was booming forth from the tower.

His task was accomplished. He had driven in the large nail nearly to the head. With the hammer still in his hand, he turned to leave the gloomy burial-ground—turned quickly—was seized by the neck—was checked suddenly from behind—and fell, in a fit or faint, insensible to the ground.

Within the Writers' Buildings the revelry continued.

"The wager will be won," said one; "he

will return forthwith—a hundred rupees easily earned."

"I would not do it for a thousand," said another.

"That was he, as he shut the door behind him, that leads into the corridor," suggested the first.

No, it was but the wind.

"A glass to the ghost of the wooden tomb!" and, in heedless mirth, a bumper was quaffed all round, with much laughter.

"He delays long," is whispered round the table, as one after another peeps at his watch, and discovers that it is past twelve—he had been half-an-hour gone, and more. They drank, laughed, told tales again; half-an-hour more glided by. He had been more than an hour away! and the wind still blew and the rain still fell, sheet-like, as before. Faces that had been joyous grew more and more grave; flushed cheeks became pale; the mirth had given place to anxiety and alarm.

A few minutes more, and they issued forth in a body, with servants and lights, to see what had become of their friend.

They entered the church-yard. They advanced near to the wooden tomb, and there, upon the frowzy grass, lay their late boon companion, half shrouded in his boat-cloak,—insensible.

They examined his cloak. It was nailed to the tomb. In his hurry and agitation, he had driven the nail through the fold of his cloak, as he struck it home with hard, quick blows into the timber. He had turned, alarmed, agitated, excited, to depart—the cloak had grasped him by the neck, and, overpowered with sudden emotion, he had fallen sideways upon the ground.

When his companions lifted him from the ground, they found that they bore a corpse in their arms. He had fallen in a fit, from which he never recovered. Excitement and terror had killed him.

CHAPTER XII.

PER PORRINGER TO ADEN.

It is with pleasure that the exile of a few years turns his back upon the scene of his banishment, and commences the journey that is to lead him to the land of his birth and of early associations. Beautiful as may be the country; magnificent the buildings; picturesque the views, he leaves them all behind, without regret and without a sigh. Even the discomforts of a steamer, and the incessant tremor in which the luckless voyager is kept by the vibration of the machinery, are disregarded and made light of. The eye is fixed on a far distant shore, which presents attractions far superior to any other—attractions that the mind feeds upon during the long voyage without fear of satiety.

The Overland Journey from India to England—if one may be allowed to apply that term, as it is usually applied, to a journey of some thousands of miles by sea, and scarcely a hundred by land—is one of considerable variety and interest. It has been described over and over again, and it is not my intention to write much of what has been so fully discussed already. One part of the route, however, and that I think the most interesting—the Red Sea—has been generally dismissed with a few words only, whilst whole chapters have been written about Alexandria and Malta, Gibraltar and Point de Galle.

No one can help being struck with the aspect of Aden, who visits it for the first time. The traveller is approaching Arabia, that land of extraordinary associations and extraordinary history—a history of fitful activity, alternating with long periods of repose: the Red Sea is on his left, as the steamer labours along, and the inhospitable coasts of Africa and Arabia are in his immediate vicinity.

Situated on an iron-bound coast, with bleak rocks and gigantic volcanic cones in its immediate vicinity—volcanic cones once terribly active, doubtless, but now mute and at rest—the harbour of Aden has, to the eye of the wanderer over the ocean, all the attraction of the oasis in the desert to the weary traveller.

Few coasts, indeed, can compare with those of Arabia in bleak sternness and repulsive ruggedness. From the very jaws of the straits of Ormuz, leading into the Persian Gulf—the "Green Sea" of Asiatic geographers—to the Gate of Tears, as the poetic Orientals have styled the entrance into the Red Sea, a name which we use, losing its beauty, in the Bab-el-mandeb; throughout that vast extent of coast, there is an almost unbroken succession of rugged rocks and precipitous mountains, dashing headlong into the ocean, with shapeless accumulations of granite and lava scattered about in every direction, on the very water's brink. Nor is the prospect much improved to the traveller by pursuing his journey up the Red Sea.

The Gate of Tears, with all its dangers, seen and unseen, safely passed—its rapid currents which sweep the becalmed merchant vessel noiselessly to destruction, and ultimately cast it in malicious sportfulness upon the jagged rocks, which seem made to pierce a ship's bottom: its gusts of wind, which blow furiously and suddenly from either side, and lash the sea to fury and to foam, as it finds itself helplessly dashed against one sharp-pointed rock after another: its ugly rocks themselves, some peering aloft to heaven, stretching their long necks out of the ocean, as if to take a survey of the troubled sea around, whilst others hide themselves beneath the summit of the wave, lurking, as it were in ambush, for the unwary ship.—

These dangers passed—and man's ingenuity has sufficed to baffle and outwit them all—the iron-bound coast of Arabia stretches in a long line far away to the north and west, still rugged, still forbidding, still dangerous-looking and repulsive. Red and white mountains of rock—bare, unvariegated, monstrous rock—still exhibit themselves upon the water's edge, some playing calmly with the vexed waves, as they lash themselves into spray all around, others retired a little from the coast, and, looking down in ugly grandeur upon the scene of commotion near their base. Such are the characteristics of the coast of Arabia.

It is not to be wondered at, then, that the voyager—as he sweeps round the bases of the rocky bluffs that long hid the harbours of Aden from his eye, and sees within the comparatively still water, and the few English colliers and Arab ships that trade to the port—feels a relief as if a load were taken off his mind, and, unoppressed by the weight of the gigantic debris of a former world, he could breathe freely once more. Not that the reader is to fancy a smiling village, and green fields, and pleasant country seats, dotting the margin of the landscape, as a companion picture to the few masts and hulls, and the peaceful harbour of which I have spoken.

By no means. As our noble vessel, one of the Peninsular and Oriental Company's Steamers, the *Porringer*, swept gracefully round the projecting bluffs, and gradually opened up the harbour within to our anxious gaze, we looked in vain for the pretty village which we had associated with the name of Aden.

"Aden, in Arabia," says the imagination, "on the very coast—with a fine harbour well-enclosed by lofty mountains—what a delicious scene it must be! The minarets of the distant mosque, sparkling in the sunshine, and the white flat roofs of the houses, with the orange trees and palms just peeping above them from the luxurious gardens of the Orientals; the coffee bushes on the distant hills so gracefully relieving the grander features of the primeval forests, and speaking of cultivation and peaceful happiness."

Peace, imagination, peace—a truce to your reverie—nor coffee-bushes, nor primeval forests, nor luxurious gardens, nor palm-trees nor orange, nor flat roofs, nor distant mosques, are here—the scene is totally different, as different from such a one as you have pictured as a scene can well be. I am still on the deck of the *Porringer*, surveying the landscape with what enthusiasm I can muster for the occasion. Right in front of us are three Newcastle colliers, lately arrived, to feed the insatiate steamers—dirty, and black, and repulsive, as colliers do look, and, perhaps, ought to look, everywhere. Eleven thousand miles of ocean which they have traversed have not sufficed to wash them clean. By the side of them are a few Arab vessels, looking as if made of shreds and patches from all others, without much distinctive character or anything particular to make them interesting—rather, indeed, the reverse, for their sailors are the most repulsive of living men.

Ladies or gentlemen who travel in Egypt or Arabia must not be over-nice—if they wish to see the lands of the sun, they must take them as they find them—to us, however, it does seem a refinement of indecency for those brawny black wretches — black almost as negroes—to wear a woollen jacket that covers their shoulders, and buttons over their hairy breasts, partially concealing them, whilst they leave all the rest of their ugly persons naked in their massive, muscular development. And in this costume, *proh pudor*! they will crowd to the sides of their vessels, or by the banks of the canals in Egypt, to watch modest Europeans going on their way rejoicing.

I have seen such a monster actually offer to assist an English lady into a boat to take her ashore, and, instead of turning and flying into the sea, the lady had the good sense smilingly to accept the proffered assistance, and graciously to reward it! When one hears of an Australian native—half-monkey, half-man — getting a soldier's coat, and, with a stick over his shoulder to represent a musket, marching soldier-like through the streets of Sydney or Melbourne,—innocent the while of any other particle of clothing,—one does not feel so much astonished at it. Sydney and Melbourne lie east of refinement, but in Arabia and Egypt, and the Holy Land, one looks for better things, and does not expect to be shocked so outrageously.

By the side of these few Arab vessels, lying rather behind them, is moored the Bombay steamer, the *Agility*,—a steamer proverbially slow, even for Bombay,—which, by dint of leaving that port the day after the *Porringer* left Calcutta, has contrived to arrive at Aden in time with her passengers and mails, which we are now to take on to Suez. A few boats pass backwards and forwards in the harbour, rowed for the most part by those brawny Arabs in their easy *negligé*. These boats are of various sizes and shapes; and when they have been added to the colliers, the native coasting vessels, the *Agility* and the *Porringer*, the entire contents of the harbour have been enumerated.

But the shore? Well, we are coming to that. Before us rise huge masses of rock, principally of a brick-red colour, as though an Australian brick-fielder had just swept over them, covering them with the reddest possible dust. Here and there a whiter portion of the rock may be faintly discerned—not that the contrast is striking, but on looking attentively one *does* perceive that the entire masses of rugged rock-mountains, with their jagged pinnacles, are not quite uniform in colour. In other places, indeed, it is slightly darker, not by any means approaching to black, but a decidedly dark red, like brick for some time exposed to the weather.

At the base of these forbidding mountains, red dust, like sand, is strewn, sinking into the waves in shingle and rock. Rocks and sand are before us, sand and rocks are behind. On our right hand rocks and sand alone are visible as far as the eye can reach, and sand and rocks on the left. Fantastic in form, varying in outline, with even some varieties of colour, too, amongst them, but still the same—rocks and sand every where, sand and rocks on all sides. One irregular flat-roofed building alone breaks the monotony of the shingly, sand-covered beach—it is on our right hand, and is a kind of hotel and store, where, at enormous prices, various articles, eatable and other, may be procured.

But the town, the village, the port—Aden? Surely the one house on the sandy beach, shingle-covered, with rocks and sand all round it, does not constitute the town? exclaims some energetic and impatient reader. Certainly not. Hidden behind a rocky promontory, with an ugly shed peeping out towards the beach, is the Custom House, or the building which answers the purpose of such, and a few Arab huts are to be found, I believe, in its immediate neighbourhood. But even these do not constitute the village of Aden. Far away, in the crater of an extinct volcano,—three miles away at least,—the village lies, snugly imbedded in a huge amphitheatre of stone, and scarcely have our Arab friends, in their untrammelling costume, landed us upon the beach, than we desire to visit it, and are determined, indeed, to make the attempt. Till to-morrow morning the *Porringer* will have the black stream, which feeds her fires, pouring into her—till daylight she cannot leave the harbour, so that we have plenty of time.

But how are we to get there? How to make our way from the hotel to the village imbedded in the rocks, three miles away? Walk, suggests the unsophisticated reader; nay, good reader, walking in Arabia, in the south of Arabia, within almost hailing distance of the hottest part of Africa, will not do. A walk of three miles from Charing Cross to Bayswater, or through May Fair, is practicable enough, in winter or summer, but a walk of three miles in the south of Arabia at midday is a totally different thing. Besides, even were it safe or practicable, who would think of walking in Arabia? is it not the land of camels and dromedaries, of horses and mules, of he-asses and she-assès?

All around the hotel, their feet sinking deeply in the sand and shingle on the beach, are animals prepared for the road. Horses, and mules, and donkeys with strange-looking saddles on their backs, and stranger bipeds at their heads, are looking mournfully at us, as though well aware that their mission for this day, at all events, is to scamper over the well-known road, if road that can be called which is *no* road, to Aden, each with one of us on his back. There are side-saddles, too, for the ladies—yes, decent, Christian-looking side-saddles, evidently not Arab—for Arab ladies do not require such—they wear the bloomers, and ride accordingly.

A more awkward collection of quadrupedal animals than that which is drawn up on the beach before us, it would not be easy to discover elsewhere. The length of the ears of the horses astonishes the new-comer; their bony frames, too; one might almost be inclined to suppose that rocks and not bones distended their knee-joints, and produced the angularities of their outer surface. "Good horse, saar!" says the conductor of the steed, and, to show off his paces, jumps on his back and scampers madly over the shingle and the sand, and between huge masses of rocks, in an eminently reckless manner. He has come back, however, safe and sound, and whilst the ill-used animal mildly blows himself into wind again, his dismounted rider repeats his eternal "good horse, saar!—go to Aden, saar!" which words, indeed, compose his entire available stock of English.

"One is a long distance from the ground on such an animal as that," muttered my fat friend Mealy, as he stroked down his fierce-looking moustache, and wiped his mild eyes free from dust.

"And, of course, has further to fall than from a donkey's back?" I asked.

"Yes, of course." replied Mealy; "they tell me the road to Aden is all climbing up rocks and amongst stones—in fact, that there is no road at all. I shall certainly take a mule or a donkey."

"And I'll try Rozinante," said I, jumping on his back, to the great delight of the grinning Arab, who now proposed to accompany me on foot, continually exclaiming, notwithstanding all I could say, "Good horse, saar!—go to Aden, saar!" propositions which he kept uttering in every key and in every variety of intonation from the moment he had brought the animal towards us, until we actually set off for Aden. It was useless to correct him, however, or to attempt to check him, for he did not understand a word I said; so at length

I accommodated myself as best I could to the muttered and shouted ejaculation, "good horse, saar!—go to Aden, saar!" constantly ringing in my ears.

Having inspected a mule which he found dead lame, Mealy at length determined on trying a stout-looking donkey, and mounted accordingly. We had expected to see noble animals of the asinine kind in Aden, for were we not in Arabia? and who has not heard of the superiority of the Arab asses? of their height and strength, their beauty and their docility?

The passengers by the *Porringer* must have been singularly obtuse, however, or the asses in Aden were an exception to the rule, for we could recognize no difference in outward appearance between them and the every-day donkey in England or India. Our fellow-passengers were now widely scattered over the beach, some mounted on horses, some on mules, some on asses; some trying the mettle of their steeds by reckless galloping over the uneven and stone-strewn shore, others carefully picking their steps along, but all with their animals' heads turned towards Aden, and all with a wild-looking native behind, who was either fluttering along at a hand-gallop after the labouring steed, or quietly quarrelling and abusing another Arab as the two walked after their more sober employers. Those only who had seen Aden before, remained on board, or hired boats from the shameless Arabs to explore the harbour and its shores.

We were a polite company, we passengers by the *Porringer*, and so the ladies were accommodated with the best steeds, and some of them became them well, although their absurdly long riding-habits did not suit the road, and greatly puzzled the Arab attendants. These latter wretches were constantly making plunges at the saddles to see that all was right, and as they dived under the ladies' riding-habits and were lost for a moment in the folds, there was great fun and great screaming —fun on our part, screaming on that of the ladies.

"You go, sare! how you dare pull my leg dat way?" cried out a French countess of our party, after one of those intermittent plunges, at the same time shaking her whip at the offending attendant.

"Ver good saddle, ver good horse, mame," said the attendant, soothingly, quite ignorant of the cause of offence.

"You take care, sare, not for to come near my horse again," said the countess; but blackey was already deep in a wordy warfare with a neighbouring Arab, and heeded her not; nor, had he heard her, would he have been much wiser as to her wishes.

The Count Rotamotin, who rode by her side, was rather amused at the occurrence than otherwise, and contented himself with laughing heartily at his wife's discomfiture.

"You don't speak English well enough, my love," said he, soothingly, "for this man to understand."

The Countess was indignant, and remained silent. In a few minutes she cantered off gracefully, the Count accompanying her, leaving us far behind.

"Shall we try a trot?" said I, to Mealy.

"I have no objection to make the trial," was the reply, "although I fear it will be a vain one."

A smart cut of the whip sent Rozinante off into a subdued canter; he did not know how to trot, had evidently never been taught; and donkey, with Mealy on his back, not liking to be left behind, exerted himself to the utmost to keep up with us.

"Hurra! for long and thin, and short and stout!" shouted some uproarious fellow-passengers as we darted past them, our Arab attendants bounding over the shingle and sand in a wonderfully careless, easy-going manner, with bare feet, too—my self-constituted groom still muttering at intervals, *sotto vocè*, "good horse, saar! go to Aden, saar!"

"You and Rozinante are well matched," said Mealy (laughing at us), as he laboured on a little in the rear; "you want but the armour and the spur, and a coat of whitewash over the steed, to personate Don Quixote to the life."

"And now that you put me in mind of it, Mealy," was my reply, "what an admirable impersonation of Sancho you do make—donkey and all."

Thus complimentary on each other, we made our way pleasantly along, bantering and being bantered, as odd horsemen or energetic parties swept past us or were distanced by us.

The beach was soon left behind, and, whilst a rough, uneven mountain rose precipitately on our right, straight before us was the volcanic cone, broad-based, and round-shouldered, which contained Aden in its hidden recesses near the summit. On our left spread out as bleak and desolate a prospect as even Arabia or Africa could present. Distant hills of primeval granite, shining barely and bleakly in the rays of the sun, which coquetted with their angularities and recesses, sunk down into level plains of red sand, variegated by rocks of every hue and size, all stern, repulsive, wild and lifeless.

As we advanced into the hills, and saw more distinctly the summits which we were approaching, here and there interspersed with battlements and walls thrown up by British engineers against Arab marauders, battlements promising to make Aden what Gibraltar long has been, impregnable—as we advanced into the hills and discovered these things, I say, the extent and variety of the masses of stone which lay about us on every side surprised us more and more.

It was as if giants had been flinging rocks about in sport, and heaven had been raining shingle to fill up the ugly chasms the rough giants had left—rocks of enormous size, of middling size, of small size, some dark from continued exposure to the weather, others lighter in colour, rested in every possible way on every possible ledge and projection—some standing on narrow ridges on the hill's side, as though suddenly arrested in their descent, and waiting a favourable moment to tumble on the passing traveller; others, broadly based upon wide rocky promontories, massive, firm, immovable. Grey stones and sparkling granite, and dark trap were strewn all about in admirable confusion, all volcanic or plutonic, telling of nature's combats and the results, but no sign of vegetation, no blade of grass, no wandering creeper to relieve the eye, or whisper faintly of vegetable nature.

Here and there the ribs of a camel scattered about were eloquent of suffering and death—suffering and death endured by that most patient and most miserable of animals. Who that has heard the whining lament of the young camel, as it moves uneasily its graceless limbs about, can help feeling for it and for its race? It cries continually—it seeks helplessly about for food or comfort—food it may get, but comfort apparently never—it never gambols like the young of other animals, every movement seems to be accompanied with pain. No one ever yet saw a young camel frisking joyfully about its mother, happy in itself and the source of happiness in others, as lambs and foals are—no, its severe life is one of early misery, crowned by later suffering and a wretched death.

The tourist who has visited the deserts of the Indus or the dreary confines of the vast Sahara of Northern Africa, will find the camel still the same; and that its life is just as wretched on the elevated plains of Thibet, and amid the salt deserts of Persia, every traveller's account assures us. There is something inexpressibly affecting in those memorials of the most patient of animals, which one meets so constantly in the dreariest places of Oriental travel—the bones of the camel are landmarks over the desert, they are like the wreck at sea, that speaks of a gallant vessel broken up and destroyed—who shall tell with what misery and hardship the tale of its loss, if rightly told, would abound?

A strange sight it was to see this dreary region of rocks and sand, dotted over with life and vigour—men and women, of various, and for the most part, of far distant climes, with horses, mules, and asses, all busily urging on their way, and almost all in one direction—a long string of camels, the nose of the one behind tied to the tail of the one before, alone making its way, slowly, solemnly, silently along, in the opposite direction.

The camels' bones were unheeded even by the camels themselves, and, as they journeyed on laboriously, one could not help fancying that they had too many sorrows of their own to attend to, to waste a thought on those of others. Some of our fellow-passengers were now climbing the narrow gorge through which alone entrance can be obtained into the strange caldron-like valley in which Aden lies imbedded,—they and their steeds dotting the sides of the eternal hills curiously—the only signs of life where all else was sternly bleak and wildly desolate.

CHAPTER XIII.

A LUNCH IN THE CRATER OF A VOLCANO

At length it came to our turn to ascend the rugged hill before us. At its base, however, a strange-looking cavern on our right attracted my observation, and, as it was inaccessible to the quadrupeds, I dismounted and climbed to it. There was nothing particular either in its aspect or situation, and was of far less extent than I had anticipated. I therefore speedily descended, and found Mealy sitting on a rock waiting for me. He, too, had dismounted, partly to relieve his donkey, and partly to cool himself. He looked as if he were moralizing inwardly upon the vanity of human and asinine life.

With a huge pith hat covering his head and eclipsing his features, his rotund figure cased in white, looked like a bag of flour thrown carelessly on the rock with a white umbrella above it. He was supporting his chin on his hands, and his elbows on his knees, his eyes resting mournfully on the plump donkey which stood before him, motionless, and reflective perhaps, as himself. His Arab groom was lying at full length by the ass's head, whilst my Rozinante was held at some distance by his owner, who reclined uneasily on the sharp rocks. It was altogether a picture worthy of the pencil of a Cruikshank, or the pen of Punch himself to delineate.

I sat down by Mealy, and we watched several fellow-passengers disappearing in the gorge above, whilst a Bombay soldier on guard, paced mechanically backwards and forwards like an automaton—and truly an automaton he was, wound up, clock-like, by his matutinal meal, to pace backwards and forwards under those formidable masses of masonry above him, for so many hours without cessation. A well-trained monkey would do as much with equal effect.

"There go the Countess and her husband," said Mealy, as they disappeared in the pass, "we shall be late for the luncheon;" so, springing up, he proceeded to mount his donkey.

I was speedily walking on quietly, Rozinante evidently disposed to take it easy, when I heard the sounds of blows, and imprecations too in choice English and Arabic, all showered upon the plump-looking donkey, who did not feel disposed to go. I turned round. Seated in the saddle, Mealy was belabouring the unfortunate animal with his light riding-whip, making as much impression on the tough hide beneath him, as he would have made with that implement on the rock which he had just left. His Arab groom laid on more heavily behind with a walking-stick, stopping every now and then to see what effect his blows had. They had none—a fact which, speedily discovered, was the cause of a renewal of the flagellation.

At length, seizing the bridle, Arab pulled with all his might forward, and donkey, as resolutely, threw his weight to the rear.

"Stop!" said I, "I'll bring Rozinante up

by his side, and, perhaps, he may persuade the beast to move."

For a moment the blows ceased, even the kindly wishes showered upon the asinine head were hushed. Rozinante stalked gravely with his long legs by the side of his diminutive companion; it even struck me that he looked reproachfully at him, as if such conduct were not what ought to have been expected in *his* company. The asinine head stuck out the long asinine ears as if meditating a move, and then, as we passed on, quietly replaced them on the neck. It was still no go; and, as a fresh shower of blows descended on the imperturbable donkey, I could not help laughing at his repose, and the sweltering heat into which he was putting Mealy and the groom.

At length, my groom, assistant, or guardian, whichever he might be considered, went to their assistance. Planting himself behind the contumacious donkey, he placed his back against the animal's tail, and, sticking his feet furiously into the shingle, pushed with all his might, whilst Arab number two pulled vigorously in front, and Mealy belaboured in the middle. But all to no purpose! Donkey's feet were resolutely set for a shove backwards, and the united force of the three did not stir him an inch.

"Do you know," said I to Mealy, "that animal must be remarkably strong to withstand all that?"

"And as obstinate as—" replied Mealy, his simile broken short by a fresh volley of abuse in choice Arabic, to which the donkey submitted uncomplainingly.

"You will have to dismount," said I, at length.

"I fear I shall," was the reply; "I am in an extempore bath as it is, and a continuation of this will melt me."

"And the luncheon?" I suggested.

Mealy was off in a moment.

"Good! good! ver good ass, saar!" shouted the groom when he saw him alighting; and, taking the bridle, he proceeded to turn donkey's head towards the harbour. The donkey moved round without the slightest difficulty, and his groom then proceeded to turn him dexterously round three or four times, Mealy and I admiring the manœuvre, until at length, he ceased, walked him on a little, and then showed by signs that donkey was now ready to proceed. With the patience of a martyr, Mealy mounted again, and we walked on quietly side by side, as if nothing particular had happened. Nor did donkey again exhibit his strange idiosyncracy.

Cantering quietly up the pass, we at length entered the gorge leading into the snug little valley in which Aden is situated—a gorge that nature has herself rendered almost impregnable, and which man, with the aid of rocks, mortar, and cannon, has rendered completely so. There is certainly no power in Asia to take Aden, whatever the more advanced science of continental Europe may be able to accomplish. The nation which rules the Indian ocean must inevitably be also the ruler of this rock-bound fortress, for, useful as stone is to keep out intruders, it will not do for food; and, as all the supplies for the garrison must be brought from sea, the possession of the harbour of Aden must lead to the possession of the fortress itself.

A descent of a few minutes' duration brought us into the middle of the little town. Nestled in the very centre of a semicircular valley, with jagged peaks rising on every side,

Aden is, perhaps, unique in its position. It is not likely that human necessity or human ingenuity has established a town anywhere else, in the very middle of the crater of a volcano—an extinct volcano, it is true, but still what once was a volcano, undoubtedly. One cannot help speculating, indeed, on what would probably be the effect of the volcano's renewal of its activity, and where Aden would be in that case!

In itself, independent of its extraordinary position, the town presents little that is interesting or striking to the eye of the visitor—the rugged peaks, with their well-worn summits, ever pointing heavenward, which surround it, are its chief features of interest. A detachment of Bombay troops constituted the garrison, their lines forming a distinct quarter of it. Some of the men we found had been two years in the town, without having once extended their peregrinations beyond the limits of the little valley—they were living, in fact, in a rock-caldron—a caldron in more senses than in its shape merely—and they had no desire to see what was round it.

The wildest of nature's scenes lay within

short distances on every side; the boundless ocean to the south, the rugged hills of Arabia to the north; but they recked not of such, they were perfectly contented to live as they had lived, without an eye to see the glories of creation, or a heart to feel them! Other Orientals, shop-keepers and such-like, had lived for still longer periods within the dreary confines of the rock-bound valley, some of them, indeed, ever since the English occupation of it, without once passing the frowning battlements that secured them from the lawless aggression of the Bedouins.

The educated Englishman, condemned to pass any large portion of his life in such a place, is surely to be pitied. What number of rupees or gold mohurs can recompense a man for selling the best years of his life in such a way? or be an adequate remuneration for burying himself alive in the crater of a volcano, from which he is, *perhaps*, afterwards to emerge, mentally unsuited by habits and tastes for the distant land he has left, or physically unable to endure the vicissitudes of its climate? Such a life is spent in regretting the past and abusing the present—in sighing in

Aden for what has been relinquished in England, and again in grumbling in England for the want of physical luxuries enjoyed in Aden!

The town itself presents the usual aspect of the black town or pettah of an Indian city. It has little or nothing to distinguish it from the native quarters of Madras or Colombo—the same thatched or tiled roofs—the same exhibition of articles of commerce in the verandah—the same lazy shopkeepers voluble of tongue and indolent of body — the same groups of half-naked or entirely naked children, of every shade of brown, from the whity-brown of well-milked coffee, to the deepest black of the negro.

The Muhammadans are, as usual, the most energetic of the native populace, jumping to their feet at the sight of an intending purchaser, with an alacrity that it makes the more sluggish Hindu hot to contemplate. The only hotel in the town, if hotel it could properly be called, was kept by a Muhammadan, and, as an express had been sent on previously to tell the proprietor to have a first-rate luncheon ready, we expected to find every thing comfortably prepared for our reception.

We found the Count and his lady, with three other fellow-passengers, awaiting our arrival, and, in a few minutes, were informed that our meal was ready for us. There was little at the table save English biscuits that we could eat; but, if the viands were bad, the various beverages with which they were to be washed down were good, and we complained little.

Refreshed and exhilarated by what we had taken, we proceeded to inspect the town on foot—Mealy escorting the Countess, and the rest of us following without much order or regularity. We met various groups of our fellow-passengers in the course of our peregrination, all, like ourselves, looking very red and very hot, and very much determined to enjoy themselves before being again shut up in our floating prison.

Having contrived to make the acquaintance of the Commandant, Mealy obtained a decent horse from him, with which to ride back to the shore, and therefore accompanied the Countess, telling her Arab guardian that if he proceeded to take any liberties with her feet—the lady herself said "legs," but Mealy knew that was a mistake—he, Mealy, would lay his horse-whip over the offender's shoulders unmercifully.

To enforce his words, my benevolent friend looked as fierce as possible, whilst his dragoman for the occasion (one of the Commandant's servants) was translating all that he said. The Arab explained that he had merely been putting the saddle right, as these female-saddles, as he described them, were very likely to become displaced on a road with so many ascents and descents as that from Aden to the shore.

"Leave the care of the lady and her saddle to me, sir," was Mealy's energetic and imperative reply, "or else—" and with that he carved imaginary welts out of tawny's back with the horse-whip.

The Arab said no more; the last argument being unanswerable.

With the exception of having once to stop in order to adjust the Countess' saddle, for which purpose she alighted, we reached the harbour in safety—Mealy escorting the lady and "witching the world with noble horsemanship" the while, whilst the Count and I rode on quietly behind. It was quite evident, however, from the entire displacement of the "female-saddle," occasionally that Arab's plunges into the lady's riding habit were far from useless, however inconvenient to the horsewoman. Arrived at the shore we found those abominable native sailors, in their own original costume, ready and anxious to take us on board. The shades of evening were fast gathering round us, however, and we were not particular, so, making our way cautiously into the largest boat we found in the vicinity, we were speedily deposited, in perfect safety, upon the quarter-deck of the *Porringer*, feeling tired after our journey and pleased at our return, just as if the ship were really our home, and Aden only a Kew or a Richmond in its vicinity.

The heat in the Red Sea, as we steamed rapidly through its luke-warm waters, was intense, and there was just sufficient of a favourable wind to prevent our feeling any agitation of the air whatever, inasmuch as the wind travelled *pari passu* with us—had it been against us, or from any other quarter, indeed it would have been cooling and refreshing, but no—directly up the sea it blew, keeping pace with us as easily as an English race-horse would with an Aden donkey at full speed, but not outstripping us, nor leaving us an inch behind. A truly tantalizing wind!

"Were I the Captain," said Mealy, energetically, during a melting mood one day, "I would turn the ship's head round and stop her for an hour every day, if it were only to prove that there really is a wind, and to get the vessel aired a little. What's the use of a man's constantly making an assertion and then reiterating it over and over again, if he can't prove it—particularly such an assertion as that, so easily capable of verification if true?"

"But you must remember," said I, "that we and the wind are going in the same direction, at about the same speed—hence it is we don't feel it, hence it is the smoke ascends so quietly and perpendicularly from the funnel; were there no wind, the smoke would be left behind, and we should feel the air being cut through by the vessel."

"All which amounts to this," quoth my fat friend; "that there is a wind because I don't feel it, but if I *did* feel it, there would be no wind."

"A strange way of putting it truly," was my reply, "but not the less a correct one."

"Now look here," said he, argumentatively, "here's this chess-board. I say the chess-board is here, because I both see it and feel it, but if I could feel it only, I should still be sure of its proximity to me; now to apply your lógic and the Captain's, if the chess-board could not be seen or felt it would be here, but if it were not here, it would certainly be felt. Why, sir, do you suppose that any man of ordinary sense—hang it, sir! I'm not—"

"The chess-board and the wind,"—I began interrupting him, but it was too late. Indignant Mealy had risen from his seat, and, mopping his bedewed countenance energetically, he turned and went away in a rage.

After the bleak rocky shores of the south of Arabia, and of the island of Socotra, which we coasted shortly before entering the Red Sea, the first glimpse of Mocha and its environs was a relief both to the eye and to the mind. Since we had left the tropical luxuriance of Ceylon, not a green spot of any extent had refreshed our sight. Rocks,—bare, rugged, bleak, stern, impracticable rocks—had bounded our view on every side, whether we looked towards Asia or Africa, and now, as if from the waters of the ocean, by enchantment, rose a fairy city and a fairy scene. The white roofs and the glistening minarets, and the rich green which formed a background to the picture, and even covered the hills behind, were all so unlike what we had seen, and what we had been gazing at for so many days, that we regarded the entire panorama with great interest and pleasure.

Had we landed and inspected the town, our impressions of it would have been different I was told—narrow, filthy streets, the hot sun drawing up reeking pollution and the most abominable complication of vile smells to be found out of Lambeth, from the offal-strewn lanes and byways. But all this we were spared—of all this we could see nothing from the shore,—nothing but the white house-tops shining joyously in the twinkling sun-shine, nothing but the glistening minarets with their picturesque heaven-pointing ornaments, nothing but the vivid green of the trees contrasting so richly with the bleak red and brown of the rocks and the yellowish green of the sea. It was a bright spot in the bleak panorama passing before us, such as the eye and the memory love to dwell upon—a bright spot suddenly disclosed and rapidly lost, lost before we had been satiated with gazing upon it, and hence the more regretted.

The very name, Mocha, is so associated with coffee, that our excellent Captain astonished us that day at dinner, when he informed us no coffee was now exported, or had for a long time been exported thence—that the cultivation of the shrub there had gradually been diminishing, and that the production was not sufficient to supply the demand of the neighbourhood.

"Then where does all the Mocha coffee come from?" asked twenty voices in a breath.

"I'm telling you a simple fact," replied Captain Spoon, blandly, "I do not pretend to explain every thing connected with it. This I am sure of, the Mocha coffee does not come from Mocha, so I suppose it comes from somewhere else."

This was allowed to be a very sensible supposition, and the matter was set at rest after sundry "*dear me's!*" and "*well now's!*" accompanied by looks of virtuous surprise—calling things by wrong names astonished us all.

Chess, back-gammon, draughts, cards, and even quoits, formed the chief amusements on board the *Porringer* during the weary voyage up the Red Sea—yes, quoits too, quoits made of rope, instead of iron, and pitched into circles instead of at a peg, a very inferior game to the original, but still sufficiently amusing and scientific to wear away an idle hour when one is in anticipation of that most melodious of sounds in an "Overland" steamer, the dinner bugle. No man can fail to recognize ever after the tune of the "Roast Beef of Old England," who has steamed from Ceylon to Suez, so eagerly are the notes listened for, so musical do they sound to those who for four or five weary hours of oppressive heat have not known what to do with themselves.

Day after day the same wearisome monotony of rocks and sand presented itself, sometimes nearer, sometimes more distant, but constantly the same. Doubtless, the shapes of the rocks varied, although even that fact some were hardy enough to dispute; but that was the only change—in every other respect it was like a vast panorama of red and white rock-mountains, relieved by red and white shingle and red and white sand, stretching along interminably on either side.

Even the excellent view afforded us, as we entered the Gulf of Suez, of Mount Sinai, and the interesting group of which it forms the centre, was scarcely sufficient to rouse our curiosity or excite us to animation. Like the rest, like a thousand others that we had left behind —only a little more distant and more loftier— its tall jagged cliffs and precipitous summits stood bleakly, desolately, prominently forth, clearly traced upon the glistening, reddish-blue of the sky behind, without a single peculiarity to distinguish it from the numerous similar mountains we had passed. But what it wants in physical features association supplies—none who allow that association to act, can pass it without peopling the base of the rugged mountain with a vast multitude, their straggling cattle gleaning a scanty subsistence in the adjacent valleys, whilst they peer anxiously into the mysterious cloud that envelopes the summit, into which cloud their law-giver has passed, and in which he has disappeared.

Such a scene is easily traced upon the surrounding desert by the pencil of the imagination, and he who has once traced it there, will not willingly let the remembrance die. Nor will he regret the fatigue or *ennui* of a monotonous voyage, if it leads to such consummations as a distant view of the wondrous Sinai, and opens the portals of a land so famed in Biblical and classical history as the land of Egypt.

As we gazed upon the wilderness in which, for so many years, the wandering Israelites journeyed to and fro, preparatory to entering upon the Promised Rest, we could not help remarking to each other, that, in such a place, it was no wonder they should long again for the flesh-pots of Egypt, or look back with sighs to the banks of the Nile and the verdant country they had left. Those who feel astonished at the ungrateful conduct of the Israelites, have but to take a comparatively easy voyage up the Red Sea in order to persuade themselves that murmuring, discontent, and rebellious reproaches were the natural results of their position—that content and gratitude would have been unnatural and therefore improbable. The blessings of freedom they were by no means disposed to weigh against the material advantages of Egypt—the iron of slavery had entered into their souls, and was still rankling there.

CHAPTER XIV.

THE OMNIBUSES OF THE LAND OF GOSHEN.

The bleakly monotonous voyage from Aden to Egypt is fitly ended by the desert city at which the voyager lands. Suez, like Aden, is a city *sui generis*, not probably to be found paralleled elsewhere. Yet it is most unlike Aden. Here there are no frowning mountains of volcanic rock, no wild scenery that puts one in mind of the *debris* of giants' battles. All is level, or merely undulating, far as the eye can reach—undulating sand, unvaried desert. For miles out to sea from the town itself, the water is so shallow, that the boatmen who convey the passengers a-shore from the steamer, are as often pushing their unwieldy craft along with their hands, whilst they wade over the soft yellow sand, as they are sitting quietly within it, rowing, or walking to and fro, shoving it on with long poles.

The extremity of the Suez Gulf of the Red Sea sweeps, shallowing gently, over miles of fine sand, and where that sand first appears permanently raised, Suez has been built. The wide desolation of the desert surrounds it, a horizon of sand and stone meeting the reddish blue of the sky on three sides, whilst on the fourth the arm of the sea is visible, stretching far away to the south, one side of it bounded by the inhospitable rocks of the wilderness of Sinai, the other by the no less sterile shores of Africa.

Not a drop of fresh water is to be found in the vicinity of Suez; for miles the luckless traveller will find no trace of such, let him search never so diligently on every hand; all is sand, and stone, and sea—bleak sand, ugly stone, and a dangerous sea, a sea over which the Simoom of the desert wafts its blighting influence too often, filling every crevice of the exposed ship or steamer with clouds of fine sand, striking down in a fainting fit the strongest and the most muscular, and carrying off to the wide bourne whence no traveller returns, the weaker or the more enervated.

Suez itself looks more like a city of the dead than of the living. Its flat-roofed oriental houses crumbling to decay, with here and there a sickly shrub forced into a kind of dying life by man's obstinacy and perseverance, are so indicative of desertion and misery, that one can scarcely fancy himself in a city or a town containing a living, breathing population, men, women, and children, such as constitute towns elsewhere. Casting the eye over the apparently illimitable desert that surrounds it, a train of camels, — those toiling desert-ships,—is seen winding its way along in single file, most gloomy-looking, most melancholy.

There is something in the very aspect of the burdened camel that appears to tell of pain and suffering: the long, ungainly legs shambling about, the huge joints bending as if with springs; the rolling burden now thrown on one side, now on another, as the two legs on each side are simultaneously raised and then simultaneously depressed; the raised head and drooping neck, bent in, not proudly arched upwards like the horse's, all are characteristics of patient endurance and long acquaintance with suffering, such as one pities and commiserates. Wending its way toilsomely and slowly over the desert, the nose of the one attached to the tail of the other, the train of camels makes its way along without a sound, almost without the appearance of life, a few men with long staves walking by the side, or else mounted uneasily on the burdens, dozing amid their merchandize.

The whole is a scene of truly oriental character, quite unlike what one is accustomed to in the West. One expects such a scene in the desert, and wonders it is so like what, from a child, he has pictured to himself; it is but the realization in actual life of what his imagination, guided by sketches and descriptions, has often bodied forth in the mind.

A vast number of camels were in waiting upon the beach, ready to receive the luggage and the mails, and to take them to Cairo. As we landed from our Arab boat, we saw them lying about on every side, chewing the cud peacefully, occasionally waving their long necks about from side to side in monotonous motion. The attendant Arabs were seated on the sand in circles, some gambling, others discussing political matters—the last incursion of the Bedouins, the effect of the new Tanzimat, or the contrast between the rule of Mehemet Ali and Abbas Pacha in Egypt; others, again, repeating to each other alternate tales, tales similar to those of the Arabian Nights' Entertainments, and merrily did the long beards wag in laughter as they concluded.

Our caravanserai — the Suez Hotel, as it was styled—was what might have been expected, a large and somewhat ruinous building, inclosing a square in the centre; the lower rooms mostly intended for cattle or merchandize, the upper as habitations. Round the square, on the inner side, ran a balcony or verandah, communicating with all the rooms, the favourite lounge of servants and gossips, who could hence descry what was going on in the court below, and the opening of any single apartment.

We had a breakfast at this nondescript establishment—a breakfast at which one might fancy some of the workmen from Babel were the parties appeasing their hunger. French, German, Spanish, and English were spoken at the table—those that had Hindu servants addressed them in Hindostannee, whilst one gentleman from Hong Kong, with a Chinese valet, was great in the uncouth tongue of the celestials, and did not fail to sport it on such an occasion; his servant spoke English far better than he spoke Chinese, but that did not matter, Chinese he would speak, and he did,—after a fashion.

The servants of the establishment swore at each other in choice Arabic and vulgar Egyptian, and in the midst of all this, we bolted our meal like Americans, knowing that the omnibuses were to be soon ready to take us over the desert.

French, German, Spanish, English, Hindostannee, Chinese, Arabic, Egyptian, clattered, and grated, and rushed against each other on the quivering air, whilst knives and forks, and cups and saucers, with all the other paraphernalia of a civilized breakfast, clicked and rung and sounded continually, joining the Babel chorus. What an amount of work the unfortunate air in that long, barn-like room had to accomplish! Verily, if one *could* feel pity for such an object, *it* was to be pitied—so tortured, and twisted, and gyrated and vibrated, elaborately tortured, intricately twisted, vehemently gyrated, and incessantly vibrated.

The omnibuses were soon ready—omnibuses to convey us over the desert to Cairo!—the thing sounded strangely to the uninitiated, but was a fact, notwithstanding. Outside the walls of the town—for even Suez has what serves for such, hard walls for Bedouin men and Bedouin horses to knock their heads against—outside of these, we found the omnibuses awaiting us. Each of these conveyances was intended to hold six, and was drawn by four horses, helter-skelter over the wide waste, no road made, no road required.

We had drawn lots for the omnibuses before leaving the *Porringer*—the very evening indeed that we presented our address to Captain Spoon, informing him what a noble ship he had, and what a kind man he was, and how he conveyed us in perfect safety to Suez. These new and entertaining facts related to him, he wrote to us to say how grateful he was, and how grateful the officers of the ship were, and how happy he was, and how happy the officers of the ship were, and how proud he was, and how proud the officers of the ship were. This imposing ceremony completed, slips of paper with six names on each had been handed in—the six who wished to be together in an omnibus for a twelve or fourteen hours' ride—these slips were mysteriously placed in a mysterious urn—a soup tureen—and violently shaken and intermingled by Mr. Crabby, the purser. The fair Mrs. Plugget was then requested to insinuate the ends of her fingers into the mysterious "urn," and to draw out one of the said papers, which she did heroically, although very much at the same time as if she suspected a snake were in the said mysterious "urn," and great was the laughter as she drew thence a piece of paper containing six names,—a singular fact, particularly when it is remembered, that there was one with only four, and that all the rest *had* six.

Then the six on that paper were thus settled to go in the first omnibus, and mightily did they congratulate themselves; for stopping in Suez is neither interesting nor agreeable. The heroic Mrs. Plugget pulled out another and another paper, and Mr. Crabby, whom, with the other officers, we had been just assured was so happy, looked red and worried as he wrote the names hastily down on a sheet prepared for the purpose, begging and beseeching of Mrs. Plugget not to be in a hurry, all which mightily increased the hilarity of the company. But the laughter became outrageous, when Mrs. Plugget pulled out her own paper almost last, that on which her own name and party were written, and although offers were made by devoted bachelors of an omnibus near the beginning of the list, she would not hear of such a thing, she positively would not, and insisted on enjoying the full luxury of her misfortune —a misfortune which she had anticipated, nay, foretold more than once.

Thus had it been decided as to the order in which we should leave Suez—batches of four omnibuses at a time left the inhospitable town, with six passengers in each. There was an interval of some hours between the departure of each, and as it took four batches to clear us all off, it was evident that some would be enabled to study the curiosities of Suez at their leisure. Great was the merriment of those first off, as they contemplated the long faces of the *détenus*, and with wonderfully lachrymose sympathy did they bid their more unfortunate fellow-passengers *farewell*—the unfortunates turning disdainfully on their heels, and sullenly retracing their steps to the "Hotel," as party after party swept off.

Baron Rotamotin (whom the English sailors insisted on calling "rotten mutton") and his Countess had been fortunate enough to secure seats in the first batch—Mealy and myself went in the second. As we had none of the fairer members of the human species to take care of, we had made up a party of our own, in which we had collected those of the more agreeable kind whom we could obtain, apart from the trammels of family and party. It was pleasing to have for our long journey, of more than seventy miles over the bleakest of all bleak deserts, companions who would not complain of a little jolting, or object to a cigar.

To those in rude health, who do not care for a little fatigue, the drive across the desert is interesting and amusing, save when the dust-storms prevail. We fortunately escaped this infliction, although for the most part prepared for it by green veils depending gloomily from our hats. To the invalid, or the nervous, however, this strange wild jaunt is a perfect torture—over mounds of sand and over obtruding stones the vehicle rattles along with its four wild Bedouin horses at full gallop, the still wilder Bedouin coachman urging them on faster. The invalid feels his head and his heels playing, as it were, at hide-and-go-seek with each other, as he is jolted now to one side and then to another, now rising abruptly over a rugged rock, and now sinking into a profound abyss, in the most reckless and apparently insane manner. The nervous individual again feels confident that such reckless driving can but end in an upset, calls out to the driver energetically to be cautious, and he, shaking his beard and nodding, without understanding a word of the entreaty, assures the excited passengers that he'll make them go, whilst he cuts up the leaders more furiously than ever. It is of no use, and sinking back in martyr-like resignation, nervousness resigns itself to its fate.

After a time, however, and when, over rocks and sand and camels' bones, the omnibus has still driven on unscathed, at the same wild rate, nervousness begins to take courage, and looks forth at the bleak desert again — the coachman is evidently running a race with the Jehu of another omnibus, descried at some distance. The vehicles approach — there is a good little piece of hard ground ahead, which both wish to take possession of, and from afar, the two vehicles, rattling along at a hard gallop, gradually draw nearer and nearer—"they will certainly dash against each other," says nervousness, as he watches, with agonizing eagerness, the rapid approximation—"Coachman! coachman! you will certainly upset us!" he shouts, unable longer to control himself; "*do* be cautious!"

"Coachman" is the only word the grinning Arab understands, as he exhausts his vocabulary of abuse on the male and female relatives of his rival. It is an appeal to him,—as he understands it,—to drive quicker, and not to allow them to be beaten by the worthless son of his mother who drives the other vehicle.

"Bismillah!" he replies, "but the knave shall not beat us—be not afraid my lord—our horses shall walk over his unsavoury carcass before he gets a-head."

With this comforting assurance, nervousness

is obliged to rest content—not that he understands a word of it, it being spoken in Bedouin Arabic, but he fondly flatters himself that he has drawn the driver's attention to the danger, and that they are therefore safe. As he sees the huge whip gyrating over the vehicle, however, and descending forcibly on the hind quarters of the leaders, who are plunging manfully along, regardless of consequences, he sees that his efforts have been vain, and resigns himself to his fate again.

Had any one taken a peep into our vehicle, as we were thus hurled over the inhospitable wilds of one little corner of Africa, he might have doubted whether the individuals within belonged to any recognized type of humanity. Few, very few, think of shaving on board ship —in long voyages men become more natural, and less dandyfied and puppyish—by the time Egypt is reached, therefore, there is a stubbly growth of a fortnight covering lip and chin,—a growth of all varieties of hue and shade, that looks anything but picturesque or interesting. The six who occupied our omnibus were as hirsute a community as one was likely to find out of Germany; and when, to the nascent beards and moustaches, are added the various hats and veils that covered and partially concealed these brush-looking faces, the entire picture will form anything but an every-day scene.

Some men were deep in the widest possible wide-awakes, the edges tortured and twisted, and convoluted and squeezed into a vast variety of patterns; others wore straw hats, some purchased at Moses and Son's, others made on the banks of the Ganges at Monghyr, and others by Chinese in Canton; wide-awakes and straw hats were in the majority, but one unfortunate individual of the party had a regular white beaver hat—that is, it had once been white, but having dropped into the sandy water at Suez, was now in part of a sea-green hue, the rim, however, for the most part, retaining its original silky brilliancy. In front of all these head-dresses depended the indispensable veils, green and blue, through which glimpses only of the odd faces within could be obtained by our imaginary inspector.

I would venture to assert, that a sharp French gend'arme, or an Austrian inspector of passports, would have found our little company a hard nut to crack. So accustomed are we to see veils on the soft attractive faces of the fair sex alone, that, after we got fairly into the desert, and began to inspect each other, it was some time before we could do so without laughing.

Not that we ever discovered the utility of the appanages — we had all been solemnly warned, however, on no account to go across the desert without them, and accordingly we wore them. Having made a similar remark to a mercantile friend, who had frequently been backwards and forwards, and knew the line as well as a London omnibus conductor knows the streets on his route, the reply was—"Ah, it is evident you did not cross at the proper time—in November they are of no use—you should go across in June, when the dust-storms prevail, in order to experience the utility of the veil." I have never since felt disposed to try the experiment, and must, therefore, continue to protest, that as far as mine and my friend Mealy's experience went, the veils were useless.

At convenient distances in the land of Goshen, houses have been erected along the route, at which refreshments are prepared for the voyagers, and excellent accommodation and excellent dishes, considering where we found them, were to be had in these houses. The keen desert air gave us all excellent appetites, and irrespective of conventionalisms, for once in our lives we found ourselves sitting down to dinner and enjoying it heartily, on one occasion only, at two o'clock in the morning. It is a positive fact, that although at such an outrageous time, the dinner tasted as well, and was as much relished, as if it had been then only the orthodox Indian dinner-hour of half-past seven. On the whole, with the exception of the wild way in which the vehicles were driven, and the total want of any thing like a road, we found the arrangements admirable, and rather enjoyed than otherwise the arduous undertaking of "crossing the desert."

Arrived at Cairo, we took up our quarters at the Hotel d'Angleterre, a large, commodious house, in which we found only a very small instalment of the vermin nuisance we had been led to expect. Perhaps, as in the case of the veils, we did not arrive at the proper season; but certain it is, that there were not those "fearful swarms of every kind of vermin" of which we had been premonished. This was a disappointment, and, as Englishmen will grumble, Mealy declared that having made up our minds to endure the plague of insects, it was too bad to cheat us out of the luxury of being enabled to complain of them afterwards. However, we had to endure the disappointment, and slept all the sounder in consequence.

I say we found there only a small instalment of the plague we had expected to encounter in all its virulence. The majority of us found nothing of the kind to complain of, but a few declared that they had lost their sleep, or, at least, a portion of it, from the attacks of the parasitic insects with which their beds abounded.

It is not my intention to describe Cairo—it has been too frequently described already. Every one knows all about the citadel, and the mosques, and the Egyptian women, and the Turkish and Arab shops, which form its chief attractions. Every one has heard how narrow some of the streets are, and how a loaded camel coming down one of them, sweeps all before him, making the passengers precipitately retreat into archways and shops, to avoid being knocked down by the swinging load that moves from side to side upon his back.

Every one has heard also of the poetical cries of the Egyptian salesmen, as they recommend their wares to the passers-by,—although but few Europeans understand them when they hear them. Every one has heard of the Mameluke's leap, and the Pasha's palace; and, in fine, who has not read accounts of the ascent of the great pyramid, until he has almost wished Egypt were prohibited to Englishmen? We hear, too, of the marvellous effects produced upon weak nerves by the first sight of the pyramids; we hear of enthusiastic ladies and gentlemen of "fine nervous temperaments," being thrown into a kind of wonderment-*coma* by the vastness of the structures and the imposing length of unvaried wall, which appears to stretch out to infinity.

All this is very pretty, and sounds very well; but, although neither a resident of Manchester, nor in any way connected with the cotton trade, I will venture to say, that one of the lofty chimneys of the manufacturing districts of England, if gently tapering towards the top, and isolated at the bottom, will give the observer who stands near its base a better idea of infinity than the great pyramid of Ghiza—the best idea that brick and mortar *can* give of it.

Our intention being to remain in Cairo for a fortnight, and inspect its often-described *lions*, Mealy and myself bade our fellow-travellers farewell ere they quitted the hotel for the river steamer that was to take them to the canal leading to Alexandria. The Baron Rotamotin and his amiable wife, Mrs. Plugget, and Mr. and Mrs. Hondhy from Ceylon, we saw them all depart, and felt lonely as we returned to our apartment when the last batch of them had been driven from the court-yard, so strangely were we affected by the loss of the society of those of whom, three weeks before, we had known nothing.

A short paragraph ere I conclude, anent the slave-market of Cairo. We had not been many days in the city, ere our dragoman proposed an expedition thither; and we assented with pleasure, wondering that we had not thought of it before. We were taken on donkeys as usual, through an infinite variety of narrow streets, brushing the knees of the male and female riders that happened to meet us in our journey, and often astonishing the honest pedestrian by catching him in the spine with our knee or foot when our dragoman would insist on a trot or gallop. We were at his mercy, and were forced to submit; jolting and jostling, and being jolted and jostled, we made our way along to the entrance of the slave-market. Turning down a narrow court, dismounting from our Egyptian donkeys, and following the dragoman through a half-ruined gateway, we stood at length within the slave-market of Grand Cairo.

A square court-yard was before us, round which rose buildings of no great height, the front, as usual, in the south and east, protected by a low verandah that ran quite round the enclosure, supported on rude wooden pillars. Seated in the sunshine were groups of slaves, principally Nubians, men, women, and children, some in little clusters, some singly, some playing upon the court-yard, the sun's rays dancing upon their jet-black skins. A few grave-looking Turks, the owners of the slaves for the most part, were enjoying the chibouk in other parts of the enclosure, and eyed us with anything but friendly glances as we inspected their wares, knowing well that curiosity, not commerce, had brought us there.

"There is no misery, no squalor," we repeated to each other in a breath; "they all seem happy and contented." "Do they generally look thus?" we asked of the dragoman.

"It is the same all the days I have come," was the reply, in dragomanic English.

The black articles of merchandize looked at us and smiled, the children, for the most part, continuing their games without heeding us; old men and young ones, old women, matrons, and girls inspected us attentively, and talked incessantly as they did so. We walked round the yard, and peeped into the places where they lived within the verandah. They were infinitely more comfortable and less filthy than the dwellings of the labouring classes in the south of India. The clothes the poor wretches possessed were neither very voluminous nor very fine in quality, but they were more than sufficient for their ideas of decency, and the hot sun of Africa prevented them feeling the want of more; a scanty cloth round the loins was all the covering they had, and they were content with it. The children were naked, and happy and healthful apparently, as children ought to be.

"Tzaffa!" called out a fat pursy Turk, who was diligently fumigating in the corner of the yard; a graceful young girl of fourteen or sixteen years of age bounded to her feet as she heard the call, and going towards her lord, salaamed respectfully as she approached him. She was elegantly formed—her figure might have served as a model for the sculptor, so firm, graceful, and undulating in its outlines—but her face was Nubian, and contrasted disagreeably with the fine form. Receiving some order from her fat master, she went into an adjoining room and brought him something he required. He took it from her hand without a word. Making a low obeisance, and returning to the group she had left, she sat down again, and commenced talking immediately.

We knew nothing of Tzaffa's history or of her character, but she interested us much, and was frequently afterwards, when we were far away from Cairo, a theme of conversation. Often did we speculate what her fate had been, and what the feelings with which she endured it. Tzaffa! Tzaffa! the name alone was sufficient to interest us.

We left the slave-market of Cairo with the conviction that thousands of our own countrymen and countrywomen—that tens of thousands of the natives of India—were more, far more, to be pitied, than the Nubian slaves there exposed for sale.

PAGES OF CEYLONESE HISTORY.

It would be well for Ceylon and its inhabitants were its history better known to Englishmen generally, and were its affairs brought more prominently before the British public. No one who has visited the island, can help feeling an extraordinary interest in all that appertains to it. Unfortunately for its people, however, its history is not so intimately connected with any portion of that of Greece or Rome as to render the island an object of interest to the classical student. It was but faintly known to the Greek and Latin geographers as Taprobane—they had some indistinct idea that some such island, rich in pearls, cinnamon, and elephants, existed somewhere in the recesses of the Indian Ocean — and that goods came from it that had been conveyed from a far more distant shore, that of China.

Few untravelled Europeans, indeed, realize to themselves the size of Ceylon. They probably look upon it as a sort of counterpart of the Isle of Wight, or Malta, and are possibly incredulous when informed that it is very nearly of the same size as Ireland—Ceylon containing 24,600 square miles, and Ireland about 28,800. They have their doubts, too, when told that it once contained at least five millions of inhabitants, and can still exhibit ruins of cities, once of vast extent, and of buildings that almost rival the pyramids of Egypt in size and age.

But that which more than anything else evidences the greatness of Ceylon in by-gone times, is the fact that it has a continuous history of itself, which extends from five hundred years before Christ up to the period of the Portuguese invasion in 1505 A.D.—a history proving that the people of Ceylon were once a powerful and refined nation, and that too, long ere Julius Cæsar had invaded Britain, or the Celtic inhabitants of these islands had learned the rudiments of civilization. Southern India and the Eastern Peninsula were successively the scenes of the warlike exploits of the Ceylonese in their days of greatness—their conquests, it is true, were but transitory, still, however, the gaudy pagodas of Burmah and Siam bear testimony to the truth of Singhalese history, for to those countries Ceylon gave its own religion, Budhism ; and they have ever since retained it. In the hope that a perusal of some of the facts of this history may induce the reader to seek fuller and more explicit information on the subject elsewhere, I here present him with an epitome, originally compiled, after considerable research, for an Indian periodical. It will be considered by many *dry* reading, I doubt not—hence its position at the end of the second volume.

The Chinese, Burmese, and the natives of India are all claimants for the honour of having originally peopled Ceylon. It appears most probable, that, when the neighbouring shores of the continent were occupied, the narrow island-studded strait between would be passed, and the rich plains of northern Ceylon be provided with inhabitants. Fable identifies it with the scene of the contests between Rama and Rawana, the heroes of the great Hindu epic, entitled the *Ramayana;* but, leaving the region of fable, which it might be curious, but would scarcely be instructive to enter, we naturally turn to the religious books of the island for its early history; and of these books there is no lack.

The founder of modern Budhism, Gotama or Gaudma—impelled by the reputed sanctity of the island, we are told, a sanctity celebrated long before his time—visited it, to raise from their degradation the debased inhabitants. Of this indefatigable reformer many wonderful anecdotes are related, as having occurred during his visits to the island; and of these, not the least miraculous, in the eye of the Budhist, is the fact of his having known by intuition the places hallowed by the touch of former Budhas—knowledge which his admiring disciples could neither dispute nor deny. Anxious to connect still further the history of their country with the life of their great man-god, the Ceylonese historians inform us, that on the very day of Budha's death, the founder of their subsequent royal dynasty landed on the island.

This founder, Wijaya by name, is stated to have been a prince driven by his father, the king of a district of modern Bengal, from his home and country for his misdemeanours. With a considerable band of equally reckless characters with himself, he directed his course to the sea, and having sailed from Bengal, attempted to land on a part of the coast of India, where he was violently opposed. He next directed his vessels to Ceylon, and there succeeded in making good a settlement (554 B.C.). By a fortunate alliance with the daughter of a chief, he established himself more securely; and she, violating patriotism and paternal love for the advantage of her newly-found spouse, aided him in a cowardly massacre, whereby the chief rulers of the island were destroyed, and Wijaya left supreme.

He was not long in taking every advantage of the superiority he had gained, and by sending his followers to found cities, throughout the island, of which they were to be the chiefs, dependent only on him as their feudal lord, he fixed himself securely in the sovereignty, 540 years before the Christian era. His long reign of thirty-eight years was embittered but by one misfortune,—he was childless, and the fair kingdom he had gained was in all probability about to pass soon into the hands of another family. Perceiving this, and anxious to prevent it, Wijaya sent to his father, whose favour his achievements had now won for him, requesting that Panduwasa, his younger brother, might be sent to succeed him.

A voyage from Ceylon to Bengal was then something like what the circumnavigation of the world would be now, and Panduwasa did not arrive till a year after the death of his distinguished brother. Fortunately for him, a minister of Wijaya, possessed of the rare virtues of moderation and fidelity, had preserved the government for his master's successor, and instead of having to re-conquer the kingdom, as under other circumstances he might have been obliged to do, he seated himself upon a peaceful throne. The Budhist historians inform us that he married a cousin of their celebrated prophet Gotama, and thus again they connect the history of the island with that of the founder of their faith. Unlike his brother, Panduwasa left behind him ten sons and three daughters, and connected with one of the latter, Unmansit, a romantic tale is told, which I shall lay before my readers.

On Panduwasa's death it had been prophesied by certain Brahmans that the offspring of Unmansit would destroy his uncles and dethrone the reigning king Abhayo, who was one of these uncles. This the superstitious princes believing, had their unoffending sister, who is represented, of course, as having been exceedingly beautiful, closely confined. But "love laughs at locksmiths," saith the proverb. A prince of the royal family caught a glimpse of the fair captive, whom he also wooed and won. The consequences of their intimacy could not be concealed, and, to avoid open disgrace, Abhayo and his brothers were forced to consent to a marriage, on the condition, however, that should the offspring prove a son, he should be immediately destroyed.

The offspring *did* prove a son, but, with the aid of her faithful attendant, the same whose assistance facilitated the former intercourse, Unmansit saved his life by the substitution of a female infant, lately born, and introduced into the apartment clandestinely.

Abhayo discovered the fraud, sought to destroy the boy, but in vain, as he had the favour and protection of the priests. Yet the consequences of his endeavours were by no means unimportant. Looked upon as the child of destiny by the people, Pandukabhayo, the persecuted youth, soon found himself at the head of an army, and after a long and wasting war, succeeded in dethroning his unnatural uncle.

During his and his son's reign, Ceylon appears to have been rapidly advancing in improvement and civilization—the capital city, Anuradhapura, was embellished with works of art and architecture, the remains of which may still be seen, nearly 2300 years after their erection;* villages and towns were starting up in districts which the tide of population had probably never reached before; the country was divided into districts, over each of which civil and judicial magistrates presided; tanks and canals were constructed to facilitate cultivation, and, in fact, the island was advancing with rapid strides to prosperity and eminence.

* A description of some of these ruins will be found in *Forest Life in Ceylon*, vol. ii. chap. 6.

I shall now pass on to a remarkable fact in the history before me—that of the introduction of Budhism in a systematic form. This happened in the reign of Tisso the First, about 300 years before our era. Tisso being about to enter into alliance with Dhammasoko, a King of India, noted for his enthusiastic love of Budhism, sent him a present borne by the chief of his nobles, in return for which, the religious Dhammasoko sent, along with presents, advice to Tisso "to take refuge in Budha, his religion, and his priesthood." Not content with sending advice alone, however, Dhammasoko persuaded his son Mahindo, a high priest of the Budhist faith, to accompany Tisso's ambassadors to Ceylon, and his reception by that monarch was such as to leave him little ground for regret at his determination.

Mahindo entered upon his proselytizing career with zeal and success. Multitudes flocked to hear his discourses, numerous priests were ordained, colleges were established, temples reared, and Budhism finally installed as the religion of Ceylon. The females were not to be outdone in the career of piety. They requested a priestess to raise some of them to the priestly office, and, in accordance with their request, a sister of Mahindo was sent for and obtained, who should establish a sisterhood of nuns, and thus put Budhism on its proper footing in the island. These communities, although essentially a part of the faith, have been long suppressed in Ceylon, although, I believe, they are still to be seen in Burmah.

With Sanghamettra, the female high priest, came also a branch of that holy tree under which Gotama had attained his Budhaship (the bo-tree, or *ficus religiosa*), which was planted in Anuradapúra, on the spot where, at the present day, the wandering tourist may observe the spreading branches of "the great bo-tree at the Maha wiharo," amidst whose branches—safe in that sacred retreat—thousands of monkeys and other animals disport.

Tisso was not backward in exhibiting his faith in Budhism, by the erection of many splendid buildings devoted to its service. The remains of some of them, especially those of the Thuparamaya Dagobah, may even now excite our admiration. Ten years after the death of Tisso (B.C. 256), we for the first time hear of the Malabar race interfering in the government of Ceylon, and the event is an important one, inasmuch as it was but the prelude to numerous instances of incursions and rapine committed by the same race.

Suratisso, the reigning prince, took into his service, during a period of profound peace, a large body of mercenary cavalry, commanded by two Malabar chieftains, called Sena and Gutika. These generals so well ingratiated themselves into the favour of the whole army, that on their raising the standard of insurrection, Suratisso found himself completely deserted, and ended his life and reign by his own hands. Sena and Gutika, now supreme, divided the island between themselves, and reigned, with an iron rule, for upwards of thirty years, when a counter revolution replaced the sceptre in the hand of Asela, a prince of the royal family.

Asela, however, was not allowed to reign in peace. Elala, a Malabar leader, landed at the mouth of the Maha Velli River with a large army, marched directly towards the capital, was met there by Asela, and gained a victory, which gave him the crown of Ceylon. This he enjoyed for a lengthened period, and it was not till old age had weakened his intellect and unnerved his arm, that he found a claimant for the throne in every way worthy of him as an enemy. The royal family had fled to Rohona, and a descendant of Tisso's brother, who held that, the south-eastern district of the island, as his province,Gaimono by name, alone dared to oppose the usurper.

Youth, lofty hopes, and a vigorous intellect were in favour of Gaimono; a settled government, full treasury, and former renown, were the supporters of Elala.

But Gaimono was no ordinary opponent: his measures were full of boldness and vigour, without rashness. Fort after fort fell beneath his arms; and in a decisive engagement with Elala, he killed the latter with his own hand, and then occupied his throne. A relation of Elala's, who came to his assistance with an army of thirty thousand men, was equally unsuccessful, and, on defeating him, Gaimono found no one able or willing to dispute his sovereignty. His piety now became as conspicuous as his military prowess had been; and of his religious exertions, sufficient remains exist to satisfy us that the Ceylonese of that period were considerably advanced in architecture, sculpture, and refined taste, whilst the size of some of these monuments, and the vastness of the tanks which he excavated, may convince us that the city during those years must have been populous and magnificent.

The particular account which the native histories afford us of the construction of one of these buildings is such, that most students have doubted its correctness, whilst those who have not examined the evidence, have positively pronounced it an exaggeration. As in other instances in this history, however, where truth is concerned, an extended investigation has, in this case, but confirmed those accounts. We are told that it was erected on sixteen hundred stone pillars, and of these the greater number are still standing, whilst fragments of the rest lie near their original situation.

We are also informed that the interior was decorated in a way which might lead us to believe that the fancy of the writers heightened the description, but this has also been confirmed by the narrative of the Chinese Budhist, Fa Hian, who in the fifth century visited

Ceylon, and whose narrative has been translated and published in Paris. Him we can scarcely suspect of any motive for exaggeration, or, if we did, we must still account for his description tallying with that of the *Mahawanso* and *Ratnakare*, the native histories.

Besides the temples and other religious erections attributed to Gaimono, we read of hospitals for the sick being established throughout the island; roads formed, and officers for the preservation of order appointed by his directions and exertions. The reign of Gaimono is one of the best evidences we possess of the state of the country at this early period, a subject on which I cannot dilate at present.

I shall pass over a few succeeding reigns, in which there occurred apparently no event of material consequence, till we come to that of Walagambahu, who ascended the throne about one hundred years B.C. By an invasion of the Malabars, who were now, fatally for Ceylon, too well acquainted with its riches, he was driven from his throne, and obliged to conceal himself in a remote district of the island: for fourteen years this exile continued. Chief after chief of the invaders having during that period been rulers, and usually falling by the hands of their successors. These disturbances, we might imagine, would have afforded some opportunities to the dethroned monarch to expel the invaders, but this does not appear to have been the case, and for that long period the island was a prey to anarchy and confusion. On reascending his throne, a scheme of the monarch's, formed in exile, was put into execution, and that was to have the discourses of Budha, then but orally transmitted from one generation to another, committed to writing. For this purpose, a meeting of the oldest and ablest priests was called. Different versions of the sermons of the prophet were collated and compared, and after a lengthened investigation, the voluminous Pitakattaya and their commentaries, the Atthakatha, the sacred books of Ceylonese Buddhism, were committed to writing.

Two of the dagobahs, whose remains at the present day most prominently attract the visitor's attention, owe their erection to the piety of Walagambahu, and one of these (the Abhayagiri) was originally upwards of four hundred feet in height, equal to the elevation of the topmost pinnacle of St. Peter's at Rome.

The next remarkable feature which the history of Ceylon presents to us, is the reign of a monster of wickedness, in the person of a Queen Anula. She was the wife of Walagambahu's son, and put an end to the life of her husband in order to reign alone. One victim after another was raised to the dangerous seat vacated by his predecessor, and these appear to have been chosen on account of their personal appearance, to gratify the depravity of the insatiable Anula. In this way five victims were dispatched in the course of as many years, until the world at length becoming weary of her, she was dethroned and executed.

Her successor had no easy task in bringing order and regularity out of the confusion worse confounded caused by the irregularities of Anula; and it was not till three or four peaceful reigns had passed, that the kingdom attained its former prosperity. "Happy is that people whose annals are tiresome," was the exclamation of a philosophic and thinking mind; and if I were asked to point out the period of Ceylonese history when the country appears to have been most flourishing and contented, I should certainly select the most uneventful period of its history — the first five centuries of our era. During that time, order and peace for the most prevailed. Tanks and roads were formed, Budhism was in its glory, the royal family established, and every thing promised a long career of prosperity.

We have positive evidence as to the flourishing state of the kingdom at this period, both in a material and intellectual point of view. The first is confirmed in a curious way, both in the far East and the far West, by a Budhist priest of China, and a Christian priest of Rome. The Budhist, Fa Hian, formerly referred to, visited Anuradhapúra, the capital, in the fourth century, and tells us that nothing could equal its magnificence and extent.

Numerous magistrates, nobles, and merchants, he informs us, dwelt in it. The houses were spacious and handsome, the public buildings magnificent and highly ornamented. The streets and roads were broad and straight, whilst at the corners, numerous lecture rooms were erected, in which the doctrines of Budha were daily expounded. The very fact of a distinguished Chinese Budhist proceeding to Ceylon in search of the authentic writings of his prophet, shews the importance of the island at this period—so much for Eastern evidence. The Western is to be found in the writings of St. Ambrose. A Theban, he informs us, visited Ceylon and the Malabar coast of India in the fourth century. There he was detained by a Malabar prince, subject to the king of Ceylon, for six years, and he only regained his liberty on a rebellion of the tributary, which was punished by an army sent from the island, and that army delivered him. In speaking of this event, he describes the king of Ceylon as "*the great king*, who lived in the island of Taprobane."

From the writings of Cosmas Indicopleustes, it also appears that at this period a very extensive trade was being carried on between China and Ceylon on the one side, as well as between Ceylon and the Persian Gulf on the other. From these facts, as well as from that of the buildings whose remains now exist, having chiefly owed their origin to this period, I conclude that for two centuries preceding, and five centuries succeeding, the Christian era, the island was populous, powerful, and flourishing. Nor does literature appear to have been neglected, inasmuch as to the time under review, Ceylon owes its best historical, scientific, and poetical compositions, of which, however, the first only can be appreciated by the English reader, none of the others having yet been translated.

Some romantic stories of the various kings who reigned from the fifth to the eighth century, compose the chief part of the history of these periods. I shall neither stop to relate them, nor to investigate their truth; suffice it to say, that from the violent deaths, the numerous insurrections and invasions which followed, it may naturally be concluded that the prosperity of previous periods was being gradually merged in the turbulence of the succeeding, and that a gradual decline in the arts of civilization and refinement was contemporaneous with a more scientific mode of warfare, and more attention given to that destructive art itself, than to the arts of good government or the wants of the people.

The period of the transference of the seat of government from Anuradhapúra, the ancient capital, to Pollonaruwa, appears to have been coeval with the decline of the former town. This event happened about the latter end of the eighth century, and from that time may be dated the neglect of the buildings and the gradual dilapidation of the former capital. Indeed, shortly after, the fact is stated of a person having been deputed by the king at Pollonaruwa to proceed to Anuradhapúra to repair and restore the buildings of the latter town. From this period, too, may be dated the rapid decline of the island in power, prosperity, and population. Inroads from the coasts of India, and attacks from bands of roving Malays, became more and more numerous and frequent—insurrections multiplied in the mountainous districts of the island, and everything was in a state of turbulence and disorder.

In this condition it can be easily imagined that numerous bands of soldiers were scattered over the island, and that, in fact, its inhabitants were assuming a military character. Such being the case, nothing was wanting but a military leader of eminence to render it a conquering country, and this it found in the twelfth century, in the person of one of its most enterprising and talented monarchs, who was certainly the greatest military leader Ceylon has produced. Of the birth and boyhood of this wonderful hero, Prackrama, numerous miracles are recorded with the utmost circumstantiality, whilst a particular account is also handed down of his youthful education.

The Budhist faith, logic, grammar, poetry, and music are all mentioned as subjects in which he became extraordinarily proficient, whilst horsemanship, archery, and the management of elephants were not neglected. When he had gone through the whole circle of the sciences, as then taught by the most learned priests, travelling was considered still necessary to fit him for the duties of his station. On returning to his native land, he received the throne by the voluntary resignation of its possessor (Gajabahu)—a resignation which appears to have been made, however, in favour, not of Prackrama himself, but of his father, Wickrama. A dispute arose in consequence between the two claimants, which ended in the accession of the son; and shortly after, a reconciliation took place between him and his father, which happened just before the latter's death.

On obtaining quiet possession of the kingdom,

Prakrama entered upon an enlightened career of improvement, which proves him to have been no ordinary character. The formation of roads, canals, and tanks, which are particularly mentioned in the native annals, and numerous remains of which are now visible, prove the utility of his exertions. Libraries (chiefly of Budhistic works) were collected for the colleges of the priesthood—the poorer classes were aided in reclaiming waste lands—and, if native authorities are to be credited, the whole island was rendered prosperous and happy by his exertions.

This state of peaceful progress, however, was soon disturbed by the notes of warlike preparation.

A tributary princess, in the most hilly and remote district of the island—Rohona—was determined to oppose the advancing reforms of Prakrama; and Subhala, the lady in question, having once taken the resolution to resist, prepared to oppose her superior with vigour and determination. The account of the warfare is handed down with sufficient minuteness to enable us to form some judgment of Ceylonese tactics at the time.

The fortified places, we are informed, were surrounded, by her orders, with large and deep moats. The roads leading into the province were rendered impassable to elephants and cavalry, by being strewed with large trees, and stakes fixed firmly in the ground. The uncovered sides of the hills were defended by briars and brambles plentifully scattered over them. These preparations completed, Subhala posted her army in the immediate vicinity of a fortress which commanded the only accessible road into her territories, and there awaited the attack. Prakrama, on his part, was not idle—a force greatly superior in numbers to any which the Rohonians could bring into the field, was dispatched under Rakha, one of his most experienced generals, whilst the king himself remained to superintend the improvements progressing by his directions.

Rakha advanced with all the celerity circumstances would admit of, to meet his enemies. Harassed as his troops were by the obstacles in their way, they yet surmounted them all with great bravery, notwithstanding the opposition of the Rohonians, and at length a general battle was offered and accepted. By a skilful disposition of his forces, and a judicious choice of ground, Rakha was enabled completely to overpower the more impetuous but less cautious mountaineers—a defeat and rout were the consequences. The Rohonians attempted to throw themselves into the fortress formerly mentioned, but Rakha was no sluggard in pursuit. Both parties entered together, and the fortress was taken in the *melée*.

Scarcely was this great advantage gained, when Rakha found his communication with his own capital intercepted, and his army actually besieged in the fort which he had taken. Strong reinforcements were sent to his aid by the king, and at length so overpowering a force marched into Rohona, as to preclude the possibility of further resistance on the part of Subhala. Surrounded in her capital, and unable to resist, she accepted the terms offered, and by an absolute submission saved her life and tributary title.

An imposing ceremony was conducted at the capital by Prakrama in consequence of this victory, during which the native historians, one and all, inform us, that a miracle was exhibited — a special mark of Budha's favour. This miracle consisted in the occurrence of a thunder-storm, and a copious fall of rain, at the very time when the gorgeous procession, with Prakrama at its head, was proceeding to the temple of thanksgiving; and yet, wonderful to relate, not a drop of this copious shower touched a single thing engaged in the procession, although it fell plentifully around! The confidence with which this miracle is related, and the reiteration of it by the various native historians, is a curious fact in the history of the native character.

The court at Pollonaruwa, however, speedily found that their thanksgiving was premature; the submission of Subhala was but a prelude to a vigorous preparation for a renewed contest on her part, and scarcely were the rejoicings at an end, when the trump of war again sounded in rebellious Rohona. Of the campaign which ensued, we are not supplied with the particulars so minutely as in the former case. All that can be gathered from history is, that it was obstinate and bloody—that the Rohonians lost two battles, both of which were obstinately contested, and in the latter of which twelve thousand Rohonians were slain or taken. The siege and capture of Subhala's capital was the last act of the tragedy, and there is reason to believe that her temerity, when led as a captive before her conqueror, caused her death.

The peace of the district was subsequently ensured by the vigorous measures of Prakrama, and these were generally so successful, that profound tranquillity reigned throughout the island. It was not till after the year 1169 of our era, the sixteenth of his reign, that the monarch found it necessary again to assemble his forces and to face an enemy. Now, however, they were to be turned against a foreign foe—not to be engaged in civil commotions. The king of Cambodia and some other provinces, in the Burman Empire, had roused the just resentment of Prakrama by plundering certain Singhalese merchants and slighting his ambassador. To avenge these insults, the king strained every nerve to fit out a naval expedition, capable of grappling with the numerous ships of his enemy, and of conveying his army to the eastern peninsula. By these exertions a fleet of five hundred sail was quickly prepared, an officer of renown was put at the head of the expedition, and the armament was dispatched. They sailed to Cambodia, landed at a port called Kúsuma, whither the enemy advanced with precipitation on the first intelligence of their appearance. A battle was fought, in which the Cambodians were totally defeated, and Adikaram, the general of the Singhalese forces, followed up his advantages by an immediate march to Camboja, the capital, which the precipitate haste of its king had left utterly defenceless. This was speedily taken, and with it all the treasures and resources of the sovereign. The fortified places were surrendered in consequence, a viceroy and annual tribute appointed, and the whole country was declared subject to "the great and glorious Prakrama-bahu, King of Ceylon."

Thus successful in his first expedition against a foreign foe, Prakrama next turned his arms against the kings of the district in Southern India, called in the native annals Pandi and Solli—on the Malabar and Coromandel coast. The motive of this invasion is but faintly exhibited, as some real or fancied grievance. Endeavouring to land at Madura, the general of Prakrama found a force so considerable drawn up to oppose him, as to render the disembarcation impracticable. The expedition then proceeded up the coast to Tellicherry, where they again found a force prepared to oppose them—they made the attempt, however, to land, and, after a hard-fought battle, succeeded in driving the Pandians from the shore. One action after another succeeded, but generally so much to the advantage of the Singhalese, as to put the greater part of the country into their possession. In the last and most decisive combat they were thoroughly successful, and the consequence of it was the submission of the entire country. The reigning prince was dethroned, and his son, as a tributary of Prakrama, was placed upon the throne.

Such are the principal details handed down to us of the reign of Prakrama the Great. He died in the year 1186 of our era; and had his measures been imitated by his successors, Ceylon would have been in a different condition when first visited by Europeans. A period of anarchy and confusion followed, however, in which the foreign conquests were lost, and many of the internal improvements neglected. But one short interval of nine years elapsed, in which a step was made in the right direction.

With this exception, the entire course of Ceylonese history from 1186 to 1505, was one of rapid retrogression. Civil wars, domestic commotions, and external aggressions, combined with the apathy of the natives; all conducing to reduce the island from the flourishing state in which Prakrama left it, to the condition in many places of an uninhabited wilderness. The tanks were neglected, the embankments of the canals were allowed to fall in, the bridges were unrepaired. Every foreign invader extorted from the wretched inhabitants and the weak princes every particle of wealth they could not by subtlety conceal, and Malabars, Moors, and Malays, all found it their interest to make incursions into Ceylon. The evils of a disputed succession commenced the decline, the aggressions of foreign foes increased it, and the natural apathy of the native character allowed it to continue.

That the people who inhabited Ceylon at the time of Wijaya's invasion must have been barbarous in the extreme, we should have concluded from the facts of that invasion, had it never been asserted by the native historians. The attainment of supreme power by the chief of a band of but seven hundred followers, and the extension of that power into the remoter provinces, proves at once, that the native princes were at variance with each other, and not in any case capable of effectual resistance. It is true that the means employed by Wijaya for the establishment of his authority were those of cunning and artifice, not of open force—yet still the civilization of himself and his followers must have been infinitely superior to that of the natives, or he could not have succeeded in his enterprize; and in what the civilization of Bengal, whence Wijaya came, then consisted, we are pretty well aware from the Hindu annals.

From this period, then, we may date the introduction of improved habits and manners into the island, an improvement which, from the dispersion of Wijaya's followers, would gradually extend itself in every direction. The three centuries which followed, till the reigns of Sena and Gutika, the usurping Malabars, although not wholly undisturbed by warfare, were yet eminently fitted to promote and extend the improvement already begun. The establishment and embellishment of towns seem to have been the first object of their exertions, and the remains of the more important of these, which still exist, prove what their population and perseverance must have been. The faith of Budhism, so congenial to their dispositions, received a great proportion of their attention, and in the erection of buildings in honour of the faith, many of the kings delighted to pass their days.

But with Prakrama this state of things, promising as his civil and military abilities had made it, ended—the Ceylonese, by habits, religion, and disposition, were essentially unwarlike, and they relapsed on his death, into that lifeless apathy or irresolute and fitful disturbance so common in the East. Anarchy, civil war, foreign invasion, and weak princes, completed the evils which had arisen on the death of Prakrama, and at the beginning of the sixteenth century little else was visible but the wreck of that which had once been a magnificent and flourishing kingdom.

On the testimony of both eastern and western writers, the conclusion arrived at is, that the trade of the island at one time was extensive and lucrative. Ceylon was the entrepôt for the commerce of China on the one hand, and Arabia and Persia on the other. Hither, merchants from the east and west of Asia came, mutually to exchange the commodities and productions of their respective countries—a traffic which must have considerably enriched the country in which it was carried on. Of this trade the Moors on the western, and the Malays on the eastern side, appear to have been the principal carriers; and from the accounts which they carried back with them of the island they had visited, probably arose those Moorish and Malayan invasions, which we have noted as having become exceedingly numerous in the thirteenth, fourteenth, and fifteenth centuries. To this trade the discovery of the passage round the Cape of Good Hope by the Portuguese put an end; and as that people supplanted the Moors on the coast of India, so did they also in the traffic of Ceylon.

The gradual decline of the country in civilization and population, is admirably depicted in the ruins of the various cities, which, at the different periods of Ceylonese history, became the capital of the island. The remains of Anuradhapura, the earliest capital, as far exceed those of Pollonaruwa, the succeeding seat of government, in vastness, elegance, and beauty, as those of Athens exceed the Egyptian Thebes in the latter respect—nor is Pollonaruwa less distinguished, if compared with the succeeding capitals. These, together with the ruins of roads, bridges, canals, and tanks unoccupied or disused, perhaps, for fourteen hundred years, are the substantial proofs which we now possess of what the island and its inhabitants once were, as well as the verifications of the accounts of native annalists, which, without this indubitable testimony, we might be disposed to doubt.

Some idea, then, of the state of the island at the period when the Portuguese first visited it, may be gathered from what has been said; yet, to make this idea clear and distinct, it will be as well to notice in a few lines the different classes of inhabitants which it contained. The northern parts, from their proximity to the southern coast of India, were most subject, of course, to the irruptions of the Malabars, and hence it followed that, in that quarter of the island, they had become as numerous as, or even more so than, the Singhalese themselves. It was this continual increase of a foreign and hostile race in the very heart of their dominions, which, probably, caused the gradual removal of the seat of government to the south and east by the later kings; the first capital, Anuradhapura, having been situated in the very centre of that division which the Malabars had at length occupied as their own. The general prevalence of the Tamil language, and the Hindu system of religion in this province ever since Europeans have been connected with the island, up to the present time, prove the fact of their occupation.

Besides these, however, a wild race, subsisting on the produce of the chase, and destitute of habitations, also existed; totally distinct in almost every respect from their nominal masters—the Singhalese proper. These were, and still are, called Veddahs or Beddahs, a barbarous wandering tribe, ignorant of the simplest elements of civilization.

The district chiefly occupied by them is a wild, unopened portion of forest and mountain land towards the east and south of the island, whilst they are also to be found, or, at least, were to be found at the period we speak of, between the level plain which skirts the sea on the north-western coast, and the open districts of the interior, where, at an earlier period, numerous large cities had arisen. The supposition seems probable that these remarkable tribes, thus shut out from the rest of mankind, in inaccessible mountain and forest land, are the descendants of their primeval inhabitants, whom Wijaya and his band conquered, and who were gradually driven into the more inaccessible districts by the occupation of the best parts of the country. The conjecture is, at least, as probable as any other with which we are acquainted on the subject.

We have stated that the trade of Ceylon on the western side was principally carried on by the Moors, and of this tribe many enterprising merchants had settled in the island, who gradually engrossed in their own hands the entire of the transit traffic of the interior, and, by the favour with which they were received by the kings, became at length an important and influential class. At the present time, and during the occupation of the Portuguese and Dutch, they form the most enterprising and energetic class of the native inhabitants.

Ceylon had been faintly known to antiquity by the accounts of Pliny and Strabo. Amidst much inaccuracy and exaggeration, its chief features and most remarkable characteristics are to be found in one or other of their accounts, as well as in the allusions to be found in the works of other classical writers. Thus its abounding with elephants was referred to by Dionysius, the geographer, when he speaks of *μητερα Ταπροβανην Ασιηγενῶν ελεφαντῶν*. Onesicritus and Megasthenes described it as abounding, the former in elephants, the latter in gold and large pearls, according to Pliny, (auri margaritarumque grandium fertiliores quam Indos). The later writers, such as Ammianus Marcellinus, and Cosmas Indicopleustes, added little to the knowledge formerly on record, with regard to the island, nor was the information picked up respecting it by Marco Polo extensive or accurate.

He appears to have been the first, however, who noticed and described the remarkable mountain styled Adam's Peak, on which he informs us the tomb of the progenitor of mankind had actually been found! Ludovico Barthema, of Bologna, at the end of the fourteenth century, describes the inhabitants as by no means warlike—their arms, he informs us, consisted of spears and swords, but declares that in their contests little blood was shed, from their cowardice (perchè sono vili). His account, which is, at least, amusing, is to be found in Ramusio's collection. Nicolo de Conte, a Venetian, and Jerome de Santo Stephano, a Florentine, also visited the island previous to the first arrival of the Portuguese, but without adding any thing of importance to previous accounts.

It may be concluded, then, that of the extent and population of the island, its inhabitants, productions, and condition, little was known in Europe till its *discovery* (if I may use the word) by Lorenzo d'Almeida, in 1505. Francisco d'Almeida, the father of the naval officer just mentioned, was then governor of Goa, in which the Portuguese had established themselves a year or two before. Some Moorish vessels of which he was in pursuit, d'Almeida was informed had been seen in the neighbourhood of the Maldives, and thither he dispatched his son Lorenzo with a considerable force. Strong westerly winds, however, set in before his vessels had reached the place indicated, and the result was his being driven near the coast of Ceylon, where he anchored opposite to the town now called Colombo. No sooner had the Portuguese shewn themselves on shore, than information was at once conveyed to the king that "a race of men exceeding white and beautiful" (such is the description of the native annalist) had landed, "wearing boots and hats of iron, and never remaining at rest." "They have tubes" (said the same account) "which make a noise like thunder, when it breaks upon Jugandere Parivata, and even louder; and a globe of iron shot from one of them, after flying some leagues, will break a castle of marble or even of iron."

This curious account filled the court with alarm, and the question of commencing upon them immediate war, was at once proposed in a council called for the purpose. After some discussion, however, it was resolved that an ambassador should be dispatched in disguise to investigate the disposition of the new arrivals,—no acts of violence on their part having yet been heard of. His report was, that they seemed peacefully disposed; and his advice, that an embassy which they were about sending should be favourably received. This prudent counsel was adhered to, and on the arrival of Lorenzo's messenger, presents were mutually given and received; whilst the Portuguese would have us believe that in the treaty which followed, the Ceylonese monarch promised a large annual tribute of cinnamon. This weighty matter determined, Lorenzo erected a pillar in commemoration of the conquest of the island, and of its entire possession by His Majesty of Portugal! With so little scruple was the principle of *appropriation* then adopted!

At the period of this visit, the Portuguese historian, Ribeiro, informs us that there were then in the harbour "many ships of Bengal, of Persia, of the Red Sea, and other places, whence they had come to trade in cinnamon and elephants," a circumstance which, if it can be credited, and I see no reason why it should not, proves that a considerable trade was still carried on by the natives of the coast. During thirteen years which succeeded this expedition of Lorenzo, and which appears to have been an interval of internal tranquillity, we hear nothing more of the Portuguese in connection with the island. At the end of that period, Lopez Suaar Alvarengo, with nineteen vessels of various sizes, anchored in Colombo, and proceeded to erect a fort. The natives were not disposed tamely to submit to this act of invasion, and they accordingly vigorously but ineffectually opposed it. The invaders had a force sufficient to overcome all the opposition their feeble enemies could offer, and from being attacked, Alvarengo soon became the aggressor.

No army that the Singhalese monarch could bring into the field could withstand the charge of the well-disciplined Portuguese, and submission, with the promise of a tribute, was the only course left him to adopt. Nor was the invasion of their country the only evil the Singhalese had now to deplore; for on the death of Prakrama the Ninth, in 1527, the sword was drawn by rival claimants for the throne, and the country was plunged in civil war and bloodshed. The singular moderation and ability of a third party, a chief of considerable power, and a member of the royal family, at length succeeded in quelling the commotion, by raising the direct heir, a minor, to the throne, to the exclusion of the rival combatants.

An important siege of Colombo by the natives, however, had preceded this war, in which, so strictly did they blockade the city, and with such resolution did they meet the sallies of the besieged, that, but for a reinforcement of men and provisions, which opportunely arrived from Cochin, the fort would, in all probability, have been taken.

A quarrel between the reigning prince and his brother, which occurred some time after these events, and which was followed by the revolt of the latter, was the cause of a measure of the utmost importance as regarded the future prospects of the island. This was no other than the enlistment, by the reigning prince, of the Portuguese in his service, to aid him in quelling the insurrection. The desire of Buwaneko, the prince of whom we are speaking, was to adopt a favoured grandson as heir to his dominions, a design opposed by his brother. In order at once to secure the most strenuous exertions of his new allies in his favour, and to ensure the succession of his grandson, he sent an ambassador to Lisbon, with an effigy of the youthful aspirant and a crown, praying that the King of Portugal himself, John the Third, would be pleased, with his own hands, to place the crown upon the image, and thereby pledge himself to support the measure he so much desired; a ceremony which was accordingly performed, amid great display, in the Great Hall of the palace at Lisbon, A.D. 1541.

The death of Buwaneko the succeeding year, afforded an opportunity to the Portuguese of putting their promise into effect, and accordingly the youth alluded to, under the title of Don Juan, was raised to the vacant throne, nominally as the independent prince of Ceylon, but really as the puppet of the Portuguese. He found himself opposed, however, as his grandfather had been by the prince who resisted his accession, and that with an ability and energy which quickly altered the situation of events. The western coast, it is true, was in his hands, but the greater extent of the interior acknowledged the rebel leader. The death of this leader, shortly after he had succeeded in defeating a combined army of the nominal king's and the Portuguese forces, was far from relieving either from the difficulties of their position, for he left behind him an able, resolute, and determined son, willing and prepared to continue the conquest. This son was consequently a distinguished character in the history over which we are travelling, and under the title of Rajah Singha, *the Lion King*, frequently caused the invaders to tremble for the security of their footing in the island.

Anxious to take advantage of the death of their enemy, and ignorant of the resources of Singha, the Portuguese at once dispatched a force to take Kandy and subdue the interior. In one of the passes through which their course lay, Singha planted a powerful ambuscade, and there, at its extremity, drew up his forces to await his enemies. A bloody combat was the result; but when the Portuguese saw themselves at length hemmed in on every side, and their retreat cut off, all confidence was lost, and besides a large force of native auxiliaries, 1700 Europeans perished in the battle. Reinforcements from Goa, however, soon enabled the authorities at Colombo to fit out another expedition for conquest and revenge, which it was determined should be sent up the river Kalany, to avoid the distress caused by marching in the low country. Singha was prepared for them; the victories of his father and himself had now given him a small force of artillery, of which he took the utmost advantage. It was posted in a convenient position on the banks of the river, and, on the appearance of the invaders, a fire, well directed and violent, was opened upon them, which they could neither pass through nor effectually oppose. A retreat was the consequence; and so well were the measures of Singha taken, that before they reached Colombo, they were exposed to another attack almost equally destructive.

Excited by these successes, Singha now undertook the siege of Colombo, but had scarcely entered upon the enterprise, when he heard of a rebellion in Kandy, which he was obliged to withdraw his army to subdue. A course of cruelty and barbarity on his part to the members of the royal family succeeded, which makes one shudder at the horrors related; and of this cruelty the bitter consequence recoiled upon himself when he least expected it. A second time the siege of Colombo was attempted; for nine months the fort was strictly invested; their provisions were exhausted, the soldiers disheartened, and every thing promised a speedy surrender, when news was brought that the son of a prince murdered by Singha,—a youth baptized by the Portuguese under the title of Don John,—had assembled an army, and was making rapid progress in the neighbourhood of Kandy. To his infinite chagrin, Singha was once more obliged to raise the siege and march against this new foe.

Don John slowly retreated to the south and east as Singha advanced, and a lengthened warfare ensued, of which no particulars are recorded. Of this warfare, carried on at a distance from the capital, the Portuguese took advantage to raise a new claimant, Don Philip, to the throne, a measure which for ever alienated from them the alliance of Don John; the latter took the first opportunity of passing to Kandy, and there he cut off his new rival by poison, and disarmed the Portuguese. Scarcely had this tragedy been transacted, when Singha was advancing rapidly upon his enemy. Don John speedily had his forces, now recalled, put into order of battle, and at the pass of Kaduganava the final conflict of this long-continued struggle was fought. There, for the first time, the lion king was thoroughly defeated, and at a very advanced age, even upwards of a hundred years, it is said, he died a few days after the battle, of a wound received in it. Such was the end of Singha, one of the few native princes who, by innovation on the military tactics of his predecessors, became a formidable opponent even to European warriors. This event occurred in the year 1592.

During all this time the weak and imbecile Don Philip was in the hands of the Portuguese, flattered by those around him with the *title* of King of Ceylon. Him they were unwilling to part with; and accordingly, on having, by aid from Goa, been enabled to fit out another expedition against Don John, they put his descendant, Donna Catharina, the lineal heir of the crown, at its head. But the war with

Singha had made Don John a soldier, and while the Portuguese general, De Souza, to whose nephew Donna Catharina was affianced, was advancing from the north, in all the fancied security of contempt for his adversary, his opponent was quietly awaiting him at a pass on the road, into which the Portuguese forces entered with fatal confidence. The event was what might have been anticipated. "Suddenly from every side the shrill chank and dissonant tom-tom sounded. Before, behind, on the right hand and on the left, their enemies leapt forth, and clouds of arrows, balls, and spears descended upon them: it was a moment of fearful carnage; nothing was to be done by bravery, nothing by genius, nothing by flight. Every man was cut down in the place where he stood, and of that powerful army not a living being was saved but Donna Catharina."

Even she was reserved for a fate worse than death—Don John forced her, by the indignities she suffered, to accept of him as her husband, and thus constituted himself "lawful heir to the crown." A second expedition was equally unsuccessful, although not accompanied with such dreadful loss to the invaders.

Shortly after its termination (for I must hasten on in my survey), we find the Dutch for the first time engaged in the affairs of the island. Admiral Spilbergen arrived with three vessels at Batticaloa, on the eastern coast, and thence proceeded to the capital. There he was very favourably received by Don John; permission was given by him to the Dutch to build a fort on the coast, and to carry on a free trade in cinnamon and pepper, on condition that they should wage a war of extermination against the Portuguese.

The death of Don John soon afterwards, in 1604, left the interior once more a prey to disorder and bloodshed. Donna Catharina found herself quite unequal to enforce obedience, and, still in the prime of life, looked about for a successor to her late husband. But two princes of the royal family appeared eligible from their influence and authority, and the matter was quickly determined by the murder of one of them. Senerat, the bolder and more wicked of the two, on the murder of his rival, presented himself to the queen, and with the consent of the nobles, she accepted him as her consort. Nothing of much importance subsequently occurred till the year

1612, when Boschhouder, a Dutch naval officer, made his appearance in Kandy, and there had the strange offer made to him of at once entering into the service of Senerat as admiral and general The proposal was accepted, and Boschhouder proved himself, on various occasions, of infinite service to the Singhalese monarch in the quelling of insurrections and training of his forces.

The death of Catharina, in 1613, appears to have greatly shattered the stability of the Singalese throne at this period; and were it not for the prudent advice and conduct of Boschhouder, the Portuguese would probably have succeeded in reducing the entire island. As it was, they expelled the Dutch from Cottiar, near Trincomalee, and built a fort there and at Batticaloa, for the protection of their trade on the eastern coast. Into the particulars of Boschhouder's embassy to Europe on behalf of Senerat, in 1617–19, we cannot enter; suffice it to say, that the unfortunate death of that officer on his return to Ceylon, prevented Senerat from availing himself of the aid he had obtained from Christian IV. of Denmark.

The death of the nominal sovereign, Don

Philip, at the age of sixty-two, shortly prior to this event, gave to the Portuguese, according to their historians, a valid title to the whole island—that monarch having left it to them by will. It was not till 1630, however, when they had collected a force, which Senerat was not likely to have the means of opposing, that they resolved to take advantage of this bequest. Constantine de Saa, an experienced officer, was put at the head of this expedition, and by the caution and prudence of his operations seemed to ensure its success. The pass of Wellane, where the troops of De Souza had been cut to pieces by Singha the First, was that by which De Saa advanced upon Kandy. Here Senerat had erected a tower, the siege of which occupied some time; but it was finally taken, and thence the road to Kandy lay before them open and undefended.

Senerat, distrustful of a general engagement, had retreated to the south-east as De Saa advanced, whilst the king's son, afterwards the second Singha, harassed the march of the Portuguese in the rear. It was not till the invaders had advanced into the heart of a woody and difficult country, with a very much diminished force, that Singha, at the head of his own and his father's army, succeeded in surrounding the army of De Saa. The native auxiliaries of the Portuguese could not, of course, be trusted, for on the very first opening of a fire they deserted to the enemy. The European force thus encompassed was left to defend itself in the midst of innumerable enemies, and in the centre of an almost inaccessible district. For two days the Portuguese bravely defended themselves against the host of enemies that surrounded them, but at length, wearied with slaughter and continued fighting—with their leader mortally wounded, and no hope of escape, even if they cut their way through their enemies—they surrendered at discretion. The consequence was, the death of all those who refused to join the ranks of the king.

Senerat, after this brilliant exploit, the success of which he mainly owed to his more able son, lost no time in undertaking the siege of Colombo, then badly defended; but the arrival of reinforcements from Goa and Cochin rendered his expedition fruitless. Shortly after, in 1634, he expired, after a prosperous reign of thirty years, the prosperity of which, he owed, however, to Boschhouder in the early, and Singha in the latter, part. The son of Catharina, by Don John, had, of course, a prior claim to the throne on the death of Senerat; but this claim the warlike Singha was well prepared to oppose, and accordingly he had himself crowned at Kandy with the usual solemnities, whilst his rival, Wijayapala, fled to the Portuguese. They were willing, but for some time were unable, to attempt a diversion in favour of the fugitive prince; and when they did so, the usual difficulties, the inaccessible nature of the interior, and the numbers of Singha's forces, conspired to overthrow the project and defeat Wijayapala's hopes, whilst they gave Singha an additional force of artillery, of which he well knew the importance.

Anxious as Singha was to drive the Portuguese from the island, he was yet aware that his own forces and the powers at his command were not sufficient to accomplish this. He therefore sent an embassy to Batavia, asking the assistance of the Dutch to enable him to accomplish his undertaking. A treaty was entered into between the two powers, by which the Dutch promised their assistance, Singha bearing the entire expense of the expedition, on the condition that all the fortified places in the island were to be finally given into his hands. Accordingly, in 1639, a force from Batavia was sent to the eastern coast, which speedily reduced Batticaloa and Trincomalee, fortresses which Singha, with a very questionable policy, immediately destroyed. The following year, Negombo and Galle, on the western coast, were also taken, on the capture of which, disagreements broke out between Singha and his allies, from the non-fulfilment of their promises, on the part of the latter, which ultimately led him to look with as much suspicion on their proceedings as on those of his former enemies. A desultory warfare between the two contending European powers in the island was the consequence,—into the particulars of which I cannot now enter.

In 1646 an armistice was concluded, which continued in force till 1654, four years after which the Dutch found themselves sufficiently strong to undertake the siege of Colombo and Jaffna, the only remaining Portuguese possessions in the island. The former of these endured a long-continued blockade, but was at length compelled to yield by famine, during the continuance of which siege, occurred one of those horrible instances of maternal barbarity and cannibalism sometimes recorded—to satisfy the cravings of hunger. A few months afterwards, Jaffna was invaded and taken, thus completing the expulsion of the Portuguese from the island. The effects of their possession will probably never be eradicated. They have left their religion and language indelibly impressed upon the natives, forming, in this respect, a curious contrast with the Dutch—who, although they possessed the same districts for 130 years, have scarcely left a trace of themselves behind.

With the Indo-Portuguese language one can even now travel throughout the entire of the maritime, and a large proportion of the interior, provinces, whilst a knowledge of Dutch would be of as little service as a knowledge of French or Italian; and it is similar with their religion. Roman Catholicism now disputes with Budhism the majority of professors—whilst of the Dutch Reformed Church there are not probably three full congregations in the entire island. This contrast is remarkable, although perhaps not difficult to account for, when we consider the difference in character of the two nations—the lively, accommodating, proselytizing Portuguese, and the avaricious, stolid, and independent Dutchmen.

Thoroughly convinced, of course, as Singha must long have been, that the Dutch had no intention whatever of performing the stipulations of their treaty with him, we cannot be surprised on finding him now treating them as enemies. They, on their part, however, were content to defend themselves from his fury, without attempting, as the Portuguese had done, to mix themselves up in the contentions of the natives, at the same time that they hoped, by the obsequiousness of their conduct, and the numerous embassies with presents, which they sent, to conciliate at length his favour. His treatment of these embassies and the ambassadors was such, as the more mercurial Portuguese would not have tolerated without an attempt to be revenged. He frequently detained their ambassadors without reason, imprisoned some, and left others at large—at one time he accepted their presents, and then maltreated the bearers of them; at another, he would neither receive them, nor grant an audience as they desired, but threatened destruction if they did not instantly leave his territories. Such was the relationship which subsisted between the two powers. The Dutch were content with the extent of their possessions, and directed all their thoughts to increasing the profit which the commerce of the island yielded. They were merchants, not soldiers; and as every source of income was made a governmental monopoly, the character of their possession was rather that of a trading company's depôt, than of a political dependency.

In 1672 the French are first heard of in connection with the island. During that year a fleet of fourteen sail anchored near Trincomalee, under De La Haye, who sent three ambassadors to Kandy. These were favourably received by Singha, who being anxious to see the new comers embroiled with the Dutch, gave them permission to build a fort at Trincomalee. De La Haye was soon after obliged to leave for India, but before doing so, he dispatched a M. De Lanerolle to inform Singha of his departure, and of his intention speedily to return. De Lanerolle arrived at Kandy—

refused to violate "*la grandeur de la grande nation*," by acceding to the forms of the Singhalese court—and after an exhibition of childish punctiliousness and blustering bravado, so irritated Singha at length, that he was thrown into prison, where there is every reason to believe he ended his days. De La Haye never returned—he was met by the Dutch admiral, Van Goens, and totally defeated, in a naval encounter; four of his vessels were captured, the rest dispersed, and Trincomalee was taken again, and again occupied by the Dutch.

The death of Singha, in 1687, after a lengthened reign of nearly fifty years, gave the Dutch that peace and security which they so much desired. His successor, Suria, was naturally of a religious and peaceable disposition, so that whilst the Dutch were prosecuting their commercial schemes on the coast, he was endeavouring to restore Budhism to its pristine grandeur; in order to do this with effect, he invited twelve priests of the highest order of the hierarchy from Siam.

During the twenty-two years over which his reign extended, the Dutch government drew large sums from their monopoly of cinnamon, which they controlled and regulated by a system of policy admirably adapted to ensure the success of their intentions; that is, to raise and prepare the spice at the smallest possible outlay, without any punctilious regards to the rights of the native proprietors, and to sell it afterwards at the highest possible rate.

In 1707, Suria was succeeded by Kundisala, his eldest son, whose unwarlike disposition, like that of his father, gave a long rest of thirty-two years (the extent of his reign) to the enterprises of the Dutch. His character appears to have been as bad, or even worse, than that of any other prince of his line. Drunkenness, cruelty, ignorance, impetuosity, and revenge were the chief and most prominent characteristics of his disposition, and by the exercise of these qualities he at length fomented a rebellion amongst the nobles, which would probably have ended in his dethronement, but for the interference of the Dutch. In an embassy dispatched by the latter, to condole with him on the death of his Queen, they described her as his "high-born, excellent, and all-accomplished consort;" a proof that if a compliance with the Eastern arts of flattery and dissimulation would have secured their conquests, they were far from despising them.

In the characters and conduct of the Dutch governors, we find a striking proof of the necessity for a rigid system of supervision over colonial rulers. Without a free press, or an intelligent population beneath them, and at a distance so considerable from the supreme government, some of them launched out into a series of barbarities seldom read of in the annals of civilized people. Thus, one of them, Vuist by name, determined to render himself, if possible, an independent sovereign, and for that purpose proceeded to the persecution and destruction of every Dutch officer whom he supposed likely to oppose his schemes; whilst the patriotic opposition of those officers was visited by a barbarous refinement in cruelty on their unoffending wives and daughters. At length, in 1729, three years after the commencement of his government, a few patriotic soldiers banded themselves together, to arrest the monster. He was accordingly seized and conducted to Batavia, where he was tried, and suffered for his crimes.

Another, and that the very governor who succeeded Vuist, bent on aggrandizing himself, took a monopoly of the rice trade into his own hands, and, as a very great proportion of the rice consumed in the island is imported, obliged the unfortunate natives to buy it at his own price. Grain was refused to all—even to those formerly in comparative affluence, whose whole resources had been previously expended in purchasing it, famishing as they were,—unless they could bring the stipulated price. It was not till 1732 that this heartless villain, Versluys, was obliged to relinquish his infamous traffic, by being deprived of the government. A few exceptions, and some of them highly honourable to the Dutch character, are to be met with in the history of their governors, amongst which the names of Falck, Van Goens, and Van Imhoff are honourably distinguished. By their exertions, the agriculture of the maritime provinces was improved, and pepper, coffee, and cardamoms added to the exports of the island.

It was in 1766 that the first English embassy from Madras arrived at Kandy, Mr. Pybus being the ambassador. On this occasion the friendship of the English for the reigning prince was dwelt upon, and assistance offered against the Dutch, in the war which had just then broken out between the two powers. This assistance, however, the Madras government found itself afterwards unable to give, and the Kandian court was left to carry on the war on its own resources. This measure on the part of the English was exceedingly unjust and impolitic,—unjust, because war was not then being waged between Britain and Holland; and impolitic, inasmuch as a promise was made which was never fulfilled. In 1782, however, under the governorship of Lord Macartney at Madras, war having been declared with the Dutch, that nobleman dispatched a land force under Sir Hector Munro, and a fleet under Sir Edward Hughes, to attack the possessions of Holland in Ceylon. With this expedition Mr. Hugh Boyd, one of the reputed authors of the Letters of Junius, was dispatched as ambassador to the court of Kandy. The fort of Trincomalee was speedily invested and taken, and on the departure of

Mr. Boyd to Kandy, the admiral found it necessary to proceed to Madras for repairs. Before his return a French fleet had arrived in the harbour, taken the fort, and so fortified it, that on re-visiting it, Sir Edward did not consider that prudence would warrant an attack. Mr. Hugh Boyd in the meantime went to Kandy, and on his return to join, as he supposed, his comrades, fell into the hands of the French. Such was the conclusion of the second attempt at interference made by our countrymen.

The third, which occurred in 1795, was more successful. General Stewart, in the course of that year, attempted, and succeeded in, the reduction of Trincomalee, after a siege of three weeks, the only siege his enemies endured in the contest. The Dutch forces were at this period totally disorganized—their forts were continued scenes of riot, dissipation, and mutiny, whilst the officers had not power to check these disorders. Shortly after the reduction of Trincomalee, General Stewart advanced against Jaffna, where he met with no resistance, the fort being surrendered on the first summons. Early in 1796, Negombo was similarly surrendered, on the occupation of which, the British forces lost no time in advancing against Colombo. The only opposition here met with—such was the supineness of the Dutch authorities—was in a single sortie of a regiment of *Malays*, headed by M. De Raymond, a *Frenchman*. This sally was vigorously repelled, and before all the dispositions for a siege had been completed, the fort was surrendered. Galle, Matura, and Batticaloa, followed the example of the capital, and thus, without a struggle from its European occupants, the rich maritime provinces of Ceylon were yielded to the British. The possession of the interior, however, was not so easily and bloodlessly obtained.

Such was the inglorious termination of the Dutch occupation of Ceylon. If their conduct and proceedings in that island are to be taken as a sample of their colonial government, I can only say that any territory which comes under their control is to be sincerely commiserated. The military despotism and religious bigotry of the Portuguese were certainly not so injurious to the native character as the commercial rapacity and total selfishness of the Dutch; and although we find them taking some steps to procure the conversion of the Singhalese to Christianity, we find them also taking the surest means of inoculating them with hypocrisy, by preventing any but *professing* Christians from obtaining employment in their offices.

The next object of the British, on obtaining possession of the Dutch settlements, was to remove those injurious impressions which existed in the breast of the reigning prince against them. These suspicions had been engendered by the previous embassies, which had so fatally miscarried, and in the expulsion of the Dutch without any communication made to him on the subject. The professions of the ambassadors were received coldly, and answered unmeaningly, nor was it till Rajadhi's death (which occured in 1798), that the sentiments of the Kandian court underwent a change. The first Adigar, or prime minister, Pilame Talawe by name, resolved to take advantage of the death of Rajadhi for his own aggrandizement. He, therefore, elevated a youthful illegitimate son of the last prince to the throne, conscious that he should thus obtain the real, whilst his creature held the nominal, sovereignty. The other members of the royal family were imprisoned by the usurper, and Múta Samy, the Queen's brother, alone succeeded in reaching the English. On the arrival of Mr. North, afterwards the Earl of Guildford, to assume the governorship of the British possessions in the Island, Talawe was not slow in opening a communication with him, promising, if encouraged, to murder his sovereign, and assume the crown as a tributary prince. These proposals, in the open injustice of their original formation, Mr. North did not encourage, but proposed that the King and court should reside in the British territories, whilst Talawe should govern as Viceroy at Kandy. To this neither the King nor Talawe would agree, and the negociations accordingly ended in no important result.

In 1802, however, a difference arose between the Kandian and British authorities, which produced a wasting and destructive war. The plunder of some Mohammedan merchants proceeding from the coast into the interior, was made the ground of demanding satisfaction by the authorities at Colombo. This the Kandian court would not give; and accordingly, early in 1803, General Macdowall and Colonel Barbut were ordered to advance on Kandy from Colombo and Trincomalee, respectively. They arrived at, and took possession of, the town, which was completely deserted, and there they proclaimed Múta Samy King of Kandy and of the interior. A treaty was then entered into with him as an independent sovereign, which contained numerous stipulations in favour of his new friends. Amongst these, one article declared that a tract of land stretching directly through the heart of the Kandian territories from Trincomalee to Colombo, should be ceded in perpetuity to the English for the construction of a road, and another, that a British force should be stationed at Kandy, to secure the new sovereign from the violence of his mountaineer subjects.

While these transactions were proceeding at Kandy, Pilame Talawe, the general of the native forces, was hovering about the town and cutting off the communication with Colombo. So well were his measures taken, that in a short time the roads to the interior from the coast were impassable to small detachments, and Kandy became, in fact, a blockaded town.

In this condition he again opened a communication with the British general, offering to deliver up the young king, Singha, to his enemies, and to make a suitable provision for Múta Samy, if the Viceroyalty were given to himself by the British. These were the very proposals formerly offered by the British, and were now only renewed to lull General Macdowall into security. They had the desired effect. The general was rash enough to trust that a man would be true to his enemies who had proved false to his country; and before the stipulations were fulfilled, he led a large proportion of his troops to Colombo, sending Colonel Barbut back to Trincomalee, and leaving an officer, incapable of command, Major Davie, in charge of the garrison at Kandy (about 1500 strong), with the unfortunate Múta Samy.

All the subsequent disasters are to be traced to this fatal proceeding. No sooner had the respective detachments reached their stations, than Talawe, still further to delude the authorities at Colombo, held a conference with Mr.

North, at which the treaty was ratified, and a *promise* made to deliver up the unfortunate Singha within a stated period. Now it was that Major Davie ought to have found out the necessity for some measure, on his part, to ward off approaching danger. Large bodies of armed men were seen concentrating in the neighbourhood of Kandy; the stragglers from the town were being cut off, and every thing portended a determination on the part of the natives to make a vigorous attack upon the capital.

Yet the most supine indifference was betrayed by its defenders, until at length a formidable attack was made upon the town. This the garrison was unprepared for, and it was with some difficulty that their commander could obtain an armistice, in which he proposed a surrender: the conditions of the surrender were, that the town should be delivered up, with all its military stores and baggage, and that the troops (about 1500 strong), with their arms alone, should proceed to Trincomalee. The same evening the melancholy march was commenced, one hundred and twenty-six soldiers in hospital being left to the barbarity of their enemies, every one of whom was murdered.

From Kandy to the ford of the Mahavelli river, on the road to Trincomalee, is a distance of about three miles. When they arrived at it, the river was found to be so swollen by the late rains, as to render passage without boats impossible. These, however, were not to be obtained. Major Davie and his little band stood in irresolution on the bank, whilst their taunting enemies occupied the hills around.

Next morning, negotiations were renewed; and such was the destitute condition of the force, that the Kandians had the effrontery to demand the surrender of Múta Samy for torture and murder, as the price of their assistance to enable them to pass the river! whilst, more extraordinary still, Major Davie had the barbarity to comply with their demand! Múta Samy, the unfortunate victim of what I grieve to call by its right name, British treachery, was delivered to the barbarians, and suffered the agonizing and lingering death of impalement. Will it be believed that this was done —this act of treachery consummated—before the Kandians had fulfilled their part of the unhallowed compact? Múta Samy was in their power, was already suffering for having received British protection, whilst the pusillanimous Davie, with the men he had the misfortune to command, were still on the left bank of the river. He asked for the fulfilment of their agreement; they laughed at his folly, and proposed that he should conduct his troops unarmed back to Kandy. What were they to do there? Davie knew not. What hope of safety did that hold out? none whatever; and yet the wretched man agreed to it without consulting his brother officers, without informing the troops of his being about to offer them up as a sacrifice to his insensate folly or cowardice, and Kandian cruelty. The fatal order was given—"Ground your arms!"—the soldiers, ignorant of the compact agreed upon, did so, nor did the officers dare openly to resist, although they remonstrated with their superior. The arms were removed by the Kandians, the soldiers marched into a defile, the three superior officers, Major Davie, Captain Rumley, and Captain Humphreys, were separated from them, and the unfortunate force was then murdered—butchered in cold blood—unarmed and defenceless as the men were, by the mercenary Kaffirs in the Kandian army. Major Davie and his brother officers lingered on, and at length died in hopeless captivity.

It is related in Ceylon, although I cannot vouch for the truth of the report, that on the occupation of the interior in 1815, Davie was still alive, but, aware of the execrations heaped on his head by his fellow-countrymen in the island, dared not reveal himself, and lived with a Singhalese wife in the savage style of a native in the remote part of the large tract to the east of Kandy, called Bintenne, where even at the present day the face of a white man is not seen once, perhaps, for many years.

There was in the whole transaction but one redeeming trait, and that was in the conduct of a Malay officer, Nouradin by name, who happened then to be with Major Davie. The abilities and energy of Nouradin were known to Talawe, and he, in consequence, made him the most splendid offers if he would consent to desert the British service. This Nouradin refused to do; and even when the force had been captured, and the same proposals renewed, with the information that his refusal of their acceptance would be followed by instant death, his answer was, that he preferred *that*, to treachery and desertion. He was immediately afterwards beheaded.

The retaking of their capital proportionably elevated the spirits and hopes of the Kandians, and the war which succeeded these events, and continued unremittingly during 1803-4, and 5, was conducted by them with more than their ordinary vigour. It was a desultory series of partial actions on the confines of the British territory; nor did it present any feature, save the extraordinary march of Major Johnson, to merit particular detail.

This expedition was one of the most remarkable which occurred during the whole war, and forcibly illustrates what could be done against such enemies by a small force under a resolute commander. With a body of three hundred men, he marched first from Batticaloa, on the eastern coast, to Kandy, a distance, probably, of ninety miles, the greater part of which march lay through the territories of the Kandians, and was defended by their troops.

Arrived there, he found the force he expected to co-operate with him from Colombo had been otherwise engaged, and that the hills surrounding the town (exactly as on the former occasion) were occupied by the enemy. The town is situated in a valley completely encircled by hills, and—with a small lake, partly artificial, in its immediate vicinity,—completely fills up the valley. To remain there, subject to continual attacks, would have been to risk the gradual destruction of his force, and its slightest diminution would have left little hope of safety. He was therefore obliged to undertake the same march which Major Davie, with a superior force, had been unable to accomplish, and that in the face of an enemy, rendered confident by the late massacre. His little band took the road to Trincomalee, one hundred and thirteen miles distant, fought their way along, crossed the river, notwithstanding the utmost opposition of the enemy, and continued their march, day after day, subject to constant attacks both by day and night, until he brought the majority of his gallant little army safe into the fort of Trincomalee.

In 1805 an armistice was proposed by the king, which the English governor did not oppose, and this, without any formal treaty, lasted till 1814. In the mean time, however, the proceedings at Kandy demand our attention. It is not to be supposed that Wikrama and Pilamé Talawe could continue on the same footing as had formerly subsisted between them. On the cessation of hostilities, the king was determined to shake off the yoke of his Adigar, and shewed this determination so openly as seriously to alarm Talawe. A proposition of the minister's, to marry his son to the natural daughter of the king, was the cause of his dismissal from his offices and honours to retirement in his own district. This Talawe could not patiently endure—he accordingly fomented a rebellion, failed in his enterprise, was apprehended, and beheaded. This occurred in 1812, the same year that Mr. North was succeeded at Colombo by Sir Robert Brownrigg.

On the death of Talawe, Eheylapola, who had been second Adigar, was appointed to succeed him, but did not long escape the jealousy of the king. In self-defence, Eheylapola excited an insurrection in Suffragam, but was defeated by Molligodde (the king's general, and now second Adigar), and fled to the English. Wikrama's rage was ungovernable when he heard of this escape, and with the barbarity of a savage, it was visited on all whom suspicion could taint. One circumstance, the last and crowning act of barbarity, will suffice. The final scene of this domestic barbarity was horrible in the extreme, and, if I wound the feelings of my readers by relating it, I must be excused for my strict adherence to truth,—*προς ταυτα κρυπτε μηδεν*. The unfortunate wife and children of Eheylapola were still in Kandy, and under the power of the inhuman tyrant whose actions I am relating. They were condemned to die. Before one of the temples of the gods, in the market-place of Kandy, they were doomed to suffer, and were led forth by the gaoler who had them in charge. The lady advanced to meet her fate with resolution; she proclaimed the legality of her lord's conduct, and her own innocence, and hoped that the present sacrifice might be for his good. She then told her eldest son, a lad of eleven years, to submit to his fate; the poor infant recoiled with horror from the sacrifice, when his noble brother, two years younger, stepped forwards with a determined mien, and told him *he* would shew him how to die. *One* blow was struck, and the head of the youthful hero was rolling at their feet; the barbarity was not to end here, however. The severed head was thrown into a rice mortar, the pestle was placed in the hand of the unfortunate mother, and she was told that if she refused to use it, *she should be disgracefully tortured.* The poor woman stood for a moment in irresolution, but disgrace was worse than any inward struggle. She lifted the pestle up, and once she let it fall. One by one the same harrowing scene was repeated, until all were gone, and at last the poor infant at her breast was torn from its resting-place, where, in unconscious innocence, it knew nothing of the awful scene that was transacting around it. It, too, was beheaded, and the milk which it had just received, flowed forth to mingle with its blood.

What an awful recital!—who can portray to themselves the poor mother standing irresolute, under such a dreadful trial, without feeling the liveliest pity at her fate, and the strongest resentment against her heartless persecutor? What must have been the agony of that temporary irresolution, which was only ended by her inflicting a blow upon the lifeless and bleeding head of her own son! Whatever may be the evils of the British power in Ceylon, we may yet congratulate ourselves with the certainty that it can never sanction cruelty such as this.

In the latter part of 1814, the barbarous treatment of some native merchants from the coast, by the Kandian tyrant, caused an interruption of the amicable relations between the two powers in possession of Ceylon. Compensation was again refused, and in January of the succeeding year, a considerable force was again moved towards Kandy. In the proclamation sent forth by the British government at the commencement of this final invasion, a very just distinction was drawn between the tyrant himself and the population (noble as well as plebeian) of the districts he governed. In that document it was distinctly declared that the expedition was against the tyrant and his power, not against the people whom he called his subjects. Numbers of the more influential chiefs came over to the British on the occasion, and every thing portended the conclusion of the authority of the Singha race in Ceylon. Even Molligodde, the king's prime minister, and the only general of ability whom he possessed, as soon as he had succeeded in placing his family beyond the reach of Wikrama, came over to the invading force, and lent his utmost exertions to second their intention.

On the 14th February, the head-quarters of General Brownrigg were established in Kandy: no resistance was attempted,—deserted by his own subjects, and only defended by his Malabar body guard, the king was obliged to fly, without having even the hope of effectual resistance to cheer him. Measures for his immediate pursuit were instantly taken—two days after the entrance of the British force into Kandy, his wives and treasures were captured, and two days afterwards (on the 18th) a party of Eheylapolà's followers discovered the king himself. His guard fought bravely in his defence, but were overpowered by numbers, and finally Wikrama fell into the hands of that man whom of all others he had most deeply injured.

Eheylapola was not backward in shewing his enmity to his conquered oppressor. The king was bound hand and foot, and treated with every indignity, till rescued by the British, who released him from his bonds, and shewed, in their subsequent conduct towards him, something of the courtesy of civilized warfare. The following year he was conveyed to Madras, and thence to Vellore, where he died on the 30th of January, 1832, of a dropsy. Such was the fate of the last independent king of Ceylon,—the last scion of a family which had governed the island for two thousand three hundred years!

No time was lost by General Brownrigg in taking measures for an immediate settlement of the government of the country. A conference was held in the audience hall of the palace of Kandy, on the 2nd of March, between the British general and the late prime minister, together with the other principal officers of Kandy, at which Sri Wikrama Rajah Singha was formally deposed, his family and relatives for ever debarred from the throne, and all the claims of his race declared to be extinguished. The country was declared to be henceforth under the government of the British sovereign—the laws of the country still in force—and the usual royal dues and revenues still to be levied for the support of government. Such were the principal heads of the treaty, by virtue of which the British power was recognized throughout the entire of the island.

The Kandian chiefs were not yet prepared, however, thus peaceably to surrender their authority. For two years they silently made preparations for a final struggle, and in 1817 the standard of rebellion was unfurled; a priest of the royal family became a competitor for the crown, and in a few months it was evident that the British must either relinquish their authority, or re-conquer the country. Every district of the interior was soon in open insurrection—the small detachments of the British forces scattered over the interior were cut off, and but for dissension amongst the Singhalese chiefs, Kandy must have been evacuated.

When this measure was in contemplation,

news was brought of another aspirant for the throne having appeared—the former one was captured by his opponents, and thus—their enemies disunited and destroying each other, —the British found little difficulty in gradually winning back their lost ground. Nothing could be more destructive to the country than the state of things in 1818. A war of extermination was carried on in every quarter by the three contending powers. Districts were laid waste —villages burnt—the inhabitants slaughtered, and the crops destroyed; and this, not in one quarter alone, but over nearly two thirds of the extent of the island. At length the principal native chiefs on both sides were captured —the war became fitful and irregular, until an event occurred, which at once put an end to the contest — the capture of the celebrated Dalada relic, the tooth of Budha. When it was known that this relic, the most precious thing in the world in Singhalese estimation, was in the hands of the British, resistance was at an end.

In a convention held shortly after in Kandy, at which Sir R. Brownrigg presided, the interior was finally placed under British jurisdiction. Thus was one of the fairest gems added to the crown of England—"the pearl-drop on the brow of India," "the emerald isle of the East."

Into its history under its British masters it is not my intention to enter here; suffice it to say, that, with occasional and partial checks, it has been making rapid progress in wealth, civilization, and general prosperity.

THE END